SCIENTIST SPIES

A memoir of my three parents and the Atom Bomb

SCIENTIST SPIES

A memoir of my three parents and the Atom Bomb

Paul Broda

For Angela Alexander, with best wishes

Paul Broda.

Matador
5 Weir Road
Kibworth Beauchamp
Leicester LE8 0LQ, UK
Tel: (+44) 116 279 2299
Fax: (+44) 116 279 2277
Email: books@troubador.co.uk
Web: www.troubador.co.uk/matador

ISBN 978 1848766 075

British Library Cataloguing in Publication Data.
A catalogue record for this book is available from the British Library.

Typeset in 12pt Garamond by Troubador Publishing Ltd, Leicester, UK
Printed and bound in the UK by TJ International, Padstow, Cornwall

Matador is an imprint of Troubador Publishing Ltd

For Cleo, Andrew, Linda and Maresi
and
In memory of my three parents and of Cecil Powell

CONTENTS

FOREWORD

Too often history is portrayed in blackish and whitish terms of heroes and villains. Alas, Alan Nunn May has been dumped in the category of 'villain'. In his profoundly moving account, which goes far beyond family loyalty and filial piety, Paul Broda challenges conventional wisdom.

As a freshman undergraduate, straight from National Service in the British Army of the Rhine, I was invited by a fellow student in Gonville and Caius College, to go as his guest to a talk that the Master was giving on Atomic Weapons. I blush now at the gauche temerity with which, with all the prejudices of current conventional wisdom, I asked Sir James Chadwick, Nobel Prize winner 1935, about the wickedness of Nunn May. Ouch! 'I knew Alan extremely well. I do not support what he did. But, he did it for good motives. And, because of what he did, it may just be that your generation will be spared an atomic war. None of us can know.' We should be careful before rushing to condemn.

In Glasgow, in the 1960s, I was a close friend of the distinguished geneticist Guido Pontecorvo, who spoke in similar terms about his brother Bruno, who defected to Russia. So did Brian (Lord) Flowers about his sometime boss at Harwell, Klaus Fuchs, who, like Nunn May, gave secrets to Russia.

In March 1964, as members of a Scientist/Labour Politician visit to the Soviet Union, we were taken by Dr David Schoenberg, Director of the Mond Low Temperature Laboratory in Cambridge, to see his friend Piotr Kapitsa in the elegant home of the Russian Academy of Sciences. Flanked by Academicians Kirillin and Millionshikov, the President, Professor Keldysh, looking at Kapitsa, said to us, 'It is a good thing for humanity Piotr and his friends helped us to get atomic weapons more quickly than we would otherwise have done.' It was widely thought that the Americans might have been tempted to make a pre-emptive nuclear strike. Maybe Alan Nunn May had a role in preventing such a catastrophe.

Nunn May's story is told in detail using his own words, including his fascinating vignettes of life in the Cavendish Laboratory in the Thirties. There is an immediacy to his treatment of the politics and the science in the fog of war, which graphically portrays the context in which he took his fateful decisions. These included the occasion of his passing information to the Russians in 1942 that was never detected by the authorities. Nunn May was very prescient about the dangers of dirty bombs, and on the US's desire to keep atom secrets under its sole control, even after the War, and even from Britain.

Paul Broda is able to combine this story with that of his father Engelbert Broda, who has only recently been identified as a spy for Russia of equal importance to Nunn May. He builds up a picture of the lives of his father and mother, and describes how they came to Britain in 1938 as refugees who had experienced the violence and fear of Fascist Germany and Austria, and had also been in Russia. He shows how upbringing and events shaped both Nunn May and Broda as communists, and how in turn this made them especially concerned that Russia, the ally that was suffering so much, was being kept in the dark about the Atom Project. We see that both men acted from deeply held convictions and for no personal reward.

Interesting people move in and out of the story, and events with huge consequences are interspersed with a frank treatment of the protagonists' own personal lives. This includes accounts of both the author's own early life and of Nunn May's years as a convict, a story in its own right with a counterpoint in his MI5 file of the period. Finally, Paul Broda reflects with affection on what each of his three parents made of the rest of their lives. Just one hundred years after their births, this surely is an ideal moment for their voices to be heard.

Tam Dalyell

INTRODUCTION

Very late in 2002, my stepfather Alan Nunn May was in hospital with heart failure. His doctor said: 'Professor May, if some event happens, how hard do you want us to try to revive you?' Alan looked him in the eye and answered very clearly: 'You see, I was a spy for the Russians, and I haven't quite finished my memoirs, so please do what you can.' At the end of the bed, I nodded affirmation to a bemused junior doctor. A few days later, Alan came home and he then asked us to take down a statement, and after making minor corrections he agreed to it. Two days later, on Christmas Day, just a few days before the fiftieth anniversary of his release from prison, he returned to hospital, and he died there early in the New Year. He and my mother Hilde had been married for forty-nine years. After the funeral I gave the broadsheets a precis of Alan's life and also his statement. The precis gave an account of his life beyond the giving of atomic secrets to the Russians for which he was sent to prison in 1946. The statement revealed that Alan had first given them information in 1942 when in Cambridge, more than two years before he committed the offence in Canada for which he was sentenced.

My father Engelbert (Berti) Broda came to Britain as an Austrian refugee in 1938. Like Alan he worked during the War in the Cavendish Laboratory in Cambridge on the Atom Project. After his divorce from Hilde and return to Austria in 1947 he never returned to Britain, except once in 1948. He declined to explain why, saying only that he feared that he would be denied entry. This situation lasted until his death in 1983, and so I always met him outside the UK. Given his part in the Atom Project, surprisingly little information about him was available in The National Archives until 2006, when MI5 released his extensive file. This showed that there were security concerns on Berti throughout his stay in Britain and differences of opinion about the wisdom of employing him on the Atom Project. Nothing was ever proved against him, though both before and after he returned to Austria it was suggested in the file that he had been involved with Alan, whom he knew. However, material published in 2009 based on Russian archives transcribed by Alexander Vassiliev (see below) shows that Berti was indeed a spy.

In the early fifties my mother, born Hildegard Gerwing in Aachen, was a Cambridge school doctor. In early 1953 we visited friends north of London, and while there we called on Alan, who had recently emerged from Wakefield Prison and was staying nearby with his brother. Alan was being closely monitored by the authorities, so this was a discreet way to relay greetings and invitations from mutual Cambridge friends, although Hilde herself had only met him once. This was probably when visiting Berti in Cambridge from London to hand over or collect me. Alan duly went to Cambridge, and they became friends. When they married in August, the press wrongly inferred that Hilde had been waiting and pining for Alan during his imprisonment. MI5 saw the marriage as possible evidence that Berti had recruited Alan as a spy. In 2007 this was relayed by *The Times* in a delayed scoop that sank like a stone. Shortly after, many volumes of files on Alan and three on Hilde, who had died in 2004, were placed in the public domain.

With this new material, and one hundred years after their births in 1910-11, this is the moment to write my memoir. I describe Alan's motives and actions in giving atomic secrets to the Russians and discuss whether Berti was also implicated in Alan's actions. I also describe what shaped Alan and Berti to act as they did and how all three believed that individual actions, in particular resistance to Fascism, might influence outcomes. It is also an intimate account of their personal lives, including Berti's and Hilde's difficult relationship and Alan's prison life. I then show how in their different ways all three got on constructively with their later lives.

There are several family sources. In 1987 Hilde recorded an account of her life until she met Berti. I had also written a memoir of Berti after his death in 1983. On his release from prison, Alan wrote about his time on remand and as a convict. His account is totally without self-pity. Then in the Eighties he wrote a detailed memoir of his life up until his arrest that placed his actions in a wider context. Alan's memoir includes vignettes of senior colleagues who had major roles in the Atom Project and also describes scientific and political events as he recalled them and was later to research them. These form a crucial part of the story of how Alan acted as he did. Here I have used extensive direct quotation because he wrote well and revealingly, and to make clear which were his own memories and thoughts.

Together, Alan's memoirs in typescript, his letters from prison, and some handwritten material are the basis of about a third of this book.

Alan wrote: 'How should one write a biography? How to convey the simultaneous happenings on the world stage - the growing menace of Fascism and the drift towards world war - and at the same time describe the wonderful advances in physics - discoveries such as the neutron, the mesons and the rapid advances in our understanding of the structure of the nucleus - culminating in fission and the Bomb? How to combine these with my own puny struggle to make a living and to understand what was happening around me, even to make something worthwhile of my life in the midst of it all? One needs an orchestral full score showing in the bass the inexorable movement of political forces towards war, then in the staves above the lighter more fanciful flashes of scientific discovery, brilliant and captivating, but equally lethal in their overtones of fission and fusion, and then, peeping modestly through the turmoil of the heavy tympani and trombones the plaintive pleading of the soloist, like poor Till Eulenspiegel's piccolo.'

Memory plays tricks, so it is valuable that there are also contemporaneous sources for much of the story. These include Alan's letters from prison and Berti's often heartfelt letters to Hilde over more than fifty years. There are also letters from each to me and ones documenting other relationships. These sources are usually consistent with what I remember of what I was told by each of them, and then what I saw. However, some details of my early childhood have emerged that were completely new to me. There are also the MI5 files in The National Archives, which include reports and internal memos, intercepted letters, phone transcripts, and Cabinet and Home Office papers. Quotations from these files form an important part of my narrative. The language used by officials and their informants about my parents is interesting.

Thus I can present Alan, Berti and Hilde in a more detailed and personal way than would usually be possible for spies and their spouses. I can also describe their origins and attempt to show which were the crucial events that formed them. As well as the major events and the courage that took them into such dangerous waters, they had relationships, work, political and other concerns that were important to them. All three were sensitive, optimistic and humorous, with strong feelings of friendship and of family. I also owe my career as an academic scientist largely to their interest and support as I grew up. The Epilogue describes their later years and reflects on their lives and how they affected me.

I hope to convey the pervasive pessimism of the Thirties and how both Alan and Berti felt about the pre-war slide towards war and then the Phoney War. Both were Marxists; Berti had been a committed communist from his youth, and Alan joined the Communist Party in 1936. Their view of the Thirties, of Fascism in Germany and of Russia, impelled them to go outside the law to assist Russia when it became our ally. They saw that the defeat of Naziism depended on Russia's survival and then victory on the Eastern Front. For Alan, another strong reason for giving information to the Russians was the fear he had of a post-war American monopoly of atomic capability. It was as I expected when the material from the Russian files became available in 2009 that Berti, like Alan, had passed over secrets solely for political reasons, and firmly rejected payment.

It is vital to understand the reasons for their actions, and if one wishes to judge it must be with a willingness to ask, without the benefit of hindsight, what one might have done in their position. Both were young scientists, not spies, but then realised the implications of what they knew for the fate of Russia as well as of Germany, and acted on this. Those of us, the vast majority, who are never in such a fateful position should try to avoid the 'condescension of posterity', and not simply invoke what then was unknown about the full horror of Stalin as well as of Hitler, and the Cold War.

Because both Alan and Berti were resolutely silent in public, a number of errors exist in some accounts concerning them, and speculation has tended to become fact. An example is the notion that Alan was connected with the other Cambridge spies, and in particular that Donald Maclean, who entered Alan's college, Trinity Hall, the year after him was his friend or even 'close friend'. Alan made clear to me that he had no such connection, and that he never knew Maclean. I have no reason to disbelieve this, and readers will see that his path to spying did not involve the Cambridge Four.

A world-weary and cynical aphorism of Arthur Balfour's (he of the Declaration that Jews should have a homeland in Palestine) was that 'Nothing matters very much and most things don't matter at all'. This was to be a common British attitude to the rise of Fascism on the Continent of Europe in the Twenties and Thirties. Further back there had been the arms race and the system of alliances that initiated the Great War, in which Balfour himself was an important participant, then the War itself, and the Bolshevik Revolution that ensued. There was real hostility to the Soviet Union, which was regarded by many as more of a menace than Fascism. It was only interrupted when Hitler invaded Russia in 1941, and was resumed in 1945 as the Cold War.

Some recent writers have taken the start of the Cold War to be the moment in 1945 when a Russian cypher clerk defected, resulting in the identification of Alan as a person giving atomic secrets to the Russians, and of others. But then following the publication in 2009 of the material from KGB files showing that Berti also gave information, *The Times* had an article about Berti headed 'The Spy who started the Cold War'. Because of the underlying hostility between the West and the Soviet Union, these opinions are simplistic and inflated. Moreover, in such personalised terms it is just as plausible that the activities of scientists like Alan and Berti helped to prevent a Hot War as that they were responsible for the Cold War. The balance of terror due to Russia gaining the Bomb has often been seen as having resulted in preventing war between the US and the USSR. What effect the actions of Alan and Berti actually had is unknowable because there are no control experiments in history.

In my opinion, everyone connected with the Bomb, whether as politicians, military men, engineers or scientists, had entered morally ambiguous territory. Famously Einstein himself recognised this. Of the scientists, there were those like James Chadwick (Note 1) who held that they had a job to do and that it was the prerogative of the politicians to decide how to use the fruits of their work. Then there were scientists who joined the project when it was already clear that after all the Germans had no such capability. They and others later saw it as their job to implement Ernest Bevin's celebrated remark in 1946 that if the Bomb existed he as Foreign Secretary felt powerless dealing with the Americans unless the British had a Bomb with a 'bloody Union Jack on top of it'. On the other hand, there were doubtless others who avoided the whole area.

Another view was represented uniquely by Joseph Rotblat, a Polish associate of Chadwick, who had more reason than most for fearing that the Germans had a bomb. He left Los Alamos in 1944 when he realised that the Germans had no such capability, that the Bomb would probably be used against the Japanese and, through table-talk with General Leslie Groves, the supremo of the Manhattan project, that the real importance of the Bomb for the Americans was as an instrument of US post-war policy (Note 2). It was this thought, not unique to Groves and relayed by scientists in Chicago to Alan on visits there from Montreal in 1944, that impelled Alan in 1945 to work again with the Russians. The British were being excluded from the inner secrets, and took steps to mitigate this that had included asking Alan to obtain more information from Chicago. Moreover, the Free French in the Montreal group were tacitly encouraged by both Chadwick and J. D. Cockcroft (Note 3) to act in their own country's interest, so that Jules Guéron, a good friend of both Alan and Berti, personally briefed de Gaulle on behalf of the French in July 1944.

Both Alan and Berti admired Rotblat for his stance then, and for his later work for the Pugwash Movement, for which he shared the Nobel Peace Prize with Pugwash in 1995. Pugwash (the place in Nova Scotia where in 1957 the first meeting was held) arose from a 1955 manifesto by Einstein, Bertrand Russell, and nine others including Cecil Powell, who is important in my story. It contained the immortal words 'Remember your humanity, and forget the rest'. It became a vital means for the discussion of disarmament and detente between scientists drawn largely from the nuclear powers. Later Berti was president of Austrian Pugwash. But at the time Rotblat was viewed with extreme suspicion for his departure from Los Alamos, although he broke no laws. Moreover, at the time his action had no effect on the world situation; the bombs were dropped on Japan with the support of the top scientists, J. Robert Oppenheimer, E. Fermi, E. O. Lawrence and A. H. Compton, and other scientists such as Leo Szilard could not stop this (Note 4). These scientists and others all had ample opportunity to reflect in public on their stances then.

A third position was that taken by Alan, Berti and also Klaus Fuchs, namely to go outside the law and to break the trust that had been placed in them by Chadwick, with his rather open style of management that was the antithesis to that of Groves. It was apparently also taken by a senior British civil servant, John Cairncross, and by an American at Los Alamos, Ted Hall. Of course Alan and Berti, and also Fuchs, being Communists, saw things differently from many others.

Late in life Alan wrote: 'I am often asked whether I regret venture into espionage. My answer is that I deeply regret having joined the atomic energy project at all. As one of the 100,000 or so more or less directly concerned with the development of the bomb, I must be responsible for about two of the 200,000 victims of the bombs dropped on Japan. This thought saved me during my imprisonment from regarding myself as some kind of martyr. The fact that my fellow mass murderers got off scot-free, and indeed were honoured and bemedalled, is just an example of the way justice, like wealth and happiness, is very unevenly distributed – a few get too much and most too little.

'My main job in the project had been to develop nuclear power rather than weapons, and perhaps I should console myself that this was a useful thing to have done. Ought I not be proud of having suggested ZEEP (the Canadian prototype nuclear reactor) and so ensuring that Canada came promptly into the nuclear age as the war ended? I am afraid not – nuclear power has turned sour in a big way, and our early enthusiasm now looks decidedly odd.

'So I bitterly regret that I did not turn down Chadwick's pressing invitation to join the project. As to informing the Russians, this seemed then, and does now a blindingly obvious necessity. Of course it should have been done officially, by all the obligations due to an ally who had borne the brunt of the fighting. This was pointed out at the time by many. The failure to do this was an act of treachery, first against the Russians, and also against the scientists who had devoted so many years to prepare a weapon under the impression that it was for use against the enemy, only to find that it was for use against our ally.' Thus his mature view of betrayal was not his breach of the Official Secrets Act. The present concept, that obeying orders that one knows to be wrong is no defence, was made explicit at the Nuremberg Trials at that time.

In the post-war period of nuclear monopoly by the US, it was quite respectable to advocate the use of the Bomb against the Russians while they could not retaliate in kind. For instance, it was put forward by Bertrand Russell, as he discussed in his autobiography. It is therefore incorrect to see that as a period when the world's peace was relatively safe in American hands. It is true that in a turbulent world dreadful things were going on in Russia and its satellites, that in Korea the North (and perhaps also the South) wanted conflict, and that Russia was expansionist. Who knows what the effect was of the Russians having the Bomb earlier than expected by the Americans?

Against the opinion that Alan and Berti made the world a more dangerous place is the fact that only the US has dropped nuclear bombs. We have also seen the propensity of some US governments to use air power, often involving killing at a distance populations of innocent people as collateral damage, as a preferred means of pursuing political objectives, whether in Korea, Indo-China or in more recent conflicts. They might also have used at least tactical nuclear weapons had they dared. One's view of right and wrong can depend on whether one is in the plane or underneath it, and a single view is no more likely to be uniquely valid than a single faith or a single world view.

In his introduction to his book *Spies* with J. E. Haynes and H. Klehr, A. Vassiliev writes of his earlier book: '*The Haunted Wood* doesn't contain the real names of two atomic agents - Persian and Eric - although I knew them (Note 5). It was my deliberate decision not to put the names of Russell McNutt and Bertl Broda (Eric) in the draft I gave Allen Weinstein. ... In 1996 I had no idea what had happened to them, and I didn't want to do them harm. As far as the history of Soviet espionage ... is concerned it is important to understand where I come from ... to me they are still heroes. They helped my country in very difficult times, and I had no reason to disrespect their memory or cause them any trouble if they were alive.' I thank him because it is good to read his view of Berti, a brave man who to the very end believed that things did matter. This then is my account of Alan and Berti and also of Hilde, who was so important to both of them.

PROLOGUE

On Saturday 1 August 1953 a small group gathered at the Registry Office in Cambridge. Both the bride and the groom were in their early forties. Alan Nunn May was nearly six feet tall, balding, clean-shaven and with spectacles, and looking rather intellectual. Hilde Broda was a lively and attractive blonde of medium height in a blue outfit. With them were his older brother, sister-in-law and sister, me (Hilde's fourteen-year-old son from her previous marriage), and a few friends. A cause for anxiety was the possible arrival of the press, since Alan had been the subject of intense press interest both before and after his release from prison seven months earlier. This was because he had been no ordinary convict, but an Atom Spy. Everything had been arranged in secrecy, even dispensing with the usual photographer, but banns had had to be posted. Only after the ceremony, as we prepared to return to our home for a celebration with more friends, did a reporter appear and have his request for an interview politely declined (Photo 1).

Hilde had formally and I believe sincerely asked my permission to marry Alan, and I gave this gladly, because I had liked him from our first meeting, and could see how much they had taken to each other. In this way I was included, and my liking and then love for Alan remained until his death; he was to be a real parent to me, without in any way seeking to compete with my own father, Berti. Berti had been informed of the impending marriage a few days earlier. He wrote back: 'That is surprising news! I always thought he was very nice, and so I wish you both all the best. Of course there will be external problems, but if between you everything is OK, that's much more important, of course. So, much luck. I'm also sure that Paul will like him and vice versa. I would be so happy if you have found the right one. Servus, love Berti.' And the next day: 'Just a few more words about your news of yesterday, of which of course I've thought a lot. All external difficulties can be overcome if, as I don't doubt, you are sure. I always liked him. But are you sure about your feelings, have you thought very carefully about it? I would not ask if I had not myself made such a dreadful mistake, and if I didn't have

1. Alan and Hilde at the time of their wedding, 1953

concerns whether you knew each other too little. After such a short time? Anyway, all all all best wishes from your old Berti.'

Berti had reason to be concerned as his own second marriage, made in haste to someone he hardly knew but had admired at a distance, had just ended catastrophically. But his appreciation of Alan as a person from the time when they were colleagues in the Atom Project at the Cavendish Laboratory in Cambridge and also his desire for Hilde to be happy were genuine enough. Berti might even have attended the wedding had he not felt unable to return to Britain, since he feared that he would be turned back, questioned, or detained. Before the wedding Alan's brother and sister had a tapped phone conversation in which they speculated on why they had been summoned to Cambridge. Even so, the wedding came as a complete surprise to the Security Services, and then there was a flurry of speculation on whether the wedding told them anything new about Alan's connection with Berti. From then on our letters and phone calls were of course monitored.

Immediately after the wedding party, I left for Harwich to catch a boat to join Berti in Scandinavia, and Alan and Hilde headed for Wales. At breakfast at their hotel in Stony Stratford the next morning, they saw the banner headline 'Nunn May Weds' and realised that they would be pursued, so they turned around and spent a peaceful time with friends in Essex whose house was aptly named *The Live and Let Live*. My message, '½ pint each day until further notice' (for our cat and her kittens), appeared on the front pages of the newspapers, and for a while a reporter awaited his photo opportunity on their return, provided with tea and toilet by a neighbour.

The wedding had come at the height of the Cold War, with the ascendancy of McCarthy, and the Rosenberg executions just weeks before. I was very aware even before Hilde's re-marriage that my parents were part of a minority with unpopular views, but I loyally believed and acted as they did, and defended their views when the need arose at school. This was accepted and I did not feel that my life was much affected at school or socially. This continued after Alan became my stepfather. My headmaster reassured Hilde that he would protect me from any hostility at school, but I don't know if the need arose. I have always felt that such tolerance was not to be taken for granted, but reflected a profound decency in British society at that time. I have been deeply grateful for this all my life.

PART ONE

ORIGINS

1

BERTI IN VIENNA

Engelbert Egon August Ernst Broda (Berti) had roots that were important to him. His paternal line included a famous rabbi in Prague. Eight generations back in his father's maternal line Abraham Auspitz was 'head of Moravian Jewry in the time of Maria Theresia, and for a time in disgrace with her'. The families of Brodi (Moses Brodi became Moritz Broda in about 1840) and Auspitz intermarried and became prosperous making sugar in Moravia, before moving to Vienna. Berti's grandparents married as Catholics in 1879, his grandmother Helene Bauer leaving the Jewish community in that year. They lived in the newly-built Heugasse, now Prinz-Eugen-Strasse, where Ernst Broda, Berti's father, was born in 1885. In turn Berti was born and lived there until 1938, and from 1956 until his death.

The family of Viola Pabst, Berti's mother, was Catholic. Her grandfather was a Prague railwayman and her father August was born in Moravia. August's mother was a Hawel (sic), and the Czech playwright-statesman Vaclav Havel is my fourth cousin. Viola's mother Ella Noe was born in what was Hungary and now is Romania, the daughter of a stationmaster. Viola and Georg Wilhelm (Willi) were born in Bohemia in 1884 and 1885, but August then rose to be stationmaster of the Ostbahnhof in Vienna. Berti always felt a kinship with those in all of the successor nations to the Habsburg Empire and a nostalgia for its multinational character, that also had a place for Jews. Viola went on the stage in 1898, and was successful in Vienna and elsewhere (Photo 2). Willi was, from 1911, an actor in the German Theatre in New York, and later became renowned as the film director G. W. Pabst (Note 6; Photo 3).

Ernst and Viola married in 1909 as Protestants, on the day that Ernst qualified as a lawyer. His father had died in 1905, leaving each of his four surviving children sufficient private income. The young couple were part of a well-off, well-connected and diverse set of friends and relations. Ernst's brother Rudolf was a well-known pacifist, social democrat and sociologist. One sister married a soldier and the other married Ferdinand Marek, later

„Alt-Heidelberg"
„Käthi" (Frl. Viola Pabst).

75. Verlag Atelier Woelfer, Lübeck.

2. Viola Pabst as an actress, pre-1907

Austria's Minister in Prague for the whole of the period 1918-38. Berti's parents were progressive; for a time in the pre-1914 period they acted as the letter box for a Russian exile who became well-known as Leon Trotsky. Ernst died suddenly in 1933, but Viola lived until 1971, to the end a lively and theatrical person. Engelbert was born in 1910 and his brother Christian, who was to be Austrian Minister of Justice for nineteeen years, in 1916 (Note 7).

The Great War and its aftermath completely changed their expectations, but it was not really a cruel war for the Broda family and most of their friends. Even so, afterwards the war hunger was universal and resulted in Berti's despatch to Norway in 1920, where he lived with a widow and her three sons, an enduring connection. In 1921 Ernst and Viola bought a large country house, Schloss Fünfturm in Southern Styria, that through three further owners stayed in the family for fifty years. But in 1922 Ernst lost

3. Young Willi Pabst, undated. With thanks to Daniel Pabst

most of his fortune in the inflation of the period, regained some of it but then lost it again two years later. From then on life was much less secure. He was a legal adviser on films, largely for his brother-in-law, Willi. In Berti's eyes Ernst contrasted poorly with his uncles Ferdy Marek and Willi and his godfather Egon Schönhof (Photos 4,5,6).

During the Great War both Willi and Schönhof had been outside Austria. Willi was returning to Europe at the outbreak of the war when his ship was captured by the French, who interned him until 1919. This captivity saved him from the army and also made him very radical politically. His influence on Berti was profound both on his return and later. Schönhof returned in 1921; he had been captured by the Russians on the Eastern Front, and then experienced the Bolshevik Revolution. He returned to Austria a convinced communist and as a lawyer he defended members of the Austrian Communist Party in political trials. Later he was interned by the Austro-Fascists from 1934 for about two years without trial. The Nazis arrested him in 1938 on their annexation of Austria, and murdered him at Auschwitz in 1942. Berti wrote a moving memoir on him thirty years later. Berti told me that he considered himself a communist from his encounters with these men but the outward signs were not yet obvious. His real political

4. Ernst Broda 1923

activity dated from when he started university. Schönhof took Berti on mountain trips, and Berti also climbed the Triglav in Slovenia with the young Hans von Halban, who in 1941 fatefully pressed Berti to join the Tube Alloys team in Cambridge.

At school Berti studied Latin, Greek (for which he had an enduring love) and Natural History, but not English, French or Chemistry (Photo 7). Even so when he arrived in Britain in 1938 he spoke both French and English well. In the 1920s he frequently visited the Mareks in Prague and he was also invited by Willi, already a successful film director, to Berlin. He is in a crowd scene in Willi's film *Pandora's Box* with Louise Brooks, made in 1928, the year he began his chemistry studies with a year in Berlin. In an interview in 1981 Berti merely stated that he became interested in the natural sciences, but he was already very intellectually engaged. In Germany he also spent two freezing weeks working at a lignite mine for the experience of hard manual work. From 1929 to early 1931 he was back in Vienna, and then returned to Berlin.

Paul Löw-Beer, his closest and life long friend wrote after Berti's death: 'When we met in 1928 Bertl was already a convinced Marxist and judging

5. Willi Pabst, mid-1920s. With thanks to Daniel Pabst.

from his critical attitudes to the Social Democrats he considered himself a Communist. He introduced me into the very highbrow circle of Dr Schönhof, Hans Goldschmidt and others where Georg Lukacs' *History and Class-consciousness* was being studied in a private seminar. I understood very little

6. Berti (left) and Christian (right) with their cousins Erika and Gerd Obst. c.1924

and doubt whether Berti understood much of this difficult work (the content of which Lukacs in his later years considered to be false). In those years Berti was under the influence of Schlick and Carnap – the Vienna Positivist School; he considered *Materialism and Empirocriticism* by Lenin as dogmatic. We followed with great tension the disputes between Otto Neurath and Max Adler – Berti was not sure then who was right.'

Berti's own account in a brief political curriculum vitae from 1936 held in his dossier in Communist Party archives in Russia (Note 8) states that he joined the Social Democrat students in 1928, and later became a member of both the Socialist Party and the Academic Legion (Schutzbund), and was a student functionary. It continues that in the spring of 1930 he left the Social Democrats, crossing over to Free Union of Socialist Students, which became the Red Student Group. He then states that he entered the 'Pheasant' cell of the Communist Party in the autumn of 1930. After the founding of the Wieden (Fourth district) cell he transferred there and became a cell functionary, as well as being a member of the Free Union leadership.

7. Berti at 16

2

HILDE IN AACHEN

Hildegard Pauline Ruth Gerwing (Hilde) came from an assimilated Rheinland Jewish family in Aachen. Her maternal grandparents were Eduard Meyer and his wife Pauline Salomon, themselves first cousins as was often the case in such close knit groups. They married in the face of family opposition, since there was said to be mental instability in the Salomon family. Eduard and Pauline had six children of whom Elsa (Elisabeth), Hilde's mother, was the eldest. There were two sons, Felix and Georg, and three more daughters, Dora and the twins Erna and Meta (Photo 8).

Eduard had a textile business that ran into debt, and at an early age Felix took over the business and the debts. He became an inventor and an entrepreneur, and among the inventions he developed was the flow-meter, for which there were many applications. In their late teens the twins were put in an institution for a suddenly manifested supposed mental illness. Pauline believed that their condition was the result of the first-cousin marriage and she killed herself in 1910. The twins were to remain institutionalised until the Nazis murdered them in 1942. After years of struggle Felix's company, renamed RotaWerke, became very successful. He was the paterfamilias of the extended family, and came to give support to many of its members (Photo 9). Another successful relation was Arthur Eichengrün, Felix's and Elsa's first cousin. He was a chemist at Bayer before creating his own company in Berlin. There is strong evidence that he was the true creator of Aspirin but was later denied the credit by Bayer because he was Jewish.

In 1906 Elsa had married Ludwig Gerwing, the first in the family to marry a non-Jew. They married as Catholics, and my mother was born as their only child in 1911. The marriage certificate refers to him as a businessman, but previously he had been an Army officer (Photo 10). Hilde said that Felix had several times paid off his gambling debts, and then finally

8. The Meyer family, 1889. Eduard and Pauline Meyer are holding the twins Meta and Erna, and in front are from left Elsa, Dora, Felix and Georg

in 1913 obliged him to go to Argentina to start again, leaving Elsa and Hilde to follow when he was established. However with the outbreak of war in 1914 contact was lost, so that Hilde was fatherless at an early age (Photo 11). Elsa bitterly and publically reproached Felix, so that he made her leave Aachen as the price for his continued support. Elsa and Hilde then went from one spa town to another, until Hilde was placed with friends of Elsa, the devoutly Catholic Lesmeister family also in Aachen, who had eight children of their own, the youngest a month older than Hilde. Early in 1917 Elsa too killed herself, and her final wish was that Hilde should have no further contact with her natural family. By then Herr Lesmeister had died, so the eldest son-in-law became her guardian and Hilde grew up not knowing about the Meyer family in the same city.

9. Felix Meyer in his prime, undated

10. Elsa and Ludwig Gerwing, c.1910

11. Hilde and her Meyer cousins Margot (left) and Claire (right), pre-1917

For Hilde, Maria Lesmeister was her mother, and she was treated like the other children. She spoke warmly of her upbringing and particularly of Maria Lesmeister herself. She went to the local girls' Gymnasium run by nuns, and she too was a devout and enthusiastic Catholic. However in the dire economic conditions in post-War Germany, Maria Lesmeister had to sell the homes her late architect husband had built, one by one. Hilde said the household was very busy, very poor and very economical. She had many girl friends, and the family luxury was a rented tennis court to which they invited their friends (Photos 12, 13).

Felix resumed contact with Hilde in the mid-Twenties. Hilde believed that contact was made for her support because Maria Lesmeister could simply not manage without it. After getting to know Felix, Hilde also became involved with his family. His daughters Claire and Margot were slightly older than her. He also helped the Lesmeister family, including paying for a son to set up a car workshop. This son, who was always hostile

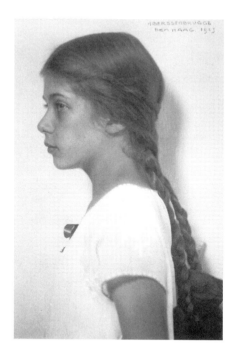

12. Hilde when in Holland to recover from malnutrition, 1923

13. Maria Lesmeister ('Mutti'), 1933

to Hilde at home, became, in her words, a vicious Nazi. At this time Hilde also became close to a nun in the Gymnasium, Sister Benedikta, who had known Hilde's mother in the period just before her suicide and told Hilde what had really happened, rather than the official version of death from pneumonia (Photo 14).

Hilde became deeply attached to her uncle Felix (Photo 15). She said that he was very loving and happy that he had access to her. He was interested in her and spent much time with her, including going together for early morning horse rides. There was also mutual respect between Maria Lesmeister and Felix. But he was paternalistic and expected to impose his will. An example occurred when Hilde was about seventeen. He held out a letter and said: 'This is from your father's lawyer. He now wants you to join him in Argentina.' She asked Felix to tell her about her father. He refused, saying that she would have to make up her own mind, but added: 'However, I must tell you that if you reply, I will never speak to you again.' So she promised to have nothing to do with her father. Probably she would have stayed anyway, but for then she accepted his autocratic use of his power. In return, Felix promised to support her at university, like his own daughters. In contrast, none of the Lesmeister family went to university.

14. Sister Benedikta, c.1926

15. Felix and Marguerite Meyer, undated

Hilde then lost her faith. One day she decided not to go to church or to pray. She was very frightened, but as nothing happened, she did the same the following Sunday. At the same time, she was angry at the vindictive treatment of Sister Benedikta when she decided to leave the convent, instancing shaving her head on her last day.

In 1929, Hilde completed school and went to university (Photo 16). She had always wanted to study medicine, but Felix vetoed this because 'being a doctor makes women cynical'. Hilde saw this as a breach of their agreement, but while outwardly accepting this veto she resolved to save so that eventually she could study medicine. She went to Freiburg to study German Literature, Art History and Sport (she held the long jump record there), to Munich and then Bonn. She was a keen canoeist on the Rhine and a skier, and she still associated with students who duelled.

A major change in her life occurred in Bonn in 1930. Until then she had no real boyfriend, but there she heard a lecture by a young psychiatrist named Gottfried Kűhnel. She got in touch with him and he introduced her to Socialism. She also fell in love with him. Kűhnel quickly became her lover; she had great misgivings about this step, but went to talk to Benedikta, who

16. Hilde, c.1931

by then was teaching. Her advice was that Hilde might as well enjoy it, because she was going to get involved anyway. So she went to live with Kűhnel and at his suggestion she worked as a volunteer in a psychiatric clinic for children. But the affair ended because Kűhnel had not told her that he was married, and his wife turned up.

Kűhnel answered many of her questions about politics and she became serious about Socialism. She also joined the Communist Youth (neither then or later was she a member of the Communist Party itself). With this new faith she went to Felix to tell him the good news. He was furious and told her to stop such nonsense. He also put a detective to work on her activities, which she did not know at the time, but she said that it would have made no difference if she had known. She said that he stopped his financial support because of her political activities and because she started to study medicine. Hilde used the money she had saved but later this became a big problem, although she gave lessons to children and had other jobs. She never, to me, held this outcome against Felix, since it was his money and she had gone against his wishes, and it never occurred to her to insist on support. There is then a gap of nearly two years in the letters from Felix to Hilde, but Hilde denied that she broke off relations with Felix. The first letter from him after this break shows that he did in fact continue payments.

Kűhnel and his wife moved to Berlin, and they suggested that Hilde should go as well. Hilde arrived in Berlin in 1930 and began her medical studies in 1931. She said that the Kűhnels tried to make her feel less bitter about his deceit, but gradually she had less to do with them. At first she lived in the household of Arthur Eichengrűn, but his wife overheard a politically charged phone conversation of Hilde's with Grete Kűhnel and, justifiably frightened of the danger such an association would have for her husband, insisted that Hilde left. Hilde recounted that at this time political life in Berlin had become quite wild, with battles between the left-wingers and the Nazis. This was when she met Berti and Paul Lőw-Beer, and also Paul's future wife Alice (Ala) and her older communist sister Beate, who were Jewish and originally from Lithuania (Photos 17, 18).

Hilde went with a man on a long trip in a sailing canoe in Dalmatia. He was Andrew D'Antal, a naturalised Briton she had met in Freiburg. In 1940 he told the British Special Branch that this was in 1932 (see later). Hilde insisted on a platonic relationship; he wished otherwise. I suppose this was before Hilde and Berti became a couple. The first dateable letter from my grandmother Viola to Hilde is of October 1932, and the first one from my father is dated 1 January 1933, so perhaps my parents became a couple in the early autumn of 1932. This is consistent with a photo of Berti and Hilde at

17. Paul Löw-Beer, c.1932

18. Alice Rabinowitch, later Löw-Beer, c.1932

Fünfturm on which Hilde wrote '1932' (Photos 19, 20). Hilde stopped the tape recording she made in 1987 at this point, saying that as Berti was then dead he could not put his side of the story. This statement partially prepared me for what I found when I went deeper into their difficult relationship, mainly through Berti's letters to her.

19. Fünfturm

20. Hilde and Berti at Fünfturm, 1932

3

ALAN IN BIRMINGHAM

Alan was born in Birmingham in 1911 as the youngest child of Walter and Minnie Nunn May. He had two brothers and a sister. Alan's father and grandfather were prosperous brassfounders. Minnie Kendall came from Truro in Cornwall, where her grandfather had been mayor. In 1913 the family moved to Barnt Green, south of Birmingham. As a child Alan had

21. The May family, c. 1917: Walter (1871-1950), Mary Annie (Minnie) 1870-1945), Edward (1897-1964), Ralph (1902-1980), Mary (1908-2000) and Alan (1911-2003). With thanks to Diana MacDonell

attacks of pneumonia and barely survived. Minnie was a believer in homeopathy, so he only had minute amounts of drugs but good nursing (Photo 21; Note 9). These illnesses made him an avid reader. He was always treated as delicate and so his schooling was mostly from governesses and later from the local vicar, before he went to King Edward's, Birmingham like his father and brothers. Alan's family was musical and sang in the church choir and, after the Great War, Walter started concerts. All young men and women had repertoires of songs to perform after dinners and at parties, and there were revues and Gilbert and Sullivan, with Walter conducting and Alan's eldest brother Ted taking major parts, and also choral productions. Alan played the piano for the family to practice their parts.

His second brother Ralph studied metallurgy at the University of Birmingham with a view to entering the family firm. He was an excellent debater and became President of the Student Union, and then of the National Union of Students. Alan borrowed his textbooks and also books on economics and politics that sowed doubts about his family's conservative views.

The family firm was damaged by fire at the end of the Great War and because Birmingham Council would not allow re-building on the same site, it moved to a modern factory elsewhere. Delays and the high cost of building led to heavy bank loans, but there was general optimism during the post-war boom. The factory started production just in time for the end of this boom. When the family firm collapsed, Ralph became Executive Secretary of the National Union of Students, a job that he held until 1939, and Alan's sister Mary took a medical secretarial post. Both Walter and Ted were in effect then sacked from their own firm through a legal manoeuvre of the other directors, but whereas Ted found a job and did well, Alan's father put his compensation into an unsuccessful milk distribution business. He then had to become a traveller for other metal firms, and the family moved to a smaller house.

King Edward's School was in the city centre. While there Alan used the Birmingham Subscription Library, of which his father was a member. This was an offshoot of the Lunar Society, founded in the mid-eighteenth century. The main book collection was on open shelves where he could browse: 'True to the traditions of the Lunar Society this contained all the radical and free-thinking classics from Tom Paine to William Morris as well as the works of Bernard Shaw and Bertrand Russell, scattered of course amongst the less provocative standard works of English literature. There was also a good collection of gramophone records and scores so that I was no longer dependent on piano arrangements to explore orchestral and chamber music. This library probably did more for my general education than King Edward's ever did.' Alan was also interested in practical work including photography and wireless.

He did quite well at school, so when the family firm collapsed he was given a scholarship. Alan wrote that he was suddenly confronted with having to make his own way in life. He became a swot, driven by fear rather than ambition, since the family plan was to article him to an accountant, but he did well enough to continue in the Upper Sixth. His description of this shows how good an education could be had then in some civic schools: 'The top maths set that year was quite outstanding. At the top were R. A. Lyttleton, A. F. Devonshire and J. H. Pearce with myself and F. W. Mottershead coming close behind. There were about a dozen more who were reasonable mathematicians. Lyttleton became a theoretical astronomer of the first rank and Devonshire made his name by an epoch-making paper on the theory of liquids with his PhD supervisor. We were given a problem paper to be worked on over every weekend that had about twenty of the toughest questions in scholarship papers covering what we had done in class and a good deal more. The top trio regularly got a mark of 95-98%, whereas I sometimes managed to break the 90% barrier, but was more often in the 80-90% bracket, usually because I just could not crack one of the problems. We had a small study of our own, just large enough to take a ping-pong table and some desks. Usually two of us would be playing while the others worked on problems. It was noisy, with plenty of argument, not at all the cloistered calm usually regarded as essential for mathematical thought. We became used to thinking out loud, throwing out ideas freely, and not being afraid of having them shot down. Although I spent a great deal of my time at mathematics I regarded physics as my main subject, but here by contrast I had virtually no competition. I did a great deal of reading. I came across Jeans' *Kinetic Theory of Gases* and was struck by the passage in which all the co-ordinates and momenta of all the molecules of a gas are represented by a point in 6N dimensional space, N being the number of molecules. Having had difficulty with the 4-dimensional space of relativity I found this quite breathtaking. There was a prize essay competition in science, and I offered an essay on radioactivity. I chose this because I had just read a Rutherford lecture of 1922. I then found Rutherford's own books, as well as other classics such as Hevesy and Paneth, Makower and Geiger and others. I won the prize, but more importantly I began early to know the serious literature on nuclear physics.

'In 1929 I entered for the (Cambridge) scholarship examinations. Every Saturday morning we sat a mock examination under strict examination conditions. King Edward's was then in deadly rivalry with Manchester Grammar School in the scholarship stakes. Besides the mathematicians there was a strong classics entry headed by J. Enoch Powell who was quite exceptional. I was awarded a Minor Scholarship at Trinity Hall, my third choice. It was clear that I had scraped home by a rather narrow margin, but I was safe from having to earn my living by becoming an accountant. We were released from examination pressure and could relax with the pleasant feeling that our academic future was assured for the next few years. It was a time for wider reading, and exploring ideas. I read a good deal of quantum theory and astrophysics and made an attempt at general relativity theory. I also made a brief return to debating. My reading of Shaw and Russell had given me a taste for paradox and voicing unorthodox opinions, and I had a certain success in debate as I found I could speak extempore while others spoke from carefully prepared notes. Later I was cured of any further ambition for debating and at Cambridge I never opened my mouth at the Union.

'In 1929 Ralph was married to Edith (Jackie) Johnson, a young actress. They set up home in Bloomsbury with a minimum of furniture. It became a convenient *pied à terre* for me when I was in Cambridge. It was a meeting place of the junior and more poverty-stricken sections of the university and theatre worlds, and I quickly felt at home there.

'During my last years at school I had become more radical. This was the time when books about the Great War such as *All Quiet on the Western Front* and *Journey's End* came out and people who had spent relatively secure lives at home realised how horrible it had been for those who had fought. They also began to realise that the causes of the War and the way it had been fought were deeply discreditable to the British Establishment. This feeling that the Establishment was not to be trusted, that any officially sponsored line of thought had to be critically examined, grew on me. I felt that my generation had been "conned" about the purposes of the War, about the peace settlement, about the Russian Revolution, the General Strike and above all about the Depression. There were so many examples of deliberate deception, such as the forged Zinoviev letter on which the Tories won the election of 1923, and the "Hang the Kaiser" election after the war, that the ruling class had lost all claims to trust and respect. I was still looking for a basic philosophy and foundation for an understanding of these questions, but I was sure that it must be very different from the conventional middle class conservatism in which I had been reared.'

PART 2

THE THIRTIES

4

ALAN AS CAMBRIDGE UNDERGRADUATE
1930-33

Alan settled on taking Part I of the Maths Tripos and then Natural Sciences Part II in Physics, which allowed two years for the latter compared with the normal single year (Photo 22). The Part I work had mostly been covered at school, but he had a weekly session with a maths coach. He also went to Part I Physics practicals that were based on manuscripts that prescribed in detail how the 'experiment' was to be conducted, a training in the scales and arpeggios of physics. To keep up his interest in Physics he went to lecture courses given by such great names as J. J. Thomson, F. W. Aston and C. T. R.

22. Alan at Matriculation, 1930. In the upper row are Alan (with glasses), Devonshire, Harvey and Pateman (at extreme right). Trinity Hall, Cambridge, with permission

Wilson. Wilson was famous as the inventor of the cloud chamber, a device in which a sudden expansion of moist air caused tiny droplets of water to condense on the ions in the tracks of fast particles which had just traversed the chamber. This instrument enabled the tracks to be seen, photographed and measured, and played a vital part in all later developments of atomic physics.

Alan then began to spend more time with friends in his own college, and especially with another physics student, Frederik Pateman, who was working class. He was widely read, and had a grasp of history and literature that was both broader and deeper than Alan's. He was also already a militant Socialist in touch with all the left wing activities in Cambridge. This was a new world for Alan, and their late night arguments had a great influence on him. He was soon immersed in reading the great classics of Socialism, and Marxism. He had been attracted to physics by the possibility of finding a consistent comprehensive picture of the physical universe, and now began to see that it might be possible to understand politics and history in the light of some grand synthesis, of which Marxism seemed to offer at least a first approximation. But he was not impelled to plunge into politics. Alan was convinced that his main gift was in physics, and that this gift was precious, and could easily be lost if he did not concentrate on it. He felt strongly about politics, but also felt that his only chance of reaching a position of any influence would be by becoming a first-rate scientist. So he read political pamphlets and attended meetings, but did little actively.

During those years the political scene was depressing and menacing for Alan. At home the Labour Government was forced out of office by the financial crisis in 1931 and succeeded by the National Government under MacDonald and Baldwin with severe cuts in all social services. Abroad, the rise of Hitler in Germany continued, while Japan's attack on China and the impotence of the League of Nations in the face of this challenge showed how weak the provisions were against the outbreak of another war. Meanwhile Fascism was in power in Italy and in Austria Social Democracy in Vienna was surviving precariously between the bloodbaths of 1927 and 1934. For Alan, only the Soviet Union offered the hope of a better future. There were many things about the Soviet Union which he found difficult to accept, and he did not regard it as a paradise on earth, or even as a fully realised socialist society, but for him the promise was there, and only there.

Alan wrote: 'I had come up to Cambridge with very vague left wing opinions, mainly centred on the danger of another World War. My generation had lived through the horrors of the first World War. Many of us had lost brothers or fathers in it, most probably believing that they were fighting for noble causes. They had come to realise that these "noble purposes" were jingoistic propaganda. We now saw the frantic scheming of rival imperialistic powers for markets, and the relentless drive towards war of the armament firms. The League of Nations had promised to be a safeguard against another World War, but it was manifestly hamstrung by the same forces that had caused the last War. There seemed little hope of avoiding a repeat of 1914-18 and what little hope there was lay with those forces which weakened the world capitalist system, and might eventually replace it by a rational and humane society.' If contact with Pateman had removed the prejudice that only middle and upper class people could be really cultured, Alan found the upper class who then dominated student life arrogant and philistine. But, he wrote: 'If I hated the established order in British politics, I had the greatest admiration for the leaders of Cambridge physics. I had now seen Rutherford and "his Boys", and nothing would satisfy me but to join their ranks. So my politics, although passionately felt, had to be relegated to my spare time.'

There were other things competing for this spare time. His Director of Studies held gramophone concerts in his rooms to which students were invited and it was there that Alan got to know the Beethoven quartets really well, by repeated hearings and following the minature score. There were also live concerts and the Festival Theatre, where Alan saw for the first time those Ibsen plays which he had read, Gogol's *The Government Inspector*, Shaw and Brecht. There were also many classic films to be seen. When Cambridge palled he visited Jackie and Ralph in London (Photo 23).

In July 1931 Alan took the Maths Tripos, Part I, and got a First. He could now concentrate on Physics. The Long Vacation was spent doing some coaching and reading – Eddington on *The Constitution of the Stars*, and the new edition of *Radiations from Radioactive Substances* by Rutherford, Chadwick and Ellis, the bible of Cambridge nuclear physics. He also tried to improve his scientific German with Herman Weyl's *Raum-Zeit-Materie* (Space, Time, Matter), in a renewed attempt at General Relativity, and Sommerfeld's *Wellen Mechanische Erganzungsband,* the New Testament of Schrödinger's wave mechanics and Heisenberg's matrix mechanics that were

23. Alan, c.1932
© Swaine

revolutionising physics. Then there was the serious business of tackling the Natural Sciences Tripos, Part II.

As no-one at Trinity Hall was qualified to tutor in Physics, P. M. S. Blackett (Note 10; Photo 24) was brought in to teach Alan and the two other physics students. Blackett was also giving the lecture course on Optics, and was running the practical class, so they had a great deal of contact with him. Alan found him a truly inspiring teacher, especially in his Optics course. For Alan it remained one of the most beautiful and satisfying parts of physics and he always enjoyed teaching it and dealing with optical equipment. Blackett was then in the middle of taking the prolonged series of cloud chamber photographs of cosmic rays in a magnetic field that led him (with G. P. S. Occhialini) to confirm the discovery of the positive electron. He was a meticulous experimental worker, always insisting on faultless technique. He once said in a tutorial: 'If you find something in your results which is a little odd, you must be quite sure that it is not something wrong with your equipment, or your technique. No new discovery can be made with clumsy or unreliable technique.' In the practical class he took the opportunity of instilling these principles. The experiments were as far as possible genuine experiments, not carefully scripted repetitions of a standard exercise, but

24. P. M. S. Blackett © Godfrey Argent Studio. The Royal Society, with permission

each involved the mastering of some basic skill – photography, glass blowing, AC bridge measurements, and in none of these was any sloppy technique tolerated.

Each week Alan and his colleagues had an essay to write, each on a different topic. At the next tutorial they read these while Blackett smoked his pipe, and he would comment. He would suggest topics for the next essay and then talk about some topic which he was concerned about – once it was the problem of designing a large electromagnet, and how the design might depend upon the relative cost of copper and iron; another time it would be the optical problem of designing cameras which could measure accurately the slight curvature of the tracks in his chamber, and how this was related to the theory of diffraction and optical resolution which they had had in his lectures. Or he would discourse on the difficulty everyone in physics now had in coping with the new ideas of wave mechanics, and the matrix mechanics of Heisenberg, how one really needed to go back to study the theory of partial differential equations, especially the great text of Courant and Hilbert on which the Göttingen school of mathematical physicists had been trained. It was teaching by inspiration rather than instruction, but given Blackett's powers of inspiration it worked. He had a very great influence on all the students who worked under him. His research students could be readily picked out by the gestures and inflections of the voice which they had picked up from him.

Alan happened to be sitting in the Cavendish library when Blackett came in with P. A. M. Dirac, and they started to discuss the positive electron tracks that Blackett and Occhialini had found in their cosmic ray photographs, and the problem of how these were connected with the positive particles, or rather anti-particles, which Dirac had predicted from his relativistic quantum theory of 1928. Alan found it immensely exciting to be present, so to speak, at the birth of the positive electron.

Rutherford's lectures on The Constitution of Matter covered atomic theory, radioactivity and the basic facts of nuclear physics, which Rutherford and his school were at that moment uncovering. 'He was a dramatic lecturer, knowing how to emphasise a point by suddenly dropping his voice to a whisper, and the drama was heightened by the knowledge that he was fresh from discussions with his team at which the next step to unravel these problems was being planned. Indeed anyone passing his office would very likely hear his voice raised in the more emphatic parts of such discussions, and see even such figures as Chadwick or (Mark) Oliphant emerge looking more than a little crestfallen. Rutherford was a very busy man and so he would hand over whole sections of his course to one or other of his "Boys". Then we would have Chadwick or Oliphant or Cockcroft each on the particular line on which they were pursuing research. This was with less drama, but more material was covered. Then there were the Wednesday tea-time Cavendish Physical Society discussions at which either a local or a visiting physicist would talk. Thus we heard Milliken and Bohr. But the greatest visiting physicist was Einstein who gave a lecture in the Senate House in May 1932. He had probably anticipated an intimate talk to a group of professional mathematical physicists. He spoke in a quiet voice in a mixture of German and English and wrote his equations on the blackboard using gothic script. The vast audience listened in silent respect but total lack of understanding. The subject under discussion was of first-class importance, but even more important was the tribute paid to the greatest living physicist (Photos 25, 26, 27).

'In May of 1932 I went home for my twenty-first birthday. The celebrations were somewhat muted, owing to the family financial crisis.

25. Lord Rutherford. The Royal Society, with permission

Indeed the main purpose of the pressing invitation I had received to return home turned out to be the winding-up of a trust which Father had established as part of the marriage settlement in 1896. This could not be done until all the children of the marriage had attained their majority. I was the last obstacle to releasing the money locked up in this trust, and so on my

26. James Chadwick
© Godfrey Argent Studio. The Royal Society, with permission

27. John Cockcroft
© Godfrey Argent Studio, The Royal Society, with permission

birthday we all went to the family lawyer in his office and signed away our inheritance. These family reunions were occasions for a family conference, at which the contributions each of us should make to the family home were discussed. Ted had by far the largest income, but he now had two children, a large house, and a Rolls-Royce, and he pleaded with all the eloquence he could muster (and that was considerable, experienced actor and salesman that he was) that his contribution should be much less than that of the others on whom fate had not thrust all these burdens. Ralph pleaded an exiguous income, and a very uncertain future, expensive life in London, etc. Mary could justly point out that as the only one living in the family home she was making a contribution in keeping it going in kind. I simply laid my meagre scholarship allowance on the table, which produced an embarrassed silence. All this was an extreme humiliation for Father, who must have felt like the family failure rather than its head and fount of authority. Afterwards Mother would tearfully thank all of us for our help. It was not a cheerful affair to look forward to.'

At the end of the academic year, June 1932, Alan sat the unofficial college exams for students not sitting University examinations. He had not prepared seriously and did badly. So he went home determined to do some serious work so as to be certain of a First Class in the finals. Unemployment figures were climbing to the peak of 2.7 million, and an interview with the university Appointments Officer convinced him that only a First Class degree could save him from schoolmastering, or worse, for life. The vacation was devoted to mastering physics, which for these purposes was defined by the content of past examination papers with a reasonable extrapolation for the next year in the light of the predelictions of the examining board.

On returning to Cambridge they had a different tutor, the geophysicist E. C. Bullard. His methods were quite different to Blackett's. He would produce an old examination paper, and proceed to work through it question by question, writing out all the mathematics in full at prodigious speed. After an hour they had outline answers to all the questions, together with comments on likely pitfalls and traps into which an unwary candidate could fall. Then they were given another paper with which to do the same in preparation for the next week. It was a frank reversion to the examination training techniques of King Edward's, but also a convincing display of the kind of total mastery of the whole range of classical physics which they were expected to attain.

In the examinations Alan had some luck. In the paper on electromagnetism there was a question on the radiation field from a dipole, a topic on which he had read original papers, and knew the standard material and a good deal more. On the night before the nuclear physics paper he had read a recent paper by Chadwick on the disintegration of nitrogen by alpha particles and several points about it intrigued him. Next day, just this topic appeared as a question. Finally in the practical examination, he noted that E. V. Appleton was an examiner, and had carefully revised his alternating current techniques and measuring circuits. This foresight was duly rewarded by a question on this, so when Appleton himself came round he could discuss the circuit he had set up without too much hesitation. The upshot was a First indeed, so acceptance as a research student at the Cavendish and a grant were now automatic. Meanwhile, Alan noted, the world had not stopped: Hitler was installed as Chancellor of the Reich, the Reichstag had burned down, the Disarmament Conference had come to an ignominious end, the Japanese had triumphed over the Chinese and what efforts the League of Nations had brought itself to make against them, and the National Government of Britain was still led by Ramsay MacDonald, who was visibly tottering towards senile ineptitude.

5

BERTI AND HILDE IN GERMANY AND AUSTRIA 1931-35

Berti resumed his Berlin studies in 1931. In his 1984 letter to me, Paul Lőw-Beer continued: 'In Berlin Berti continued his studies with great zeal and made fast progress, though he had soon joined the German Communist Party and became an active member of the Kostufra, the students' organisation of the Party. Those comrades whom he liked there he befriended deeply and much later re-established contacts with them, as you will see from his correspondence. As you know he had really no money at all; it is a fact, not just a good story, that he lived on the rolls and oils at Aschingers, a restaurant chain in Berlin, where rolls and oil were then supplied free even with the cheapest meals and therefore placed on the tables. In Berlin there were to Berti's benefit many Aschingers. In those which Berti had frequently visited free oil and later free rolls disappeared. On Saturdays Berti was nearly always invited by Willi Pabst, and, camel-like, he managed to eat there for a whole week. Having finished the organic laboratory in record time and done his exams he began his thesis in 1931 at the Institute of Physical Chemistry, Bunsen-strasse, then headed by Professor Bodenstein. Professor Gűnther was his mentor – Berti kept in contact with this upright and liberal man to the death of the professor. The same applies to Berti's friendship with many other members of the Institute. I am not sure to what extent Berti took part in cultural life in this period when Berlin was the centre of radical culture in Europe. Presumably he was too deeply immersed in his studies to find time (and money) for the theatre, but enjoyed films and of course did a lot of reading.'

Money was a constant preoccupation for Berti, and he lived hand-to-mouth, probably doing some tutoring. His letters to Hilde have references to money from Uncle Willi, for whom his father did some legal work. 'GWP has no money', 'The treasure fleet has arrived', 'Waiting for Willi' and 'absolutely no money' are some remarks in his letters to Hilde. This continued when Willi moved to Hollywood for about a year. Berti also wrote to Hilde from Vienna that things were unpleasant at home – many conflicts, raised voices, in the end about money.

Berti's own summary of his political career (Note 8) states that on his return to Berlin he transferred to the German Party, and became a cell functionary with special responsibilities as a propagandist and course leader, as well as being a student functionary. He then became leader of the Berlin student group, and in 1932 he was national leader of the Communist students in Germany.

Two events in Vienna had long term consequences for Berti. On a short visit there in June 1931 he was arrested at a street demonstration, and the charge remained active until his return to Vienna in 1933, when he was given his first conviction and a suspended sentence of a week in prison. He now had an Austrian police file. Also in 1931, he and his younger brother Christian were identified as political activists through a shooting incident that was widely reported. *The Times* and *The Daily Telegraph* accounts of the Semmelmann case constitute item 1 of MI5's extensive file on Berti. The abridged extract from *The Daily Telegraph* reads:

POLICE FIND "RED " CENTRE AT WEALTHY MAN'S FLAT. SON AS GO-BETWEEN

The police have made a sensational discovery of a Communist news centre in the fashionable Prince Eugen Strasse. The first clues were obtained among papers taken from an ex-Communist spy named Semmelmann who was shot dead in Vienna last month by a Jugoslav Communist agent named Piklovitch at the moment when Semmelmann was about to sell the secrets of the Soviet espionage system to the Jugoslav authorities. On examining Semmelmann's documents the police were surprised to find papers relating to the flat of Dr Broda, the owner both of the Prince Eugen Strasse flat and the so-called 'Five Tower Castle' in Styria.

'Red' Orders Found
A watch was kept for several weeks on the Vienna flat, and revealed

that Communist instructions were reaching this place by various means, including the post. The agent who received and re-despatched them proved to be Christian Broda, the 14-year old son of Dr Broda, and the lad has admitted to the police that he got them from his brother in Berlin. Dr Broda and this elder son are absent, and so far have not been traced. This Communist centre apparently dealt only with propaganda and espionage outside Austria. The police are unable to discover the moving spirits, and have been able only to arrest subordinates. Masses of Communist material were also found at Five Tower Castle.

Capt. Miller, Scotland Yard, noted on the file: 'It subsequently transpired that the elder was a registered member of the Austrian Communist Party. The family's town house at Prinz Eugen Strasse 14 was also visited by the police who found communist literature and papers relating to the dissemination of communist propaganda. Neither he (Ernst) or his sons were arrested.' I have no information how Ernst himself felt about his firebrand sons and the Semmelmann affair, or how that was dealt with between the family and the police.

Item 1a of 12 July 1932 is an intercepted letter between two Englishmen who were of interest to MI5: 'Cross reference to intercepted letter from Arthur Henry Ashford Wynn to David Haden Guest mentioning Engelbert Broda: "The address of the Reichsleiter of German Communist students is Engelbert Broda, Landsberg, Berlin-Grunewald, Hubertus-allee 22." ' Haden Guest was killed in Spain in the Civil War; Arthur Wynn was identified in 2009 as a recruiter for the Russians. These were the only MI5 entries on Berti until 23 July 1938. Berti told me that at this time, to his eternal regret, he had once attended a political event rather than accept what turned out to be an unique chance to meet Albert Einstein socially.

In writing about Hilde and Berti the political context is a matter of record, but there are problems in describing their own activities and their relationship. One is Hilde's refusal to give an account on tape of her life with Berti. Another is that Berti's many letters to her during their several long periods of separation in the Thirties are usually undated, were often oblique and never discussed politics. Berti would have regarded the politics as obvious, and assumed that the letters would be opened by security authorities.

An exception from 1933 was when he wrote ironically that Hilde must be proud now that her (foster) brother was in the SS, and that she could be part of the New Germany. Third, I don't have her letters to him. Although Hilde never wrote enough for Berti's needs, his letters show that she did write. But none of her letters from the Thirties and Forties or other personal ones to him from this period were among the papers he left. Among several other possibilities, Berti might have destroyed Hilde's letters, or they could have been among his papers that were taken and never returned when he was interned in London in 1939. Only two letters from that period from my mother, probably from 1932 and 1941, survive as her drafts or copies, but I don't know whether these were actually sent.

The 1932 letter, at the start of their relationship, set out at length her fears at becoming involved with Berti. It was addressed to him, and compared the good, upstanding and admirable Berti with Gottfried Kűhnel. She plainly still loved Gottfried but she committed herself to Berti because she admired his qualities and his political engagement. In the same envelope were scraps of paper on which she told herself she did not want to continue with Gottfried. Hilde was just twenty-one, beautiful, an orphan on strained terms with her uncle Felix, in a strange city, politically vulnerable, badly let down by an older married man, and probably seeking an anchor. This set the tone of the subsequent relationship. When they met, Berti was just twenty-two and also inexperienced, and he referred in early letters to loving only her, and to only seeing another Viennese communist, Eva Kolmer, in company. A reference to Gottfried shows that Berti knew of that relationship. Perhaps he believed that he could win Hilde's true love, and perhaps he did for a time. He had decided that this was the relationship for him, and though he qualified his love sometimes, he was generally firm about that.

Then on 2 May 1933 Berti wrote to Hilde: 'I have received a very lovely letter from you. I want to kiss you very lovingly. My father has died suddenly. I go to Vienna early tomorrow morning. Although in recent years we had only a neutral relationship, the news has still affected me a lot. Even though his whole life had so little youth and freshness about it one always had the feeling with him as with his dead brother – at least I had it – that he wasn't finished with life. Perhaps you can not imagine it, but this nervous drive for false activity was a sign of it. We should talk about it again. My dear dear Hilde, I would be terribly glad to have a little time alone with you. Might I perhaps fetch you on the bike on Sunday from a medieval city, Würzburg or another one, and bring you slowly to Berlin in the sunshine? Write to me immediately in Vienna, and give me a firm meeting point and a time, if you would like that. I would then just telegram you from Vienna my agreement. I long very much for the dandelion meadow, which you must show me exactly.

'Naturally I don't want to make any false judgements – but I am very sorry about my father. I hope Mother bears it well; on the phone she wept a lot. There was after all a lot with the old times that bound them. My dear wife, I long so much for you on a meadow. Altogether, you, not within walls. I will drive you very well on the motorbike. I'll write to you again from Vienna. My love, I thank you very much for the letter. Yours (how gladly yours!) Berti.

Write an affectionate letter to Mutti, OK?'

It is striking that he refers to Hilde as his wife, even though they only married in September 1935.

On the national stage Hitler's was the largest party in the Reichstag by July 1932, he became Chancellor on 30 January 1933, and the Reichstag Fire was on 27 February, followed by the arrest and later incarceration in concentration camps of many of the Communist leaders. In the following elections in March, the Nazis and Nationalists gained a majority in the Reichstag, and Germany continued on its fateful path. The parties on the Left were riven with sectarian struggles, had underestimated the Nazi danger, and were now paying for this. Also in March, the Austrian Chancellor Engelbert Dollfuss suppressed Parliament and there were anti-Jewish attacks on shops in Vienna. In contrast, Franklin Delano Roosevelt was inaugurated for his first term in March. Hilde told me that her task for the Party following the arrests was to accompany one of the very few leaders still at liberty from one safe house to another, going ahead to that night's quarters for him in case it was a trap. She said that she learned a lot from her charge, an expert on agriculture. But on the hundredth day he gave her the slip to visit his wife, and as a result was caught in a police trap. It would be interesting to establish how accurate her recall was.

Berti was also in trouble. Paul Löw-Beer recounted: 'Engelbert Broda and I were the first students to be arrested on University premises because we were communists. In May 1933 communists were being arrested, but it was still a relatively uncommon event. Engelbert Broda was half-Jewish and Protestant and didn't count as Jewish (Paul himself was Jewish). We were taken to a general police prison, the so-called Alex on the Alexander-platz. It was an enormous shock for us because of the atmosphere of fear that we experienced. From there the Gestapo took people for interrogation in the Prinzregenten-strasse, and there they were also tortured. It was the time when communists were particularly being hunted; we were communists but we were also foreigners. We too were interrogated, but not beaten. The interrogation revealed nothing and we were also not forced to give the names of others. I don't know what I would have said under torture, but I wasn't tortured. It was alleged that on an excursion to the Ruhr-gebiet we had done communist agitation among the workers. The police prison was overflowing. The veteran police officials were reasonable to us, but all the time men were brought in and showed the others their black and bloody backs. They had been tortured by the Gestapo. In the fourteen days that we spent in prison only a few were released but many went to concentration camps. But we were Austrian and relatively well connected, and that certainly saved us from torture and concentration camps. Through the efforts of my father we were released after fourteen days and expelled from Germany. Engelbert Broda returned to Vienna and I went to Prague.' (Note 11). As Paul acknowledged elsewhere it was Hilde who energetically mobilised Paul's father and also Berti's uncle Ferdy Marek, the Austrian Minister in Prague, to effect their release by a combination of financial and diplomatic influence.

Berti later stated that his time in Berlin and the increasing shadow of Naziism over Austria made him realise how deeply rooted he was in Austria's history and mentality, something which, without the Nazis, he might not have realised so soon. This emotional attachment has been widely commented on. When Berti returned to Vienna he met the new Director of the Physical Chemistry Institute, Hermann Mark, a young Austrian who had worked in Germany and then taken the job on learning that he had no future in Germany because he was half Jewish. He was a pioneer of the chemistry of polymers, including cellulose and rubber. Berti always admired Mark and was very grateful to him when he accepted him into his lab. Moreover, Mark allowed Berti to include his Berlin research work in his thesis, so that he completed a thesis of two parts, and was examined in September 1934. The two topics were first, the effect of X-rays on ammonium persulphate and second, studies on the viscosity and osmotic properties of large polymers in solution (Note 12).

A letter from Felix Meyer to Hilde in May 1933, apparently after a two year gap, shows that he had continued her allowance without interruption since she had started at Freiburg. This is a different version from Hilde's, and a later letter suggests that the money was paid through Maria Lesmeister. He wrote that, as she knew, everything had developed very differently from how they had expected. He had kept his promise to her but foresaw the time when it would no longer be possible, and also that payments were becoming more difficult as there are other relatives who would need money more than before. He asked her whether she could manage with less, but he also wrote that he would honour his promise as long as he could and that he did not want her to starve. In the same letter he reported the marriage of his elder daughter, as if Hilde had not been in close contact, and added: 'perhaps both politically and in business it will get much worse, and then everything is finished for the people I support, as well as for me, who supports so many. One should not be downcast, but also one should remain responsibly aware.' Claire had married John Hennig, the son of a Protestant pastor, and with the imminent introduction of laws prohibiting marriage between Jews and non-Jews Hennig had insisted that they marry at once.

Hilde's instant reply elicited a response from Felix: 'Your sweet lines and your willingness to bear a reduction pleased me very much, and I also gladly note your gratitude. It is a rare virtue that hopefully you will retain. I don't intend to make it 100 Marks, but propose that you continue to get 200 Marks and economise as if I had cut it. You will then hopefully add to your savings, and if a time comes when I can't continue payments, then you can keep your head above water for a time. I hope our exchange of letters shows you how things are going and where you stand.' Felix made his last regular payment in July 1934, having honoured in full his initial promise.

In his letters from Vienna to Hilde in Aachen in October 1933, Berti wrote that he was working very hard and liked the independence that he was given in the lab. He reassured her that he loved her, but was glad that theirs was not a dependent relationship and was pleased that she could continue studying in Germany. In other letters he described his daily routine as including a daily evening visit to Favoriten, a working class district of Vienna. The Russian dossier shows that this was for Party activities, and these continued, with a short leave granted by the Party because Christian was very ill in the summer of 1934. Berti held the post of Privat-Assistent to Mark and supervised a research student until May 1935, when there was an interruption for what Mark later referred to as 'the political situation'.

Hilde left Berlin for the less dangerous city of Würzburg for the winter semester 1933-34, and met Berti at Christmas in Prague. He gave her Uncle Ferdy's address, but told her on no account to write to him there, presumably so as not to embarrass his uncle. Berti's letters show that she was depressed in Würzburg and not well. With a bit more money himself from his earnings, Berti offered to send her some. Not for the last time over the next fifteen years, Berti wrote her a tough letter upbraiding her for talking of not wanting to live. He was very much of the 'pull yourself together' school and never so far as I know experienced true depression, whatever his difficulties. I think it was in Würzburg where the landlady's daughter was waiting at the street corner to warn Hilde that the police or Nazis were waiting for her. After her semester at Würzburg Hilde moved to Austria and from March 1934 she was registered as resident in the Broda family home in Vienna.

In February 1934 there was an uprising of the Socialists in Vienna against the Dollfuss regime, in effect a civil war. Berti never wrote about this but Eduard Rabovsky, another Austrian Communist, stated in his memoirs that after the uprising he and Berti hid together for several weeks with a family in the Thirteenth District. Berti did tell me of one such period, but said it was so miserable that he had completely blanked it out from his memory. By now Berti would have known many of the young Communists in Vienna as well as Eva Kolmer, perhaps including Litzi Friedmann, who married Kim Philby in February 1934, and Edith Suschitzky, soon to be Edith Tudor Hart, of whom more later. He would also have been adept at the secrecy involved in being a serious Communist.

According to Hilde, there were also elements of farce. At one point Mark interceded with Dollfuss, a war-time brother officer on the Italian front, on behalf of Berti and also a right wing student when both were detained. Then, Viola asked Hilde to visit both Berti and Christian in prison, since it was such a beautiful day, and she herself wanted to go skating, at which she was outstanding.

However, in July 1934 Dollfuss was gunned down by Austrian Nazis in his office, and was replaced by Kurt von Schuschnigg, who remained in power until 1938. There were many arrests, including that of Egon Schönhof.

Both Berti and Hilde were enthusiastic travellers (Photo 28). Berti had been to Spain in 1930, and Hilde was in Dalmatia in 1932. They used Berti's motorcycle, and his letters are full of allusions to past trips together, to excursions from Vienna into Hungary or to the mountains, and they are even more full of dreams of places to go to. Particularly when he was in Vienna completing his thesis and Hilde was in Würzburg, Berti wrote of his determination to go on a long journey. In the space of a few letters, he mentioned Greece, Santorini, Ohrid, Albania, Etna, saltpetre deserts, the footsteps of Humboldt, the eagles of the Andes, Ticino, the Carpathians, Olympia, the Gran Sasso di Italia, the Lovcen in Montenegro, and the Wildespitze in South Tirol. In one purple passage he wrote about clear light – the Altiplano of Peru, Siberia, the golden sands of Mongolia, the view from Portugal to the west, a mirror-like lake, anemones on the Triglav, albatrosses,

28. Hilde, Berti, and Christian (on left) on The Gross-Glockner, Austria's highest mountain, c.1933

Humboldt, Herwegh (a poet), the dead Communist Karl Liebknecht, and of her, and the wind through her hair. Many years later Berti wrote to me of the romance of such distant places, also seen for instance in Brecht's writings, for those in repressive Germany and Austria. In 1934 they did indeed travel. They were in Corsica, and they went down the Danube to Budapest by canoe, and on to Bulgaria. They also visited Lake Ohrid, where Albania, Yugoslavia and Greece met. It seems extraordinary that with the political turmoil in Germany and Austria, and Berti's intense involvement in both politics and science, they still made time for travel.

Hilde then went with Ala to the University of Graz for her first semester in Austria, in the winter of 1934-35. One teacher was the physiologist Otto Loewi, shortly to win a Nobel Prize, but then imprisoned by the Nazis in 1938, and made to pay over his prize money as a ransom so that he and his family could leave Austria. Ala and Hilde had a very cold room through a very cold winter. But they were close to Fünfturm, and Berti's aunt and uncle in Graz gave them food. They hitch hiked together to Vienna at intervals to see Berti and Paul Löw-Beer, and then transferred to study in Vienna. A letter from Viola to Berti in June 1935 refers ominously to Hilde being unwell; perhaps this was the first manifestation of the TB that she developed.

Berti went to prison for a month in June 1935, and that summer he was again in deep trouble. In late July, smugglers bringing communist literature across the border from Bohemia were intercepted by Austrian border guards, and revealed their destination as a flat in Vienna. A trap was set, and when Berti called on the flat he was identified and detained like previous visitors. He then jumped up and escaped down the tenement stair, pursued by police shouting that they would shoot. This became one of my favorite bedtime stories. He joined Hilde in Fünfturm and awaited the police. When they came he escaped into the forest, where Hilde met him at a pre-arranged tree with his papers and money, and he went to Czechoslovakia.

In September 1935 they married under dramatic circumstances. Hilde had been diagnosed as suffering from TB and so had to go to a sanatorium. This had to be one in Germany, since there it could be paid for by Felix Meyer, who could not send money abroad. But there was a real danger of her being arrested by the Gestapo because of her previous political activities. Berti and Hilde had intended to marry at some time, but this new situation made it urgent to marry quickly, so that Hilde could travel with a new name and an Austrian passport. Berti had to come from Czechoslovakia for the wedding, but the publication of the banns might have brought the police on his track. So he came a day before the arranged day and persuaded the pastor of the Protestant Church that Hilde had to go as soon as possible to the sanatorium. The wedding duly took place a day earlier than advertised, Berti returned to Czechoslovakia and Hilde eventually went to Germany.

Berti stated (Note 8) that while in Prague he ran the Party archives and that he went to the Soviet Union in December 1935. I don't know whether he decided to go for himself, or whether the Party sent him. He would have felt safe from the detention that Schönhof and many others were suffering. It was also an opportunity to see communism in action for himself and to contribute his talents, and his sense of adventure in travel would also have made it attractive. From the outset he planned for Hilde to visit him there.

It is painful for me to read how during their several separations he constantly reproached Hilde for not writing to him. This pattern of entreaty and reproach was a result of their separations, which in turn were mainly because of Berti's political engagement, which up to a point she shared. One can empathise that he was lonely, anxious (also for her) and desperate not to lose her. Separation to such an extent is not a situation most starting couples have to face, although it became common in the coming War. Hilde only became a willing letter writer in the Sixties, writing to me from Ghana. Her non-writing did not in itself mean that she did not then love Berti enough, but it created that feeling in him. In time it also made her feel guilty because his reproaches helped to make it become true.

In his letters Berti comes across as very controlling, asking questions that in his eyes required answers. He projected himself as loving but more mature. He was insistent on Hilde's health, on which he had opinions. He was fluent and sometimes poetic, throwing in occasional English phrases, and used several nicknames to sign his letters, particularly later from Russia. Apart from not getting letters from her and her health, his main subjects were their next meeting, how much he loved her, his outdoor activities, and family, with Fünfturm treated almost as a person. A book by H.G. Wells, *Marriage* (1912) appealed to him, but he hardly mentioned films except those of his Uncle Willi in a family context, even though he was always a keen film-goer. Throughout his life people recognised his superabundant energy, not least as a correspondent, and no-one found him easy to be with or was able to fulfil his expectations. I think the first words of Bertrand Russell's autobiography are also a description of Berti: 'Three passions, simple but overwhelmingly strong, have governed my life: the longing for love, the search for knowledge, and unbearable pity for the suffering of mankind'.

6

ALAN IN THE CAVENDISH LABORATORY 1933-36

In July 1933 Alan went back to Cambridge with four other graduates for an introductory course in research techniques under James Chadwick 'who, having just discovered the neutron presumably had some idea of what was required to do successful research'. They learned elementary workshop methods but even more crucial was the experience of the laboratory staff; the all-powerful chief technician Lincoln, who only removed his cloth cap when on the phone to Rutherford, and the mechanics in the workshop who might do for them the machining that was beyond their own capacity. The main result of the course was practice in extemporising working apparatus out of junk and derelict equipment. A major part was making vacuum lines and comparing different pumps and gauges. Most time was spent in chasing leaks since vacuums were increasingly important in physics, and hardly any experiment could be mounted without a vacuum component. Newer pumps were only for senior research workers such as Cockcroft and E. T. S. Walton. Chadwick occasionally looked in. He was very short sighted, and because of this used to glare at them with an expressionless face, while being told of any progress. He would sigh, mutter 'My God!', look at his watch, and be off.

Alan was then assigned to Chadwick, who in turn handed him on to two research students who had completed their PhD theses, and were tidying up the loose ends. The experiment on which H. Miller and W. E. Duncanson were engaged, and which occupied Alan for the next three years, was a continuation of the original discovery by Rutherford and Chadwick that atomic nuclei could be disintegrated by firing fast alpha particles at them. Those used were the highly energetic helium nuclei which come from many naturally occurring radioactive elements. Their energies were much higher than any available from high voltage sets or even cyclotrons until much later and they easily penetrated the Potential Barrier of the nucleus that was due to the electrostatic repulsion due to the electric charges on the nucleus and on the alpha particle. Rutherford and Chadwick found that coming away from these collisions were protons, high energy hydrogen-atom nuclei that were fairly easy to distinguish from the incident alpha particles.

These early experiments were difficult and tedious because the particles could only be detected as faint flashes of light from a zinc sulphide 'scintillation screen'. The observer sat in a darkened room for two hours to make his eyes sufficiently sensitive and then counted for another two hours while an assistant changed the experimental arrangement from time to time. All this was changed by the invention of ionisation chambers and electrical counting, in which the particles initiated a small electrical discharge in a gas in a discharge tube. The electrical impulse from this could be amplified and recorded, and then the numbers could be counted at leisure.

In the experiments which followed the pioneer work of Rutherford and Chadwick, it transpired that the protons were not all emitted with the same energy. Even when the incident alpha particles all had the same energy the emerging protons differed in energy by large amounts. At first this seemed to contradict the principle of conservation of energy, but then it was found that the protons were being emitted in distinct groups, each with a nearly homogeneous energy, and so the suggestion was that the nucleus produced in the reaction could either be in its ground state when the most energetic protons were produced, or in one of several excited states, each with a definite energy, when one or other of the lower-energy proton groups was emitted. Then it was shown that the emission of the lower-energy proton groups was accompanied by the emission of a gamma ray or photon which carried away the energy of the excited nucleus as it returned to the ground state.

All this was immensely important because it showed the same kind of system of quantum energy states, with energy jumps accompanied by photon emission, that Alan had learned to associate with the behaviour of atomic energy states. Now, this system or one very similar to it held inside the nucleus, only here the energy jumps were about a million times greater. Bohr's mastery of atomic structure resulted from the detailed analysis of the laws governing the atomic energy levels, revealed by the optical emission spectra and absorption spectra. It was therefore clear that what was needed was to collect as much data as possible about these nuclear energy levels, and look for any patterns which they might show when one compared the levels of one nucleus with another.

This was what Chadwick put to Alan in his briefing, only he was not given to long or very explicit explanations, nor did Alan need much prodding to see the point. He realised that he was in for years of rather boring systematic accumulation of data, what Rutherford sometimes referred to as 'stamp collecting', that was most unlikely to lead to anything profoundly new or startling. Also, since the apparatus was already working there was a strong bias against any innovations that would interrupt the flow of data and make fresh results difficult to compare with the old ones. Alan was rather disappointed, but there was nothing for it but to do the best job he could and to keep an eye open for any more exciting openings.

In his memoir Alan continued by describing the now hair-raising procedures involved in preparing their radioactive source derived from radium kept in a heavily contaminated room in the Cavendish, getting it to their experimental rig having issued a general warning to others whose experiments might be affected en route, and doing the actual experiments. These consisted of a set of ten minute runs with different experimental conditions. With small variations this routine occupied his working life for three years. To complete a single experimental curve took several weeks, and each element examined required several such curves. It was rather boring most of the time, but there were compensations since the Drawing Office where he worked was a meeting place, a sort of focus for several of the crucial developments in physics. Across the corridor was the original high tension set of Cockcroft and Walton with which they first demonstrated the disintegration of nuclei by artificially-accelerated particles, as distinct from the natural alpha particles Alan was using. Cockcroft and Walton were still operating this set, and their frequent minor sparks and electrical discharges sometimes played havoc with Alan's electrical recording. In the Drawing Office the major piece of equipment was the doughnut magnet designed by Cockcroft, which was being used to analyse the fine structure of alpha particle scattering. The main importance of the experiment for Alan was that it pioneered the development of electronic digital methods of counting. C. E. Wynn-Williams was mainly responsible for the circuits used and many other devices. His equipment gave an automatic print out of the results, probably for the first time ever. Rutherford was a frequent visitor to this experiment, in which he was a collaborator.

Chadwick had his experimental room adjoining the Drawing Office, and his door was just by Alan's equipment. Visitors who came to see Chadwick would sit waiting and maybe talk, even with a research student. Some visitors were only in transit, such as J. Robert Oppenheimer, and others were refugees from Nazi Germany seeking a permanent place to work. Another inhabitant of the Drawing Office in 1935-6 was A. I. Leipunski, a Russian physicist. He was not supposed to make propaganda about Russia, but he could scarcely refuse to answer questions, which he did honestly and straightforwardly. One topic was the Kapitsa case. Peter Kapitsa was a Russian physicist who had come to the Cavendish in the 1920s. His work was outstanding and Rutherford had secured funds to build a new laboratory specially designed for his experiments. Kapitsa went home every year, but in 1935 he was not allowed to return to Cambridge, presumably because the Russians thought he was too valuable an asset for their own science to be allowed to spend all his energies abroad. Naturally this caused much adverse comment in Britain, but Rutherford handled the matter with great coolness. He arranged for Kapitsa's equipment to be sent to him so that he could continue his experiments in Russia, where Kapitsa remained. Leipunski discussed this, fully aware that it would appear as a gross interference with the freedom of a scientist to work where he wished. But he was able to put forward the point of view of the Soviet Government, which would expect all its citizens, especially the most able and gifted, to devote their talents to the service of their country.

Duncanson and Miller left at the end of Alan's first year. Then Alan had a very stimulating new assistant, a young Indian research student, R. Vaidyanthan, who had entered physics via music. An itinerant musician playing the violin at weddings and other festivals, he came to the attention of the Indian Nobel Prize winner Raman, who was interested in the acoustics of traditional Indian instruments. He worked under Raman and took his MSc in musical acoustics, and then came to Cambridge for his PhD. Nuclear physics was quite new to him, but he quickly mastered the experimental techniques. It was the theory that worried him, since he was never content with explanations that did not go to fundamentals but were patchwork affairs made up of bits and pieces of mutually incompatible concepts. Vaidyanthan could name any note precisely on hearing it. He also found the Western system of keys and transposition of themes from one key to another unmusical. After a while he began to lose some of his disgust at the barbaric procedures of Western music, but he still found it strange, and the great emotional climaxes of the romantic composers left him cold. Bach appealed to him rather more; he could see the point of polyphonic music. He and Alan would play through the concertos in two piano arrangements.

Vadyanthan and Alan continued the experiments with fluorine, sodium, aluminium and phosphorus as targets. They chose these elements because each consisted essentially of a single isotope, so there was no ambiguity about which nucleus was being split. Another reason was that each of these nuclei could be regarded as built from the one before it by the addition of an alpha particle, which was regarded as very likely to be a basic building block of the nuclei. So it was interesting to see if there was any similarity in the energy levels that appeared in the results from these elements. They did find that the energy levels were nearly the same and then wrote up the results for publication. Alan also wrote an extended version for his thesis.

During this work Alan became interested in the general problem of detecting and counting particles and set out to master the literature on the various forms of counter and ionisation chamber. The theory as presented in these papers seemed rather crude, and so he started to work on a more thorough analysis of the phenomena involved. He did not get very far before his PhD thesis came to be written, but he later wrote papers based on this problem, and his studies on the design of ionisation chambers were the basis of much of his later work in the Atom Project. His thesis was approved and he managed a gruelling viva from Rutherford himself and Charles Ellis, who had replaced Chadwick as Alan's supervisor when Chadwick went to Liverpool. Ellis offered Alan a junior lectureship at King's College London, where he had just been appointed professor, and with nothing better on offer, Alan accepted.

Although Alan's own research work was rather routine, there was plenty of excitement in nuclear physics during those years. The great years of discovery at the Cavendish had been 1932 and 1933, with Cockcroft and Walton's first artificial disintegrations using particles accelerated in a high tension tube, Chadwick's discovery of the neutron, and Blackett's proof that the new positive electron was the paradoxical anti-particle of Dirac's relativistic quantum theory. Now there was the development of the cyclotron by Lawrence, the discovery of artificial radioactivity by F. and Irene Joliot-Curie, and E. Fermi's work on disintegrations by neutrons, especially the totally unexpected improvement obtained by slowing neutrons down. This was a paradox because everyone had up to that moment sought to make particles as fast as possible to produce disintegrations. All these new discoveries started abroad and Alan felt that the Cavendish was past its peak (Note 13).

Alan wrote: 'When the Joliot-Curies announced their discovery of artificial radioactivity in the *Comptes Rendus* in January 1934 I read the paper the morning it reached Cambridge and had repeated the experiment within an hour, it was that simple. Everyone was kicking themselves for not having done it before, especially (Norman) Feather, who had given a colloquium a few days before in which he discussed the very nuclear reactions which gave rise to the newly-discovered radioactive nuclei. He had shown in this paper that the nuclei would be unstable – therefore, he concluded, the reactions could not take place. No-one at the colloquium, including myself, got up and asked whether possibly the nuclei might be formed, and show their instability by decay by positive electron emission. It was a simple case of mass stupidity. The Joliot-Curies themselves were really no better; their discovery was purely accidental, and not in the least the result of an intelligently guided search for an anticipated result, as had been Chadwick's discovery of the neutron.

'Fermi's work on radioactivity produced by neutrons was a fairly obvious step – and here there was intelligent planning and foresight. Once he had started on this programme the Cavendish held back since there was a certain respect for the territorial rights of the first in the field. But when the slow neutron paradox was discovered, partly accidentally, but with a magnificently quick reaction by Fermi, and immediate grasp of what it meant, the Cambridge group jumped in. A young refugee, Maurice Goldhaber, went to Chadwick with a suggestion, and in a few days they had established the slow neutron disintegrations of lithium and boron with the emission of particles. But it was in this work that the greatest missed discovery of all occurred – Chadwick made a quick survey of as many elements as he could conveniently mount in the ionisation chamber he was using to see if any of them gave particles. Amongst the targets he tested were uranium and thorium – and he would undoubtedly have obtained the enormous pulses from fission particles which Frisch and Meitner obtained for the first time in 1939. But to avoid disturbance from the alpha particles emitted by uranium and thorium themselves Chadwick covered his targets with a thin layer of aluminium foil thick enough to stop the alpha particles – and the fission particles too. This was just bad luck.'

Chadwick was trying to persuade Rutherford to build a cyclotron, and to establish a more varied and powerful stock of equipment ready for use in attacking any problem which might arise. But Rutherford was very reluctant to embark on 'big physics'. He had done all his best work with very simple means, and his attachment to these was not just a Cavendish joke, but a fundamental source of weakness as physics became more and more mechanised and automated. A symptom of this was the departure of leading members of the Cavendish team. Blackett went to Birkbeck College in 1933, and a large factor in that was his treatment by Rutherford. Chadwick left for Liverpool in 1935, largely because he saw the urgent need for a cyclotron, which he set about building with help from Cockcroft, leading to a quarrel with Rutherford for his working in this way for an 'outside firm' while still at the Cavendish. 'In 1937 Oliphant went to Birmingham, also to construct his own cyclotron, and last and probably least important, Ellis went to King's College London with no cyclotron, but with me.' Rutherford died in October 1937.

During these years the political crisis worsened steadily. In 1935 Mussolini started his war of conquest in Abyssinia, while in Britain an election gave the Conservatives a large majority on a 'collective security' pledge, the falsity of which was revealed within a month by the Hoare-Laval Plan for Abyssinia. In 1936 Hitler entered the Rheinland and the Spanish Civil War broke out. Alan was only waiting for the completion of his thesis and the comparative security of a doctorate to formally join the Communist Party, believing that a well-qualified scientist was more valuable than a failed one, however heroic.

7

THE APPROACH OF WAR

Alan in London 1936-39

Kings College London (KCL) was housed in a wing of Somerset House. The Physics Department had a distinguished history; former heads were Wheatstone, Clerk Maxwell and, just before Alan arrived, Sir Edward Appleton, who had started a small laboratory in Hampstead where receiving conditions for radio were better. It had a Professor's personal flat, so Ellis moved into the flat and Alan into the laboratory. No 'big physics' was possible, so Alan started a project developing multiplying counters for detecting very small amounts of ionisation. The teaching load was heavy because Alan had to prepare a fresh course each term. In this way he covered all of the physics syllabus in his three years at KCL. The sound all round knowledge that he gained as a result proved immensely useful later in Ghana. In 1936 Alan also joined a Communist Party group in London and visited the Soviet Union. His political activity was mainly among scientists; with his union, the Association of Scientific Workers, which needed straightforward office work, and with the Left Book Club Scientists Group. There was also the sale of pamphlets and persuading colleagues to contribute to Spanish aid. Franco's revolt had started in July 1936, and within two weeks German planes were transporting his troops from Morocco to Spain. In contrast, in August the French, under pressure from Anthony Eden, prohibited the export of arms to the Spanish Government.

Alan wrote: 'In January 1939 came the discovery of Fission. My special chambers were ideal for (detecting) this, but I had no neutron sources. So I decided to study the effect of cosmic ray neutrons. I found a background of pulses which seemed to be spontaneous, although the theory predicted spontaneous fission would be very unlikely. By the summer of 1939 I was fairly convinced that this was indeed spontaneous fission, but not certain enough to publish. By that time the question began to seem unimportant in view of the political situation. Then I was invited to join a training scheme for physicists to learn about Radar, so as to man the stations, and do research on the development of the new technique. I jumped at the chance to do something effective for defence. So the fission experiments were closed down, and by August I was at Halesworth on the East Coast, and it was there that I heard of the Soviet-Nazi pact (23 August 1939) and realised that war was now imminent. KCL was evacuated to Bristol, and Ellis demanded my release from Radar work for his teaching staff.'

Berti in Czechoslovakia and Russia, 1935-36

My account of Berti's time in the Soviet Union and Hilde's visit to him there are based mainly on recalled anecdotes. Berti never wrote of this time, it was not mentioned in his CVs, and he plainly wanted it to remain generally unknown. However there was no doubt that he was there, and this has now been confirmed by his Russian dossier (Note 8). The thirty-four deliberately cryptic letters written on poor quality paper that he wrote to Hilde from there are consistent with the outline that I had. They are signed with names such as Sindbad the Land and Sea Traveller, Bori, Ostap (a roguish character in a popular and irreverent Russian novel of the time), and Old Shatterhand, a character from Karl May's novels. He refers to Prague and crowns, when he means Moscow and roubles. Moreover, he sends messages to Papa, who must have been a Party official in Austria. Berti's stay in the Soviet Union was apparently not known to Austrian or British Intelligence, but there is a passing reference to it in an MI5 minute in 1946 and the Americans seem to have known by 1955. The letters were sent to Hilde through their friend Eduard Marmorstein in Czechoslovakia, who later died in the Holocaust.

As his uncle Ferdy was in Prague as the Austrian Minister, he could not be seen to know of Berti's presence there as a fugitive, but his daughter Liesl, Berti's cousin (on both sides, as it happened) would meet him at the back door of the Legation to give him food. Berti stayed in Prague until December 1935. The story he gave when he arrived in Britain in 1938 was that he had been in Czechoslovakia until he could re-enter Austria at New Year 1937, and that he had worked in two glass works. He may indeed have done so until he went to Russia and on his return, and he would have needed money, but I have no evidence for this. A letter refers to Professor Mark being suspicious as to whether Berti really had such a job, but I don't know whether he was reassured. As mentioned earlier, Berti stated in his political CV that while in Prague he was responsible for Party archives.

Berti travelled to Moscow via Poland and found lodgings near his workplace not far from Moscow. He told me that he worked in laboratories associated with two factories. The Russian dossier refers to a Scientific Research Institue for Artificial Fibres and the Mitishchinsky factory. Berti's knowledge of polymer chemistry and his reputation as a graduate of Mark's Institute made him employable, and the letters indicate that he was given independence and worked hard, as ever. He learned to speak Russian quite well. The undated letters describe deep winter and darkness, then spring and early summer. They show that he was saving about half his pay, and that he was planning for Hilde to join him for a summer visit, and to take her either to the Caucasus or further east. He was enthusiastic about his life and friends there. But he also told me once that the police twice visited his lodgings when he was out. Perhaps these were narrow escapes.

As before, Berti pleaded for more letters and news from Hilde and about family and friends. For weeks he did not know whether Hilde had gone to Germany for treatment for her condition. Hilde did indeed spend two months in early 1936 in a sanatorium at St Blasius in the Black Forest in Germany. Her new identity served her well, but she had the acute discomfort of having to salute the medical director on his daily rounds with a dutiful 'Heil Hitler' (Photo 29). But Berti still asked her to bring a large rucksack and boots fit for climbing up to 5000 metres, which could only be in the Caucasus.

Hilde returned to Vienna and in June joined him in Moscow with a visa for a six week stay, and they travelled south (Photo 30). Berti joined a group to climb Mount Elbruz, the highest mountain in Europe, but altitude sickness prevented him from reaching the top. They travelled on the Military Highway and on the Black Sea coast. In one town, perhaps Odessa, Berti had his pocket picked, so the precious savings were lost and they were in dire straits. On the return by riverboat to Moscow an Austrian woman, who later was also a refugee in London, alleged that Hilde was a German spy, which one can see now was a possible death sentence. Berti helped Hilde leave the Soviet Union rapidly. She also fell ill again, this time probably with a

29. Hilde at St Blasius, 1936

gastrointestinal infection. There are only a couple of letters from Berti to Hilde that are from the period after she had left and he remained. He wrote that he would stop work on 30 September and expected to be in Bohemia in early October, which seems like an orderly exit. Consistent with this, the dossier states that he left by his own request in the autumn. He then remained in Czechoslovakia until the announcement of an Austrian amnesty for imprisoned Nazis that was intended to appease Hitler. However, to be seen as even-handed it was also applied to prisoners on the Left. Thus Berti was in Russia for about nine months.

It seems that Berti enjoyed his time in Russia, at least until the unfortunate conclusion to Hilde's visit. But I don't know how much he knew of the truth of the mass deportations from 1930 on, the appalling Ukraine famine of 1932-33, or of the increasing dangers within Russia for Russians and visitors alike. Typically, sympathetic visitors to the Soviet Union knew of isolated cases of disappearances and other injustices among their own circle without realising that they were part of a much larger horror. Berti would have known of the show trial and execution of Kamenev, Zinoviev and fourteen others in

30. Hilde, Berti and Øle Prestrud, from Norway, in Moscow, 1936

Moscow in August 1936. In later years Berti always put the best face on news from Russia, and for a time accepted the claims for economic progress.

Another question is whether Berti was in Russia as more than a scientist. Russian archives might reveal whether he received political training. There is an interesting comment in one of Berti's 1936 letters: 'There is no comparison with 1932; many say that the standard of living for many is indeed very very high. I'm very proud to speak fluent Czech *(sic)*. I have already often given lectures.' Had he been a witness earlier? It is possible that as an active communist in Germany in 1932 he was sent to Russia then, but at present that is pure speculation, and there is no mention of it in Berti's own political CV of 1936. I believe that Berti's view of the Soviet Union as a land of socialist promise and a bulwark against Fascism, already formed, was reinforced by his stay and kept him as a full-committed communist. It is worth noting that 1936 was the year that Alan was in Russia too, for his only visit; Alan's later attitude to the Russians was always more measured.

Berti and Hilde in Austria 1937-38

Berti re-entered Austria very early in 1937, and purged his 'guilt' for the offence of his activities in Austria in 1935 (there was no mention of Russia) by a further imprisonment of two weeks. Mark accepted him back in the Institute as a Privat-Assistent, and in October 1937 Berti obtained his first job, in a patent lawyer's office (Photo 31). The Austrian police file in relation to this application asserts that Berti was a well known Communist. He told me several times how proud he was to receive his first pay. In this period Hilde and Berti were together as a married couple. Hilde continued her medical studies alongside Ala, and they had to undergo much harrassment from anti-semitic and right wing students at their classes. In 1937 Mark took Berti with him to England to attend a meeting in Cambridge. On this visit he stayed in London with Andrew D'Antal. D'Antal told the security services in mid-1940 that Berti had held communist meetings in his flat, from which he himself was

31. Berti, 1937

excluded. D'Antal felt that he was being used, and relations became strained. He also said he spent part of the summer of 1938 with my parents at Fűnfturm, but this cannot be true because by then they were in Britain.

In this period there were passionate debates on the Left on how to oppose Hitler and the other fascist regimes, on Spain, and on the correct attitude to the Soviet Union. Berti once told me that he considered volunteering to go to Spain, but that this was vetoed by the Party. Berti and Christian bitterly fell out over these issues, and in a letter of July 1937 to a comrade in Moscow (Note 8), Berti (signing himself Albert) strove to distance himself from Christian's ('Janda's') deviationist activities, involving leading a Trotskyist youth group, and to re-assure 'Forst' and his other Moscow comrades of his total loyalty to the Party. He concludes this letter: 'If it interests you, I'm legal again and leading a middle-class existence. But in comparison that's completely unimportant.'

When Hitler marched into Austria on 12 March 1938, Berti went underground but did not know what to do in the way of resistance. A chance meeting on the street with Mark elicited the remark: 'Broda, what are you still doing here? Get out immediately.' Berti left Austria on 20 March, and reached Zűrich before making his way to England, where he arrived at Dover on 10 April. The Home Office file states: 'Wishes to stay 3 weeks, first to attend a congress of the Faraday Society at Bristol University from 11th to 13th instant, and later to visit British chemists at London University. He left Austria on 20th ultimo, and since has been doing research work at Zűrich University. He claims that he is not a refugee and will eventually return to Austria. In possession of £70.' Mark himself left shortly afterwards, taking in his car a platinum tool kit as his nest egg, according to Berti.

Hilde managed to complete her medical studies and graduate on 7 April. She then went to Aachen, where, with her foster mother and a trusted sister, she burned politically incriminating material she had left there. She then presented herself at the British Consulate in Cologne to request a visa to join her husband, who she explained was visiting Britain as a scientist. Perhaps because no Jews or communists had been applicants from Germany itself for some time, and because of her fair Aryan appearance, she was taken at face value and got her visa on 10 May, and so joined Berti. I don't know whether at this desperate time she had contact with her Uncle Felix, who was still in Aachen in great danger, but there were exchanges of information before war finally broke out.

Berti and Hilde in England 1938-39

Berti and then Hilde lived first with a refugee friend and their many subsequent addresses are given on their identity cards. By December they had found their own flat in London on Highgate Road. This was to be their home until it was bombed in September 1940, and they had sub-tenants to help pay the rent. Berti managed to get a number of extensions to his visa (Photo 32).

An important early contact for Berti was Sir William Bragg, President of the Royal Society 1935-40, Nobel Prize winner, and Director of the Royal Institution. Bragg vouched for Berti on the basis that he had been Mark's Assistent in Vienna, and Mark's own standing. Berti might have met Sir William on his 1937 visit, since Bragg and Mark shared research interests. Hilde was very fond of Sir William, and spent much time, it seems even before the war broke out, with him and his daughter Gwendolen Caroe at

32. Berti and Hermann Mark in London, 1938

Chiddingfold in Surrey. In a letter from Sir William to Hilde in October 1938 he wrote that he had not heard from her for some time, and asked whether she now had a satisfactory occupation (only later could she work as a doctor): 'You spoke one time of taking up midwifery. I should be very glad to know what happened in respect to this.' In a reference letter in early 1941 he wrote: 'I made her aquaintance soon after her arrival in England, and my daughter and I derived great pleasure from the fact that she was our guest for many months.'

The official correspondence shows that Berti (and Hilde) maintained the fiction with Sir William and others that Berti was a 'liberal Jewish refugee', and that Sir William made representations on that basis. In 1952 Hilde wrote to Berti that she had always been very unhappy about this duplicity, which for the Caroe family was doubtless a later cause for grievance, but Berti did not respond on this. He would have felt that this was a case of 'tragic necessity', but when in 1978 I sent him a biography of Sir William by his daughter, he returned it unread, writing that it would have brought back painful memories, which could have been of this deception or of the difficulties in their marriage, or indeed both.

Berti also made contact with Esther Simpson at the Society for the Protection of Science and Learning (SPSL) in May 1938. She (I shall call her simply Tess because of her later close friendship with Berti) helped hundreds of refugees and the organisation she ran still exists, now as the Council for Assisting Refugee Academics (Photo 33; Note 14). On her nominal retirement in 1966 Berti, who was unable to attend the celebrations for reasons that will become clear, wrote: 'Many people have grounds for delight on this day when you will be honoured by the large number of former refugees who have every reason to be grateful to you. ... It has not only been your power of discrimination between genuine and phoney and your sheer efficiency and tenacity that made this achievement possible. (An efficiency that I initially took, in my ignorance, as being the inheritance of generations of North English nonconformists...) The other pillar has been your human approach, your interest in the individual, your readiness to act for real persons, not numbers. Never in my life I have found that particular combination again, and I think that this combination has dominated the feeling of everybody in your sphere. ... I remember the first visit to your office – there was tea. I had been pressed by friends for a long time, and had been hesitant to call. I

33. Esther Simpson, c.1946. 'Love from Tess' on obverse
© Lotte Meitner-Graf, by kind permission of Anne Meitner

dreaded the inevitable question of my official status at Vienna University; how could I expect an Englishwoman to understand that in the 'thirties there could be no official status for a left-winger in Austria – even if he were far better as a scientist than I? But you inspired confidence. There was also the moment when – again with hesitations – I asked you whether you would like to see the baby. Through you I obtained my first real job in England – in fact the first real job as a scientist at all, in the sense that there was official status and payment (£15) every first of the month. That work (visual purple) is still the work to which I most like to think back; quiet, concentrated work by myself in a most interesting field.'

In 1938 Berti did some freelance work, including acting as a ghost-writer for an industrial chemist. Meanwhile Tess was active on his behalf, and in November 1938, through SPSL, Berti was hired by Charles Goodeve and William Lythgoe for work on visual purple (rhodopsin), a vital component of the human visual system. Berti always admired and was grateful to Goodeve, a Canadian who, as well as being a notable physical chemist at University College London, was an enthusiatic member of the Royal Naval Volunteer Reserve, who in the War became Deputy Controller of Research and Development at the Admiralty. Among other contributions he made a major one to the defeat of the magnetic mines used by the Germans against British shipping.

A more problematic contact was the Austrian Centre. This had started as a broad-based organisation used by hundreds of refugees, and was central to my parents' lives. MI5 files show that it was regarded as deeply suspect by some of the authorities as a focus of communist activity. It was indeed gradually taken over by left-wingers, in part because they were the most active and politically disciplined, to the point that others left it. A number of those running the Centre were friends of Berti's from Vienna days, including the communist Eva Kolmer as Secretary. Although a recent book on the Centre does not mention Berti, he was very involved in its activities, as MI5 knew and as his letters make clear.

Berti was also involved in the Austrian refugee Communist Party itself. Already in July 1938 the Special Branch noted these activities: 'Report re Engelbert Broda and the Austrian Communist Party Group in London. Secret. A group of the Austrian Communist Party composed principally of refugees who have come to England has been functioning in London for several months and meeting at regular intervals. Mrs Edith Tudor-Hart has now been delegated by the Central Committee of the Communist Party of Great Britain to act as a liaison between the Central Committee and this group and to assist in its control. The leader of the group is Engelbert Broda, an Austrian, whose address is kept secret from all, even Mrs. Tudor-Hart, who only knows his telephone number and communicates with him by that medium. Until last week this was Primrose 3456; since then it has been Paddington 5443. Broda is being used by the Left Book Club to give lectures to groups on political conditions in Germany and Austria. He receives a fee ostensibly to cover his expenses for each such lecture, and every care is taken to ensure that no undue publicity is given to his activity in this sphere.' In February 1939 it was reported: 'I have now heard that meetings of Austrian Communists are held at 6c Oak Court ... where Engelbert Broda is now residing.' (Photo 34; Note 15)

Hilde had kept some contact with Gottfried Kűhnel, because in June 1938 he came to Britain to try to persuade her to return with him to Germany. As she told me, she did not see him because on that weekend she

34. Edith Tudor Hart with her son Tommy, 1938
© Wolf Suschitzky, with permission and thanks

and Berti were camping with friends on the Isle of Wight, and that is when I was conceived. Letters from Kűhnel written from Germany after the War, when he had re-married, show that his first wife had died in 1938, and maybe that is when he came to London. He visited us in 1950, but that was to be almost the end of the connection.

As we know, Hilde would not record her account of her life with Berti. However, she did tell me that Berti wanted her to have another termination (she once said she had had two) as Party discipline, which he would have accepted, demanded that all comrades give all their efforts to the struggle. Perhaps he also feared becoming a single parent, given Hilde's history of ill health, and was anyway not confident about the marriage. She refused, also knowing that her precarious health made her prospects of motherhood poor in the future. In this she was supported by only one senior Austrian Party official, Martin Hornik. My second name, Martin, was for him, Paul was for Paul Lőw-Beer and my third name, Andrew, was for a Tirolese patriot against Napoleon, Andreas Hofer. Each name works in different languages, as befitted our uncertain future. I find it odd that in Berti's letters (in German) I am usually referred to as 'the child'.

Berti was absent at my birth in London on 15 March 1939, the day Hitler entered Prague. This was consistent with his earlier ambivalence about my birth, but also with some attitudes of the time. It is sadly also possible that he had doubts about whether he was my father, but that can be discounted, given the physical similarity between Berti and me. I arrived more or less on time, and Ala was with Hilde. Hilde told me of her disappointment that Berti was in France skiing with Christian one last time before war broke out. I have accepted this account until recently, and also never doubted that my father was committed to me once I was born. However, there are puzzles. First, there is no record of foreign travel in Berti's British identity papers or in government files for this period, and it seems foolhardy for him to have left the safety of the UK then for such a reason. Second, a letter from Christian to Berti in the MI5 file from 1946, the first he says since 1937, states that they had had no contact in the intervening period and were estranged.

A letter from Berti's mother Viola (who was visiting a friend) to Hilde from Paris casts some light on what Berti was doing. It is dated 17 March and congratulated her on my birth. She was glad that Hilde had Ala with her, and so was not alone. She wrote that she had seen Berti, who was there when she had arrived, but she did not know where he was then; there is no mention of Christian or of skiing. It seems that Berti's story to Hilde was a cover, and that he was indeed in France, but for another reason. It is quite possible that he was on some Comintern or Party mission. However, my former wife Linda had a different version from Hilde, that Berti was with another woman. I can imagine Hilde not wanting me know this. Perhaps this, and the memory of the two terminations, were reasons why Hilde with her baby preferred to be with the Braggs in Surrey rather than with Berti, even before the outbreak of the War (Photos 35,36).

In an earlier letter, for Christmas 1938, Viola had commented that Berti

35. Berti, Hilde, and Paul at Watlands, 1939

36. Berti, Hilde and Paul with Gwendolen Caroe and Sir William Bragg, 1940

had over a period made no mention of Hilde, and that Hilde had not written. Did this reflect problems between Berti and Hilde, or were they protecting Viola by being terse, since letters would be censored by the Nazis? In another letter Viola recounted the evidence she and Willi had to provide that their ancestry was purely Aryan. After my birth she asked whether I would be named Ernst after my grandfather (who, had he lived, would not have been able to provide such evidence), and for the christening to be delayed until she could send the family robe. Then in August 1939 she wrote with a heavy heart a last letter before war broke out.

PART 3
THE WAR

8

ALAN IN BRISTOL 1939-42

When Alan rejoined his department in Bristol in early October, most of his colleagues had been recruited into war research jobs. Although he would have preferred to stay in the radar work he had no choice, since people were sent where they were thought to be most useful. The Bristol Physics Department was in a fine building and lavishly equipped, and Professor Tyndall ran his department with quiet efficiency. Tyndall and Ellis combined their teaching and King's staff were invited to use the excellent research facilities. Alan wanted to continue his work on the anomalous background of fission particles which he had found in London, but it quickly became clear that this was not a welcome idea. The radium source he had used to standardise the ionisation chambers had been returned to the National Physical Laboratory and was now securely buried in some vault. It would anyway have been a most unwelcome addition to the laboratory since apart from the danger of contamination if it were damaged in an air raid, the background of radiation would have interfered with other experiments, notably those of Cecil Powell who was using photographic plates to detect fast particles.

Alan might have found some other means of calibrating his ionisation chambers or worked at some outstation away from Bristol, such as the caves under the Mendips. He wrote: 'But I was unwise enough to seek the advice of a distinguished theoretical physicist, and ask him whether spontaneous fission was a possible explanation for my results. He had no hesitation in dismissing the suggestion as absurd, and convinced me by a quick calculation on the proverbial back of an envelope that I should dismiss the idea. My results must have been due to some fault in the equipment. Those interested may find a similar calculation in the celebrated paper by Bohr and Wheeler to which reference will be made later. After this I did not pursue the matter any further. But I was somewhat put out when in 1940 amidst general acclaim the Russian physicists Flerov and Perzhak announced their discovery of spontaneous fission (Note 16). Otto Frisch recounts that he had a similar experience. But in his book *What Little I Remember* he apparently did not remember that I told him about my results. I dare say there were many others who nearly discovered spontaneous fission, just as there were many others who nearly discovered fission itself, not to mention almost discoveries of X-rays, radioactivity and what you will. The club of almost Nobel Prize winners is not at all exclusive.'

Thus Alan was at a loss for a project when, in October 1939, Powell invited him to join his team in developing the photographic method. 'Powell was a man of great personal charm, and even greater experimental skill, not just in the design and execution of a whole campaign of experiments. I soon realised that this was going to be a most fruitful and enjoyable collaboration.' The tracks of fast particles from radioactive substances, or from the rather modest high tension sets and cyclotrons of those days travelled a few centimetres through oil. In photographic emulsions the tracks would be about a thousand times shorter so to see and measure them one needed good microscopes. Powell had acquired a battery of the best microscopes, together with special equipment for determining the precise location and direction of the tracks. He had also persuaded the main photographic manufacturers to make special plates for him, some specially sensitive, some extra thick. In his hands the photographic method became a very powerful and versatile tool. When Alan joined his team, Powell had already applied it to the study of nuclear reactions. Later he turned to cosmic rays, sending assemblies of photographic emulsions into the upper atmosphere suspended from enormous balloons. It was for the discovery of pi mesons through this work that he won the Nobel Prize in 1950 (Photo 37; Note 17).

In 1939 Powell was preparing for experiments using beams of particles from Chadwick's cyclotron. The plan of the campaign was to carry out a systematic survey of the scattering of protons and other particles from the cyclotron by the nuclei of the light elements. The targets to be bombarded would be thin foils or in some cases gases. The camera was designed and assembled in Bristol, the special plates and the materials for the targets were prepared, and then they waited for news from Liverpool that the cyclotron was available. When the summons came they went overnight to Liverpool and set to work taking exposures non-stop on the cyclotron beam until the next breakdown, or the supply of plates or targets was exhausted. Then came the return to Bristol, and

37. Cecil Powell, 1948. The University of Bristol, with permission and thanks

the hours of painstaking measurements on the plates, until the next summons. The experiments were first reported in *Nature* in June 1940, and a full account appeared much later. Alan owed the completion of this publication to Powell because, being in prison, he could not help in the writing up. This pioneer work showed that much information about nuclear energy levels and other features of nuclear structure could be obtained in this way.

The teaching was also interesting and important because the students were about to take positions in research stations devoted to radar or magnetic mines. But if the physics was stimulating the reverse was true of the politics at that time, the singularly bitter and frustrating period of the 'Phoney War'. It was phoney for the British and French, but not for Hitler. The French were content to man the Maginot Line, said to be impregnable, but in fact easily circumvented as it stopped short in the north, leaving a convenient gap in the Ardennes for a German attack. As for the British, A. J. P. Taylor wrote that Chamberlain's government 'were at a loss to explain why they were at war or what they were fighting for. Their policy was in ruins. They had wanted to settle with Hitler on reasonable terms, or failing that, to shift the brunt of the fighting on to Soviet Russia. Now they were pledged to the defence of Poland – a pledge they could not fulfil' (Note 18).

On any rational view the situation was one of the utmost danger. Hitler might at any moment attack in the west. With the collapse of Poland, the last of the alliances that the British and French had relied on to mount an attack on Germany from the east had disappeared. They had thrown away Czechoslovakia, antagonised the Russians, and failed to rescue the Poles. The British and French discussed wild schemes to widen the war by bombing the Russian oil fields in the Caucasus, mining the North Sea shipping lanes through which Germany received iron ore from Sweden, and finally preparing an expeditionary force to help the Finns.

The Russians were not so hesitant about preparing their defences. They took up positions along the line agreed with the Germans in what had been Poland, restoring the old pre-revolution frontier. Then they secured non-aggression treaties with the Baltic States. In June 1940 when the Germans swept through France, the Russians took the further step of fully integrating these states into the Soviet system. These precautions against German attack did not turn out to be as effective as had been hoped. They were also greeted in the West as trampling on the rights of small nations and Soviet imperialism. Alan wrote: 'There was of course some justification for this, but I preferred to take all this as a welcome sign that the Russians did not take the German protestations of eternal friendship at their face value and were taking sensible precautions against which way the cat might jump.'

For Alan, it was unfortunate that the confusion in the British and French Establishments was matched by an equal state of uncertainty on the Left. At the outset of the war the British Communist Party issued a manifesto supporting the war as anti-fascist but saying that Fascism would never be effectively opposed by the Chamberlain government, which had to be replaced by 'a new government in which the key positions are in the hands of trusted representatives of the people who have neither imperialist aims, nor latent sympathies with fascism.' Alan saw this as an admirable statement of how most people felt that would have had wide support if only it had survived. But the Comintern took a different view of things, declaring on 14 September 1939 that the war was 'imperialist and predatory on both sides.' A strong reproof was sent to the British CP and after a stormy meeting of the Central Committee the erstwhile leader, Harry Pollitt, was demoted and the new line adopted. The war was now definitely an imperialist one.

Alan wrote: 'the policy of opposition to imperialist war had been one of the basic issues in the history of the international socialist movement. In 1907 the Socialist International had unanimously resolved to oppose war in a resounding declaration. When war actually broke out in 1914 this resolution was completely disregarded; the German Social Democrats voted for war credits and so did the French. Only small minority groups kept up some opposition. This collapse of the Second International was a theme which all CP members had absorbed in their training. All accounts of the history of the Third International started out from this basis. Thus once convinced that the war was imperialist every well-trained party member would immediately make an abrupt turn and oppose the war 'even to the extent of steps which might lead to the defeat of "his own" government in the war.'

This did indeed happen, but the about turn was an extremely painful operation, especially for those comrades who had joined the party when its main appeal had been its consistent opposition to Fascism and its fight to build up a united front against aggression. Many, including Alan, felt left in the lurch by the sudden switch and that the new turn in policy represented by the Ribbentrop-Molotov pact and the Russian takeover of eastern Poland was a pragmatic move, not justified by any deep Marxist analysis and forced on the Soviet leadership by events. But having taken this step on valid pragmatic grounds, the Soviet leadership insisted that all other parties should follow rigidly the policies laid down by pre-war resolutions: 'No pragmatic deviations were allowed for us, no account taken of our special circumstances. For us discipline was discipline. The results were disastrous for popular appeal and party morale. The new line became even more difficult when Hitler brought out his "peace offer" in mid-October. Having derided Chamberlain's faith in Hitler's word at Munich we were now expected to take these offers seriously, despite an inner conviction that anyone who accepted a peace offer from Hitler could expect to have his throat cut.'

Then in December 1939 came the Finnish war. Unlike the other Baltic

States, the Finns refused to accede to the Russian demands. The Russians then set about reducing the Finns by force. For the Russians this was by far the most dangerous part of the frontier, with the Mannerheim Line, prepared with the help of both German and British experts, only a few miles from Leningrad. But, however well justified from the Russian point of view, the operation turned out to be much more difficult and painful than they expected. 'There was a violent anti-Russian reaction in the west. The moribund League of Nations was resurrected to expel Russia, a step which neither German nor Japanese nor Italian aggression had called forth. The British and French cobbled together an expeditionary force to be sent to fight the Russians. They were not at all put out by the refusal of Norway and Sweden to allow them passage and the reluctance of the Finns to be involved in a World War as well as their local dispute. Our brave lads were to force their way through, making war on the Germans, Russians, Swedes and Norwegians all at once. Such was the outburst of bellicose enthusiasm released by this wonderful opportunity for mounting an anti-Soviet crusade. Fortunately all this nonsense collapsed when the Finns sued for peace in March 1940 and the Russians got all they had originally asked for and some more.'

Meanwhile Alan's colleagues and ex-students were quietly doing their best to mitigate these dangers by working to improve radar, anti-magnetic mine devices and other means of defence. His own political involvement was now at a low ebb, and although nominally still a party member, he did little beyond dutifully reading party journals. Much later he refreshed his memory of that time by re-reading *The Labour Monthly*. Even at that distance he found it difficult to take all of it seriously: 'Particularly the idea that the German working class still had a reasonable chance of bringing down Hitler if only the British and French working classes would do the same to their governments, and that anyhow the fate of the British people after defeat by the Germans would be no worse than it would be after a victory of their own ruling class. Fortunately very few took this nonsense to heart.'

Meanwhile the uranium problem had continued to simmer with occasional papers erupting into the open literature. After the initial excitement generated by Bohr's startling announcement on fission at a conference on theoretical physics in the USA in January 1939 and the spate of papers that followed, it was realised that secondary neutrons were emitted at fission and so a chain

38. Niels Bohr, undated
© Lotte Meitner-Graf, by kind permission of Anne Meitner

reaction might be possible. Governments started to show interest when prodded by their physicists, with the Germans being the first to set up a specific programme. Attempts were made to detect a chain reaction in primitive arrangements of uranium oxide and graphite, or paraffin or water but it was soon realised that things were not going to be that easy. Meanwhile an immensely influential theoretical paper by Bohr and Wheeler published on 1 September made it seem probable that it was the rare isotope U235 which was responsible for fission by slow neutrons, and provided the basis for speculations on what other nuclei, such as those of elements 93 (Neptunium) or 94 (Plutonium), would be fissionable (Photo 38; Note 19).

At this time the main interest, at any rate in France, Britain and the USA, was in the possibility of uranium reactors as a source of power. The possibility of a bomb was discounted because of an argument due to Bohr. It was held that any chain reaction propagated by thermal neutrons would develop at about the same speed as a chemical chain reaction, so the material would have time to melt or vaporise and disperse at about the same speed as a chemical chain reaction, before the nuclear reaction could be completed. The amount of energy released would only be that required to vapourise the material, which would be of the same order as that of a conventional explosive. No-one would be likely to go to the trouble and expense of assembling the materials for a reactor just to produce an explosion of the same power as that produced by the same weight of gelignite. Against this argument was the danger from the radioactive fission products, difficult to estimate, but significant. Rough guesses led to radioactive yields equivalent to tons of radium for hours after the explosion and equivalent to 100 grammes of radium months afterwards, even for the mildest nuclear bomb.

Things would be very different if the chain reaction was propagated by fast neutrons, neutrons that had the original energy they had at birth. They would be moving about a thousand times faster than thermal neutrons, before they were slowed down by collisions, and so the chain reaction would propagate so fast that the material of the bomb would have no time to melt, expand or vapourise. The whole of the nuclear energy would then be released before any expansion took place. The key question was, how readily did fission in U235 occur with fast neutrons? The only data in the literature on this point was an unpublished measurement by Tuve quoted by Bohr and Wheeler. On this basis Chadwick concluded that the amount of U235 needed for a bomb would be prohibitively large. Others were probably misled in the same way. Actually the Tuve value for the ease of fission in U235 was too small by a factor of about three.

O. R. Frisch was then at Birmingham, and had written a report on the whole field for the Chemical Society in which he repeated the Bohr argument against the possibility of a bomb. He then started to worry about the fast neutron chain reaction in U235 but he made the opposite error. He assumed that every neutron striking an U235 nucleus would cause fission. This led to a critical mass which was too small, and this triggered alarm bells, because it seemed that such an amount of U235 could be separated rather easily. He was already working on one method of separating uranium isotopes, which turned out to be ineffective, but felt sure that some method could be found. He consulted another refugee, Rudolph Peierls, who had written a paper on the calculation of the critical mass. Together they wrote the famous Frisch-Peierls report that Oliphant forwarded to Sir Henry Tizard for consideration by the government (Photos 39, 40; Note 20).

Alan wrote: 'Soon after this, in April 1940, a delegation from Birmingham came to Bristol to discuss the uranium problem. It consisted of Oliphant, Peierls and Frisch. They gave us the gist of the Frisch-Peierls report. Peierls did most of

39. Otto Robert Frisch, c.1970
The Master and Fellows of Trinity College Cambridge, with permission

the talking – he had a gift for simple and clear exposition – while Frisch sat at his side munching digestive biscuits, suggesting that he suffered from an incipient stomach ulcer, but perhaps he was just hungry. Oliphant wound up the proceedings with an appeal for help. Everything depended on finding out quickly whether the bomb would really work, and if the answer was 'yes', we had to make it before the Germans did. It was a shattering experience, even for those who had been through many discussions of the possibility of nuclear bombs before. The estimated critical mass of U235 was so small, a kilogram or two, that separation seemed eminently feasible. Once this was granted, everything else followed, and was worked out in horrifying detail in the report – the expected power of the explosion, damage by blast and by heat radiation, the mushroom cloud, radioactive fallout, and the long term contamination. The only horror missing was that it was assumed that the bomb would be delivered by conventional bombing aircraft – no-one had yet envisaged intercontinental missiles.'

Powell and Alan undertook to assist Chadwick in determinations of the relevant 'cross sections' (that is, target sizes) for various nuclei for fast neutrons. The Liverpool cyclotron was the source, and a beam of fast

40. Mark Oliphant, 1937
© Godfrey Argent Studio. The Royal Society, with permission

neutrons was aimed at a scatterer, usually uranium, but also lead and other materials were used. The intensity of the beam was measured by exposing a photographic plate. Other plates were disposed round the scatterer to measure the scattered neutrons, and to find out how many had passed through it. In each case not only the number, but the distribution in energy of the neutrons could be determined. It was time consuming work, and took many months of tedious examination of the plates under the microscope, but it was essential for any accurate estimate of the critical mass. Alan also undertook to make a prototype for a portable Geiger counter set for examining bomb craters for traces of radioactivity. This was in case the first German bomb was a dud, or they used a low-powered thermal neutron bomb, or they might even have reached the stage of having a reactor functioning and then use the fission products to make a large area uninhabitable with a 'dirty bomb'. He made a small set that worked and gave it to Ellis, his boss for that project. Alan never had any feedback on this, but much later he found in the records of the MAUD committee (Note 21) that Ellis made very adverse comments on his work. He appeared to have regarded Alan as his personal property and resented his working with Powell.

As a result of the Frisch-Peierls report there was a renewed interest in spontaneous fission, and also fission by cosmic ray particles. If the rate of these background fissions was too high then it would be extremely difficult to bring the parts of the bomb together to form a compact mass without a chain reaction starting prematurely, before the parts were close enough to generate a really big explosion. This did turn out to be the main difficulty in making a plutonium bomb. Since Frisch knew about Alan's experiments in London before the war, and he was now working with Chadwick in Liverpool, Chadwick asked Alan to let Frisch have particulars of his measurements, and the design of his ionisation chamber. This he did, and much later was pleased to find his letter and the design of the chamber amongst Chadwick's archived papers.

The Nazi invasion of Holland and Belgium on 10 May 1940 signalled the end of the Phoney War. Hitler had thrown his full weight against the West. The Maginot line proved useless, as the Germans simply went round it through the Low Countries. The French quickly collapsed and the British were cut off on their own and extremely lucky to get away at Dunkirk, even though they lost all of their equipment. Then the Italians joined in on 10 June. The main preoccupation of everyone in Britain was the possibility of invasion, which indeed hung in the balance, but for once Hitler was cautious and delayed in order to secure command of the air. Then the British were grateful that so much effort had been put into air defence – not only the radar chain, but the elaborate system of control, and of course the input of fighters and, most of all, the pilots.

Alan saw little of these battles until the main struggle on the Channel coast was over, but between November 1940 and April 1941 there were eight major raids on Bristol. Powell took his family, his precious microscopes, and his stock of plates to some friends about twelve miles from Bristol. Alan joined him in his country retreat and they would cycle to Bristol when they had classes or air raid duties to perform. Alan gave his lectures on the mornings after his firewatching duties and spent the nights making sure that the experimental demonstrations on the lecture bench worked. It was a relaxed and idyllic existence, strangely unrelated to the War, which was becoming steadily more threatening. At that time there seemed no way in which Nazi control of Europe could be broken.

During early 1941 there were repeated hints in BBC broadcasts and in commentaries that the Russian-German friendship pact was under strain. Indeed, the German takeover of Hungary and Romania and the Russian response by absorbing the Baltic States were widely interpreted in the West as signs of this. But the official Moscow line was that these suggestions were all British-American provocations, aiming to involve Russia and Germany in mutual war for the benefit of the Western powers. We now know that as early as December 1940 Hitler had given definite orders for the invasion of Russia and that a whole series of warnings, from the British and from Russian agents best placed to know, were given to Stalin. All warnings were ignored, even on the very eve of the attack, when German Communists deserted from their units and crossed the lines to give warning with the precise time and direction of the attack. Stalin's response was to order these 'provocateurs' to be shot. Even nearly fifty years later, Alan wrote, it was impossible to read of this gross stupidity without indignation.

Moreover, Stalin's preparations for the conflict were completely inappropriate. He had removed his best generals and senior officers in the purges of 1937 onwards, and even continued this process after the Germans attacked. The Russian Army was led by the remnant of conformist and mostly second-rate generals. The plan to contain the attack was inept, with major forces near the front where they would be quickly overwhelmed by surprise, while the reserves of ammunition, food etc were also brought well forward. The Red Army had been trained for attack, to carry the fight into enemy territory. Stalin regarded any studies of problems of defence with distaste, since they conflicted with his basic premise that the Soviet frontiers were inviolable.

Of course Alan had no inkling of all this in June 1941, when the news of the German invasion broke. Then came the broadcast by Churchill, promising full support to the Russians, and at once he knew that at least one cloud had been lifted. Clearly now the phoney imperialist war was a thing of the past, and they were all in it together: 'But that was small recompense for the dreadful news that kept coming over the radio. Those experts who had predicted that the German army would go through the Red Army like a hot knife though butter now seemed all too well justified. This was a horrible period to live through. The Nazis were triumphant on all fronts. The victory the British had achieved in North Africa over the Italians proved short-lived as soon as Rommel joined in. Then the Germans attacked again in Greece, there was the fiasco of Crete, and the Japanese were clearly threatening in the Pacific. This was not a reassuring background to the knowledge that an atomic weapon might be produced in a few years, and it was even odds that the Germans would get it first.'

9

BERTI AND HILDE
SEPTEMBER 1939-APRIL 1941

In the days after the outbreak of the War Berti was at the Highgate flat, and Hilde and I were with the Bragg family at Chiddingfold, perhaps as a precaution against bombing. On 12 September Berti protested that he hadn't heard anything from Hilde: 'I am glad that you have written at last, and that you are both allright. Please consider: is it really so difficult to spend five minutes every few days to write a postcard at least? I cannot imagine that you cannot spare five minutes at Watlands. Could you think it possible that Mrs Caroe does not write to her husband for seven days?' Berti was dealing with a rental contract and with new tenants, and told Hilde that she too must register at a police station and how much he regretted being designated an enemy alien. He advised her not to come back to London for the present, and told her not to write to Viola, as she would be OK, and it might cause trouble. He described how he was repeatedly phoned by D'Antal, who was very anxious because political post for Berti was being delivered to his home, and that D'Antal was so insolent that he, Berti, put down the phone. He suggested to Hilde that they break off all contact with D'Antal.

Lythgoe had the possibility of going to Oxford and invited Berti to go with him. Berti wanted to, but wrote to Hilde that he would of course also have to ask 'Uncle', presumably a political superior. He later wrote that Uncle was much in favour. At the end of September he wrote as if their relationship was in crisis, and said he couldn't get a travel permit to visit her. He expected to go before a Tribunal a few days later (which did not happen) and asked for a written recommendation from Sir William, which was quickly provided. He described digging trenches. Berti begged Hilde to come to London for a day to talk to him about their problems. Then on 6 October the Special Branch visited Berti at the flat. As a result he was interned for the first of two times. Unlike the internment of June 1940, this one only involved a minority of the German and Austrian refugees.

The Special Branch account in the MI5 file seems to equate Berti's activities at the Austrian Centre with subversion and communism. A particular problem for him was the discovery of personal letters to a Dr Faber: 'At his flat Broda had a quantity of material relating to the Austrian Centre, in the form of draft articles, reports from centres, press cuttings etc. He was asked to explain his connection with the Austrian Centre and he stated that he was the editor of the *Austrian News,* and was on the executive committee. He was asked to explain a letter dated 4 Sept. signed by E.Kolmer, in which it testifies to all whom it may concern, that Broda is a member of the Committee of Austrians in England, and the publication *Austrian News* dated 15 Sept. (11 days later) which gives on page 1 a list of the executive committee, but which does not contain the name of Broda. He was unable to explain this satisfactorily, and stated that he was on the general committee and not on the executive committee; he could not explain why his name did not appear as the editor of *Austrian News.* His name does appear on an undated list as a committee member. There is no doubt that Broda is the driving force behind the activities of the Austrian Committee and that his chief assistant is E.Kolmer … who supplies him with reports from all centres, keeps him posted as to activities of members, and is general secretary to him and the Centre. Had not an examination been made of this man's desk, it is possible that nothing would have come to light from outside enquiries to show his connection with the Austrian Centre, as during the day, he is usually engaged in pursuing his chemical studies. During the examination of Broda's property, it was noticed that there were several personal letters addressed to Dr Faber of the Austrian Centre. Broda was asked to explain this, and he stated that his wife was known by the name Dr Faber when she was secretary of the Austrian Centre – probably up to the time of her confinement. There is no doubt that his wife when in London materially assists him in his activities outside his profession. Broda was conveyed to Olympia and handed over to the military authorities against attached receipt at 7 p.m. 6 October.' There was an added comment: 'I feel that, in view of the peculiar position taken up by the Communist international and their agents in this country regarding the war, it is dangerous to allow an alien such as Broda to remain at liberty.'

This last point concerns the instructions from Moscow that the War was an imperialist one on both sides; I think that Berti was more able to follow this line than Hilde was. The file then reveals two opinions about the position of Berti and other activists and also suggests that a turf war existed between MI5 and the Special Branch. Dick White was to be much concerned with Berti and later Alan (whom much later he met under odd circumstances) and rose to be head of MI5 and later of MI6 (Note 22). Kendal headed the Special Branch of the Metropolitan Police.

22 October 39. B.2 (Dick White) to S.I.S (MI6) re Broda: 'Engelbert Broda has been interned apparently at the instigation of Sir Norman Kendal. Personally I think we shall have to decide on a policy with regard to alien communists. If we accepted them in the first place and if we have no evidence that they have abused the hospitality we have shown them by engaging in political activities, there does not seem any justification for interning them. As far as we are concerned, this is the case of Broda. On the other hand, from Sir Norman Kendal's letter of 9 October in the Home Office File, I see that he claims to have heard from a "very reliable informant of Special Branch", who has established the fact that Broda controls the secret Austrian Communist Group in this country. If S.B. have such information, surely it should have been sent to us, and I am very surprised that it has not. It may be that Sir Norman Kendal refers to the Austrian Centre when he speaks of the Austrian Communist Group in London, and the documents found in Broda's possession certainly substantiate his close connection with this organisation. But the Austrian Centre is no more dangerous an organisation than any other refugee and anti-Hitler movement, and certainly is not primarily communist. Moreover, M.I.7 appear to be interested in it and may have been backing its activity. In my opinion our policy should be to intern alien Communists only when we have evidence that they have been engaging in political activities since arriving in this country or that they are in touch with the CPGB. Any very drastic change of policy should in my opinion be taken only when it is quite clear that all Communists are on the side of Hitler in the war against ourselves.'

Writing to Tess and later in a memoir, Berti stated that he did not know why he was singled out for internment. He was being disingenuous as he (and perhaps Hilde, notwithstanding her letters on his behalf) would have known that his communist activities were the real reason for his internment. He and others were sent to one holiday camp at Clacton, and were then moved to another at Seaton in Devon, where they slept in unheated huts in freezing weather. The internees were a very mixed group, with many cultured and educated men, so that with time there were activities such as theatre, lectures and courses. Berti involved himself by teaching science and establishing language courses.

In the camp he was only partly aware of the efforts that Hilde, Tess and others made on his behalf. Tess wrote to Hilde of leaving no stone unturned. The file shows letters between Sir William Bragg and Sir Edward Mellanby, Secretary of the Medical Research Council, among others. Sir William also wrote to the Home Secretary, Sir John Anderson, referring to Berti as a Viennese liberal Jewish refugee, but was rebuffed with the terse statement that the Government had other information. Hilde told a touching story concerning Sir William and a visit she was finally able to make to Berti at Seaton in mid-November, leaving me with them. On her return, her train was delayed and she missed her local connection, causing a breastfeeding crisis for both her and me. Sir William contacted the local railway manager, who provided a special train for Hilde. Finally, the Home Office recorded a decision on 23 November 1939 to release Berti, but he was only released three weeks later, after ten weeks detention. Hilde wrote to Tess later, when she informed her of Berti's second detention: 'Do you know that had my husband not been released with your and our other friends help from the first internment he would have been on the *Arandora Star* like most refugees from Seaton?' This ship was torpedoed with great loss of life.

Berti only had six months at liberty before his second internment, and he was watched closely. This was the period of the end of the Phoney War, Churchill becoming Prime Minister, the defeat of France, and of Dunkirk. He resumed his work on visual purple. Goodeve was with the Navy and Lythgoe in Cambridge, but Berti would not join him as the equipment he needed was not available there. Then in February 1940 Lythgoe died very suddenly and Berti was on his own. In 1979 he wrote to me: 'I completed the work while I expected internment any day, in May and June, 1940, during the fall of France. So I spent some 15 or 20 hours a day in the laboratory, which had been shifted from University College to King's College. It was practically empty, everybody had gone somewhere else, and teaching was done out of London. The needed visual purple was sent to me in a darkened Dewar from Cambridge through the railway guard, and collected by me at Liverpool Street Station (or was it King's Cross?) The fundamental idea was mine, and I did all the work. I invited Goodeve to sign with me, as I liked him, and he had been helpful and decent all along, and it really had been his (and Lythgoe's) team. But by 1940 he had no time for visual purple. All subsequent work on the mechanisms of action of light on visual purple all over the world is derived from that piece of work in Kings College, though the younger generation does not know. It was, of course, George Wald's idea (he was denigrated by Lythgoe all along) that the essential step in the bleaching of VP by light is a cis-trans isomerization. This brilliant idea came to him more easily as he had spent a time before the war with Richard Kuhn and Edgar Lederer, great experts on carotenoids. Even now, you are vividly before my mind, as I found you at home in Highgate, returning from Strand, at any time of the day or the night.' Wald won the Nobel Prize for his work. A letter from Wald to Berti dated 1951 corroborates the importance of Berti's contribution.

This letter and the absence of letters from Berti to Hilde from this time show that they were together at Oak Court. But he was interned again in July 1940 with many hundreds of others and Hilde then again wrote to Tess at the SPSL: 'I know I should have informed you at once but in spite of having feared and to a certain extent expected his internment it knocked me down completely when it actually happened and I could not pull myself together to do what would have been sensible to do. It seems so hopeless this time, quite impossible to help him.' Tess was fully extended with dealing with over 600 cases on SPSL's books. The SPSL archive shows that even so she applied the human touch in such cases. Berti wrote a set of letters from his internment at Huyton near Liverpool. He was desperate to make sure that his visual purple work was published and gave Hilde detailed instructions on dealing with the manuscripts and their submission. Even more than before he organised himself and others in educational projects. In everything he put a brave face on things. He considered volunteering to be sent overseas, but resisted a proposed job in Shanghai.

It was not easy for him to write from the camp about personal matters, but one letter suggests that in a period of settled family life things had gone a bit better for them, even though or perhaps because he was working so hard: 'I hope so much to see you both before long, here or elsewhere. If sent overseas, I shall do all in my power to have you there soon. But do not worry too much, should there be delay. Give all my regards to Lunki (my nickname) and tell him not to forget me altogether. Does he walk and talk? I am looking forward for the time when he will have some brothers and sisters.'

Again both Bragg and Goodeve interceded on Berti's behalf, and he was released after thirteen weeks on 24 September. He wrote to Tess: 'Now again I have been released from internment. I am perfectly aware that again I owe my comparatively speedy release to your efforts as well as to those of Sir W Bragg and Dr Goodeve. I am grateful to you beyond words. It is a special matter to be behind barbed wire in these days. Almost all the scientists interned at Huyton are still there.' As a fervent anti-Nazi he found internment particularly difficult, and he also lost his MRC grant. During his internment, the Battle of Britain had started in mid-July and the Blitz started in early September. They lasted respectively until the end of October 1940 and June 1941. In the same period Hilde completed a course on Industrial Bacteriology at Chelsea Polytechnic, and received a 1st Class certificate in July 1940.

Hilde was unfaithful to Berti during his second internment, as he learned on his release. With all the wear and tear there had been on their relationship, that, according to Hilde, was the end for him. Berti naturally regarded this unfaithfulness, while he was interned like a prisoner of war, as a gross betrayal. She had done much to try to get him released, which he probably didn't recognise or saw as irrelevant. Hilde never regarded the person with whom she became involved, an Austrian refugee carpenter, as an alternative partner, but as a comfort in her unsettled and lonely life. The flat was then destroyed by a landmine on 26 September 1940, two days after Berti's return. The records show such a bomb on Lissenden Gardens, and Hilde told me that the opposite side of the road was obliterated. I was in the basement of our house in a solid old pram with the hood up, and that probably saved me. But the marriage was not saved and, after a period of sleeping in the Underground, Berti and Hilde went their separate ways. I return below to how they felt about each other and to their incompatibility; the letters show their attempts to mend things, and then the lengthy and distressing process towards their divorce. But for Tess, the security services, the Braggs and others, they kept up the appearance of being a couple.

After these disasters Berti found work with a consultant metallugist and then at a company in Barking that produced the juice that the Navy used to prevent scurvy on its ships. Berti alleged that over the decades the procedures had been modified to the point that no vitamin C was likely to survive. Berti also said that they made minute wood chips to make strawberry jams seem more authentic. He was there from April until October 1941, when Paul Löw-Beer succeeded him. Meanwhile Hilde had found work in a clothes factory in a firetrap of a warehouse off Regent Street. The dates I have are for seven weeks from late autumn to the end of October 1940, spanning the bombing and separation. Her job was sewing buttons on to military greatcoats. She struggled to meet the quotas, and always lamented that the buttons would have come off much earlier than they should have because of her skimping on the job.

There are two undated letters from Berti that are probably from this time. In one he wrote that the day before they had been nice to each other. He still thought that it was so sad that they were separating and that a religious person would perhaps say that before God they belonged together. In case there were any misunderstandings over the previous two weeks, he wanted to make a last heartfelt appeal for her to come back to him. He (and I) would be very pleased if they would try to regain each other's trust, even if it took time. He suggested that they should avoid getting advice from others until they got on better with each other. If she agreed he would be glad to hear from her. If not, they still should be friendly to each other and keep good thoughts of each other. He often thought of the many times when she was loving to him. But she should not phone; it would be too painful for him. In the second letter he accepted that there should be no further delay in separating. Like her he now believed that nothing was to be gained and that they couldn't make a good marriage. He said how sad he was and what a tragedy it was. For him, she remained the Hilde of earlier times, when they were like loving children. He wished that he could express his feelings in acts, and wanted her to keep trusting him. He had always been well-meaning, and never knowingly wanted to upset her. He knew it was the same for her, and they needed to be good to each other and others in the future, and be good parents.

At Chiddingfold Hilde had helped a local doctor as a volunteer, but medical degrees of enemy aliens were not recognised until, with the needs created by the Blitz, she got temporary registration in March 1941. In fact she started working as a doctor at the end of January at The Queen's Hospital for Children, Hackney Road. This hospital in the East End was bearing the full force of the Blitz, and Hilde recounted how the glass-roofed operating theatre would have its roof shattered. More happily, there was a cameraderie among the staff, and much later I took Hilde on nostalgic visits to *The Prospect of Whitby,* a pub in Wapping overlooking the river where she went with colleagues. Testimonials show the enthusiasm and aptitude with which she began her medical career.

In early 1941 I was evacuated to a residential nursery in Hitchin where things went badly for me through illnesses and neglect. Hilde was also at a low point, although coping with her job. An undated letter from Berti that seems to be from then responded to one in which she wrote that she wished she were dead. He did not try to comfort her but wrote that she must pull herself together. As a doctor she could help others, there were hard times ahead, her main duty was to her child, and he couldn't be sure how much he would be able to do for me in the future.

About this time they met and Berti made a proposal that could have been for a way for them to come together again. Among Hilde's papers was the draft of a letter that she might have sent to him. She wrote that she had begun to think that he still believed that they belonged together. Putting me in a home had been dreadful for her, and she would not have done it if he had said a word against it. Now she was using her freedom and independence to start afresh and change things that she found false, and was enjoying that.

His saying that she could not help him improve things because she did not love him enough had hit home because in recent years, when their life together seemed so bad and hopeless, she had often asked whether she loved him enough. She thought she had been a disappointment to him, and she was also bitter and had lost her trust in him. Now 'for the first time it seems to me hopeless. I realise that for years I've been a heavy burden for you. I knew that I often made life difficult for you, but I always thought that as a whole it was worthwhile for you. There is no guarantee that I won't again be a heavy burden for you, and I can't take that upon myself.' While there was something in his idea that with love they could overcome their difficulties, she couldn't just make herself love him; she needed to recover the trust she had given him. It was better not to put re-building first but for her to have time to be independent, to work and to be clearer about herself.

When they had met there was again that tone between them that she dreaded more than anything else, even though they met because they both wanted to find a way. He had spoken bitterly and scornfully of her untruthfulness, pettiness and resigned attitude to life. That was a bad start, and so she was frightened and wouldn't let it happen again; she simply couldn't bear it. Moreover, she was very mistrustful about Berti and 'E'. He had been friends with her for hardly more than a week, and his proposal would put limits on his relationship with E; she didn't understand it at all. E could have been Edith Tudor Hart, with whom Berti did indeed have a relationship that became of great interest to MI5. Hilde's letter also states elsewhere that she had a boyfriend whom she was not prepared to simply abandon as part of the proposal.

She concluded: 'I want to say clearly to you that I hope with my whole heart that we come together again. But I don't want to try before we have some chance of success. Neither of us has learned anything yet, so nothing has changed, and I don't believe that an attempt now would succeed. Let's go our own ways for now and maybe we'll learn to see things differently. Increasingly I have lost the belief that we can build something together, but I want at least to guard the possibility that it would work later.'

In their attempts at finding a way of staying together Hilde and Berti were doubtless largely thinking of me, to whom they were both deeply attached. But they did love each other, and they may also have felt that their lives as a couple had been so disrupted that if they could only have a time of peace together things might be better. Hilde's instance of unfaithfulness was the immediate cause of their separation, but maybe there had been others on each side. I think the loss of trust in Berti that Hilde mentions is more general and links with her sense of being made to feel a burden. Berti was a driven man politically and professionally, whereas Hilde craved a simpler life around motherhood and becoming a working doctor, and found political activism difficult and divisive. Moreover Berti had the trait of striving to make the wish (in this case for love) into reality by willpower, but he could not help then or later being critical and conditional in his own affections. Whereas Berti's second marriage also ended in tears, in time Hilde was to discover in Alan a man who loved her as she was, and she was truly happy with him. Meanwhile, my own life was in a sense about to be saved by Barbara Sparks.

10

BERTI, HILDE AND PAUL
MAY 1941–NOVEMBER 1942

In May the Blitz was continuing, Hilde was at The Queen's Hospital for Children, Berti was working in Barking, and I was at the home in Hitchin. An incident then affected my mother deeply. From her early days in London she had been befriended by left wing women doctors connected with the Royal Free Hospital, particularly Eleanor Singer. She was married to Sidney Fink, a Glaswegian full-time Communist Party organiser and Air Raid Warden, and they provided the London home for Willie Gallagher, the sole Communist MP, from the coalmining constituency of West Fife. After a visit by Hilde, Sidney was killed by a bomb after walking her to the Tube, and Hilde felt responsible.

The Hitchin home was bad, and Hilde and Berti sought somewhere else for me. Perhaps Gwendy Caroe helped them because I went to Barbara Sparks in Dunsfold, close by her in Surrey, and was with her from May 1941 until October 1942. From September 1941 to February 1942 Hilde was at Stoke Mandeville hospital, as part of the pioneering surgery unit for war-wounded. She had to move on because there she would faint during the very long operations, and she was then a house surgeon at the North Middlesex County Hospital from March to August 1942. In mid-1942 she herself was ill again and in June had an operation, and then spent at least a month recuperating at Dunsfold. It seemed that her illness might be a recurrence of her TB, but that was not the case.

The German invasion of Russia in June had resolved the position of Communists in Britain with respect to the war, so in the autumn of 1941 Tess could put Berti in contact with Hans Halban, who had arrived in Britain from France in 1940 with Lew Kowarski, bringing with them the world's supply of heavy water (see later). Berti and Halban had known each other as youths in Austria, and Halban was keen to recruit Berti to his team at the Cavendish Laboratory in Cambridge. Berti was equally keen to move from his job in Barking. Berti wrote to Hilde that Halban was very pressing. Berti had to obtain Auxiliary War Service clearance and the file shows that the wishes of Halban and then of Sir Edward Appleton, Secretary of the Department of Scientific and Industrial Research (DSIR) that ran Tube Alloys (the cover name for the Atom Project), overcame the very real concerns of the Security Services. However, since most British scientists had already been assigned to war-related work, when in 1941 the decision was made to support work in this new area of nuclear fission, mainly foreign scientists were recruited to work in Halban and Kowarski's group, and Berti was seen as an able recruit. Also the central military importance compared with the energy promise of the project was not yet fully realised. But it is still unclear to me why Appleton was so firm that Berti was needed. Perhaps what was at issue was a cultural difference between scientists and security men.

DSIR to Colonel Ryder, 9 December 1941. 'Mr Sams has forwarded to your department the papers about Engelbert Broda, whom we are proposing to employ on highly important and secret work being carried out for this Department at the Cavendish Laboratory, Cambridge.'

E.4(2) to DSIR, 11 December 1941. 'It is understood that the Department of Scientific and Industrial Research is considering the employment of the above named. This Department in conjunction with the Security branches has already expressed its view on the general question of employing enemy aliens without restriction on secret or confidential research work and in this particular case would point out that Mr Broda is an active member of the Central Committee of the Austrian Communist Party of which party he was Cell Leader in Vienna. Should you still feel that the exigencies of your department override the obvious security objections to this appointment, this department will be prepared to give further consideration to the grant of a permit.'

From G. W. Hogg, DSIR, 16 December 1941. 'I have referred your letter to Sir Edward Appleton, Secretary of this Department. Sir Edward Appleton directs me to say that, having given full weight to the views expressed in your letter, he feels that the exigencies of this Department do override objections on security grounds to Mr Broda's employment on the work for which his services are desired; and that it is essential to ask that a permit may be issued accordingly for his employment by the University of Cambridge, in the Cavendish Laboratory, Cambridge, on the work which is there being undertaken for, and at the cost of, this Department. I am to add that the work in question is in two parts and that Mr Broda would not be employed on the more secret part.'

E.4(2) to G.W.Hogg,19 December 1941. 'I am directed to acknowledge receipt of your letter of 16.12.1941 from the contents of which it is noted that Sir Edward Appleton feels that the exigencies of your Department outweigh any security objection to the employment of the above named. In view of this conclusion, I am arranging to send Mr Broda the necessary permit for employment at the Cavendish Laboratory, Cambridge.'

Berti started at the Cavendish on 20 December 1941, shortly after the United States' entry into the war, and some months before Alan arrived there. Berti's identity card states that he may not be absent from Cambridge between the hours of 10.30 p.m. and 6 a.m. This restriction seems at odds with his evidently frequent visits to Surrey to see me, and for his activities at the Austrian Centre. He must have had a legal way to travel as he would not have risked trouble with the police. He had also become involved with Edith Tudor Hart, and he was always open and proud of his tireless Austrian refugee activities in both London and Cambridge. Through Kaspar, an informer intimately connected with Edith Tudor Hart and the Austrian Centre, entries in the MI5 file continue to link Berti and Edith until Berti left Britain in 1947. I have been unable to establish who Kaspar was, or for how long Berti and Edith saw themselves as a couple. In Cambridge Berti was close to Kowarski and his wife Dora, and to Jules Guéron, another Free French scientist. Tess Simpson and SPSL were also in Cambridge until 1944. No letters between Berti and Tess exist from this period, but allusions to that time in later letters show their close but probably platonic friendship.

Barbara Sparks was the wife of Jack Sparks, captain of HMS *Enterprise,* who was at sea for the eighteen months that I stayed with her, and beyond. She had four sons, three from her previous marriage. After she had been widowed, she and Jack married and had a son Peter (and later a daughter). Her two eldest sons saw active service on convoys and in Burma. Barbara wished 'to do something for afflicted Londoners' and wanted a child on his own as a companion for Peter. I have the letters that Barbara wrote to Hilde, and even more important, Peter had some of the frank and detailed diary-style letters she wrote to Jack and that survived; she referred to others having gone to the bottom. As we shall see, they shed light on my state then and on both Hilde and Berti. The following quotes are from her letters to Jack unless stated, James is her name for Peter, and the punctuation is hers.

4 May 1941. 'The mother came to inspect us and we all liked her very much ... they had been bombed, the baby was in his pram with the hood up luckily as the ceiling fell on him, they all spent several nights in London's crowded underground stations, but this must have been ghastly for them, so they put the baby in a children's home outside London. They were not happy about him there, and made enquiries about getting him into a private house with other children. It was arranged that Hilda should bring the baby next day. The baby is called Lunki, and is a great disappointment. He is such a baby, and James is much more advanced, Lunki has one large brown eye and one half-closed blue one, and he doesn't speak and looks a bit vacant, we were very sad and a little alarmed. We can't keep him if he doesn't quickly improve. He looks quite repulsive poor baby, he is nearly two years old. His mother was so pathetically grateful at having found this kind home for him, she kept saying "I am *so* happy for Lunki". She is so sweet herself. Anyway she has gone so we must keep him for a while. She wanted to give us £5 a week for him. I could not accept that. The regulation amount given by the Government for an evacuee is eight shillings and sixpence a week, to feed and clothe a child. I said £5 was too much and we settled for £2. ...

'Poor Lunki gave us all the creeps yesterday. He seems to be so stupid and heavy, but today he held out his arms to me and seemed so pathetic, I have quite adopted him, and decided to do all we could to improve him. He is really too young for James, this morning they played a little together climbing up and down the sofa, he is an institution child, and no-one has had time to talk to or play with him, with the result that he has never learnt to talk and laugh and play. I think he may improve, if he does not do it fairly rapidly, I don't think we can keep him. He is only two months younger than James.

'We are getting acclimatised to Lunki, at first we thought he was dotty, but he is not. He is just very backward, the combination of measles, whooping cough, changing from German to English, not that he knows either, being buried under debris, being herded in an institution very badly run, all in four months before the age of two, is enough to make anyone look dotty, and be dotty too. He has improved but is far more bother than we bargained for. He can't even feed himself. He is very determined and nothing short of force will make him give up anything he likes. He laughs and runs now – when at first he just sat looking half-witted. Lunki's father did not turn up at week-ends, his mother comes sometimes. When papa walked in, Lunki was so pleased to see him. He looked after L. all day. He said London had a bad night and Hilda, his wife, was working in a Hackney Hospital, a bad district. He is so sweet with his baby, so humble and polite to us. If he were German instead of Austrian, he might not be so pleasant. I am so sorry to have to become involved with these enemies when you scour the seven seas looking for them to kill, it seems absurd for me to harbour them in the house, but a baby is a baby whatever its colour or creed, this one is actually a British subject having been born in England. I asked his Pop to see to it that Lunki did not drop bombs on us twenty years hence. He said he would do his best. There is a marked improvement in Lunki in two weeks he has been here. He still can't say anything but "mummy" which he calls me, he and James play well together now.'

26 May 1941. 'Lunki's parents are rather a trial, one comes one week-end and one the next, if they would come together, we would have alternate week-ends free. We like them but Lunki is awful when they are here, it makes the week-end one long yell – Hilda irritates him and is silly with him.'

June 1941. 'We have had Lunki a month now; although his improvement and development can't be much interest to you, it is interest to us. From having been a loony looking heap of fat with no ideas beyond having everything for himself and biting people who did not agree with him, now he has quite a happy normal face, except for his odd eyes, he is not quite so selfish, he is very affectionate too and is very fond of Betty (Peter's nanny) and me, he does everything James does, if I kiss James, he wants to be kissed too. Also he has more self-control over his tantrums than he used to, he will actually stop yelling if you say fiercely "stop at once", if he is left yelling, he will continue for an hour or more, but alas when his parents are here, he is quite impossible, and nothing we say can convince his parents that he is a different child when they are not there. It is very sad. I had asked his parents to come down together at week-ends, alternate ones, so that we could have a week-end without sometimes. We are very fond of the Brodas but it is exhausting having them when their child behaves like a wild animal in front of them.'

22 June1941. 'Lunki behaved abominably as usual with his parents. Is it a good or bad thing having the Germans fighting the Russians? My monthly paper kept telling us that it would never happen, and I always believed what that paper says.'

August 1941. 'We all went to the nearest wood and picked all the toadstools we could find, taking them to Berti who is an expert! I was surprised when we were all quite well the next day! Berti and I have been discussing what to do with Germany after the war. Somehow, fond of Hilda and Berti as I am, its rather like eating toadstools for me to be friends with them. They are bombing us and keeping you and R where you are, and here we are all being nice to them, and fond of them too, its a crazy world.'

Berti to Barbara Sparks, 10 September 1941. ' … We are so very grateful to you for being so terribly nice to Lunki so that he really can feel at home – I would like to say that every time I come unless I was afraid of boring you. I would be very glad indeed to show you round at our Austrian Club in London one evening. … You must not expect magnificent things there, of course, it is just the meeting place of the Austrian refugees; but still it might be quite interesting to you to have a glance on a side of their life, and to hear something about their problems and achievements. Clearly everything is quite informal there, but I hope we shall get some Austrian food there; usually it is quite good. …'

22 September1941. 'Lunki is back from a day or two with Hilda, he is becoming a very sweet little boy now, he is much more obedient than James. He was pathetically pleased to be home again after his adventures in London. Lunki has come back talking much more, he is rather pleased with himself when he does it.'

October 1941. 'Hilda was having a holiday and Betty too, so I gave Hilda the house and James and I slept in the caravan, it was lovely weather and more restful than being in the house, every time we passed the house we heard Lunki's yells. Hilda had had 6 months of very hard work and was very run down and needed a rest, Lunki's tantrums would not have helped. She looked a wreck after a few days with her son. She asked me to help with him on her last day, he was being impossible, fighting and screaming. It is very hard to undress and bath a strong child who fights and yells the whole time, and when I put him in his cot he got out, it was jolly hard and I admired the way he did it! I put him back every time without saying anything. This went on for quite a while, and I wondered who would tire first. The yells continued, it was too late for a spank, he was so hysterical, at last to my great surprise he suddenly stopped and sucked his fingers, I covered him up and he was asleep at once. James was asleep during all this, luckily. I was quite proud of my victory but felt quite shaky when it was all over. I think these £2 are earned, but I can't help feeling sorry for a couple who can't manage their child whom they both adore.'

24 October 1941 Barbara to Hilde. 'So glad the new job is nice and that everything sounds so new and clean. I am sure enemy aliens ought not to have charge of 34 innocent British seamen who will give away military secrets in their delirium. ... Lunki stopped yelling when you got to the top of the hill – he stopped suddenly ... He eats all his food and never yells for more than a minute if at all – he is *such* a good little boy, so happy and cheerful. I often wish you could be a fly on the wall and see him and I am so sorry that things can't be arranged so that he is better during your visits. He is a person with strong emotions and he gets thrilled when you come and so excited, and if he doesn't know exactly what you want him to do and how you want him to behave he just lets himself go and tries all manner of things with you that he wouldn't think of doing ordinarily – he is so sweet it seems a shame for you not to see him at his best – instead of at his worst – it must be horrid for you to have these incessant yells. I dont think you "spoil" him- perhaps it is that you are a little afraid of him and you both feel he has the upper hand from the moment you get together. ... I do feel too that its bad for Peter to see Lunki running amok on a Broda weekend! Lots of love, Barbara'

26 November 1941. 'R goes back on Saturday – I think I might go to London with him, we might do another theatre, also I shall avoid the Brodas who have been here every week-end for the last three. I would not mind them if they were not so stupid with Lunki.'

30 December 1941. 'We have Lunki back and James is much happier. Lunki is becoming so good; in fact I have only to look severe and he is an angel! One of the most surprising things in this war is the Russian Army, whoever would have thought it.'

26 January 1942. 'Bogyman Hitler is still top of the world. Churchill is always optimistic and I pin my faith on him. Lunki has started to talk and is advancing quite rapidly, he said to Betty the other day "Roger is not in his destroyer, not on his ship, he is in bed." Betty could not believe it and went

to look! We rather love him. He is so marvellous compared to what he was. Both children have picked up, I can't think where, the words "nasty Germans", which they say to anything they don't like the look of. Berti is very Jewish looking, he is not one – his hair stands on end, he has nice teeth, he always bows when he shakes hands and clicks his heels even though we are on Christian names to each other. He has a nice sense of humour, speaks fluent English and is very well informed on all political matters, he is very stubborn and rather moody. Hilde is charming, you would love her, she is very quick and intelligent, a sense of humour, very gay and will turn her hand to anything, most sympathetic and sweet and pretty, she loves people, and gaiety. Berti does not, and that is where they fall apart. When Lunki goes I am sure we shall never see or hear of them again, charming as she is, and fickle I think.'

21 February 1942. 'Your letter to James for his birthday was a great success. We sat by the fire, one boy on each side of me and read it over and over again, Lunki feels that you belong to him too – "my daddy in a ship" and Berti is "my daddy in London." They both know quite a lot of the letter by heart … I am always speculating the possibilities of you coming home.'

3 March 1942. 'Your Christmas letter posted December 4th arrived today, a very special letter … Betty and I were saying how nice to have a weekend without Brodas, when Hilda walked in! She is such a nice person in spite of my grumbling about her. She shook me by suddenly asking if I thought she was a suitable person to have charge of a child! Awful question, she insisted on an answer. I told her that she was much better with Lunki now than she used to be, which is true, but neither she nor Berti seemed to know how to treat him. Perhaps things would be better if they lived together with him. Poor Lunki, perhaps another baby would solve the problem. Austrians in England are now regarded as "friendly Aliens", instead of "enemy Aliens", Berti and Hilda say they feel inches taller. They can be out after 10 pm at night and ride bicycles, what an honour, and all kinds of exciting things.'

April 1942. 'Berti paid us a visit, he is so silly with the children. He adores them and tries so hard to please everyone. … I shall never be quite the same since the Broda invasion. I told them you might be home this year, Hilda said she would have to see about removing Lunki at a moment's notice, I asked why and she said I told her last year when he first came – that

41. Peter Sparks (right) and Paul, 1942

if you arrived home suddenly he would have to go. He was so awful then, he is a different child now. I said he could stay even if you did come home, perhaps she thinks you are not as fierce as you were, it would never occur to her that her child had become more of a drawing room specimen ... I have not heard if the reconciliation is progressing and if they really intend to set up house together in August according to plan and start off on more Lunkis.' (Photos 41,42,43)

22 May 1942. 'We have Hilda here convalescing after her operation. Hilda has been behaving very well with Lunki and Berti comes to stay too sometimes. Now they are better with their child we don't mind having them. Hilda wanted to be a paying guest here but I don't want her to, they look upon us as a hotel anyway and they would even more so if they paid. So she has offered to remake some of my old clothes for me instead of paying for their keep. Hilda is a delightful person.'

42. Berti, Peter's aunt Sylvia Sparks and grandmother Bessie Sparks, Peter (front) and Paul (rear), 1942

43. Barbara and Jack Sparks, 1938
With thanks to Peter Sparks

A letter of June 1942 from Berti to Hilde, when she was convalescing at Dunsfold, replied to one of hers. She must have said that she had been immature and perhaps more, and in return she got a detailed critique of her faults, based on this concession and referring to her as childish and irresponsible. It is written in such a patronising, self-righteous and insensitive way that one wonders at her mixture of emotions on reading it. Nothing was said in Berti's letters about the reconciliation alluded to by Barbara.

Lyme Regis, Dorset. 6 July1942. Barbara to Hilde. 'Took Lunki and Peter, Betty, Tigger for holiday. ... Lunki is prepared to walk straight into the sea up to his neck. Peter feels desperately daring if a little wave is allowed to wash over his toes. ... There seems to be lots of food here – but no fruit – the children have eggs for tea every day ... we've had meat every day ...'

26 August 1942. Barbara to Hilde. 'Lunki arrived and was welcomed with open arms by Peter. You should have heard their chatter all the way from the bus. Betty said they never stopped. ... I am so sorry you are not better but hope the sanatorium materializes. ... I am more than sorry to hear from Berti that he is taking Lunki away in October – if it is a question of L.s.d. I'd love to keep Lunki just for his keep, say 10/- a week. Tell me what you think. We shall be so sad to see Lunki go – '

8 September 1942. Barbara to Berti. 'I wasn't very clever when you said you were taking Lunki away, but now having gathered my wits I'd like to make a suggestion. May we keep Lunki til Christmas, just for nothing ... I felt I must ask if you would let him stay on a bit, and hang the £2 pw please. ...'

September 1942. 'Berti has said he is taking Lunki away on October 1st ... Berti came on Sunday to make arrangements for moving Lunki – he became very sentimental and wants to meet you very much – you must meet Berti, Hilda and Lunki, our crazy trio! bound for a bust up and, sadly, I feel that Lunki will get hysterical again quite soon.'

2 November1942 Barbara to Hilde. ' ... I was so sorry you let Berti have Lunki as he arranged it in Cambridge. I only wish you had insisted on L going to another family in Cambridge and not lead that unsettled 2 days with one person and three days with another and weekend with Berti plan – it must be so bad for Lunki. ...'

In October Berti did take me to Cambridge for two months, perhaps to show that he could manage as a single parent. It seems to me now that he did this for himself rather than for me, since I was happy and secure at Dunsfold.

During these two months he wrote to Hilde, who was lodging with friends in London, that I was doing well. But he also negotiated with her about my future. In one letter he wrote: 'In our last conversation you answered my question, when in your opinion the child would be old enough to spend the greater part of the year with his father, with "ten years". I would be grateful if you would let me know whether you stand by your word. We are agreed that the problems should be resolved as soon as possible to our joint satisfaction.' A few days later he wrote: 'I am prepared for him to be with you for the greater part of the year until we have reached a final agreement, and that he should spend two months twice a year with me. Of course it must then remain so, independent of how things develop for each of us, for better or worse. ... I don't think it is good for the child always to be with me only in holidays. I've already told you that; I don't want to discuss that at the moment. I hope that sooner or later you will arrive at my point of view, and that we can come to a good agreement for the child. I hope for your agreement for the first paragraph of this letter.'

Meanwhile Barbara was very firm in her advice to Hilde. She seemed to understand Berti's long-term ambition of re-marrying, without anyone being clearly in view, and also assumed that Hilde will find a new husband: 'You simply must fight for him – and any court would let you have him (Lunki) under the circumstances – they would probably agree to your having him entirely – but that sort of divorce is likely to be expensive – the only cheap kind is I believe where both parties are in agreement. Your only card with Berti I should think, if you haven't already tried it, is that no boy of 7 or 8 would feel "at home" with a stepmother and lots of young step brothers and sisters and a father out working all day – I don't suppose a stepmother with children of her own would either be fond of or kind to Lunki – why should she? he would be very much in the way – and Lunki would always feel it and there could be no home life and feelings of security for him in that sort of entourage – Berti wouldn't be home enough to make it so. I think as he were old enough to reason for himself he would think that Berti had treated you rather meanly, and I can imagine Lunki coming to you himself at about 14 or so earlier if he liked the man you married, and of his not having a very high opinion of Berti. I think if you had Lunki always and remained on friendly terms with Berti and allowed Lunki to stay with Berti during *Berti's* holidays – when they could go off together – when Lunki was older – and walk climb travel etc together I can see a far friendlier feeling develop between Lunki and Berti and perhaps a lasting influence – rather than the emotional feelings of bitterness jealousy and unhappiness which are certain to be his lot if the poor child is made to live with a woman who has younger children of her own and wont however hard she may try – be able to hide from him that he doesn't belong and that the household would be better without him – Lunki's only happy moments will be when Berti is home and then Lunki will feel he is possibly the cause of tension between Berti and his wife. To all that Berti may say Lunki is too young to have these feelings – but I suppose he will be 5 or 6 by the time a divorce marriage and other children come, and a child of 5 or 6 knows and feels a lot. ... Perhaps I'll come to Cambridge and take Lunki myself! ..."

We'll see how things actually worked out for us all.

11

ALAN IN CAMBRIDGE 1942

Early in 1942 Chadwick asked Alan to join Halban and Kowarski's team in Cambridge (Note 23). In 1940 they had escaped from France with the deuterium oxide (heavy water) the French had bought from Norway just before the German invasion. Joliot-Curie, who had organised this coup, stayed in France and became a member of the Resistance, but Halban and Kowarski continued the experiments in the Cavendish and had a result that seemed to establish that a reactor using heavy water could give a chain reaction (see later). Alan's task would be to develop measurement techniques with ionisation chambers and counters, and to tighten up the treatment of experimental errors, a part of the Cavendish training that Chadwick hinted was somewhat slack in the Halban-Kowarski work. Alan was unaware that his recruitment was part of the plans being negotiated with the Americans for the transfer of most of the British project to the USA or Canada, because the resources needed for it could not be spared in Britain, and the large industrial plants involved would also be far too vulnerable to attack. In the early days, the reactor part of the Atom Project was regarded as of secondary importance compared with enriching for U235, only to do with postwar power supplies. However, recent work (also see later) had shown that plutonium, generated in a reactor, could be as effective as U235 for making a bomb, and might be much easier to prepare in the purity needed. This raised the status of the Halban-Kowarski team.

In January 1942 Appleton, as head of the DSIR which was now in charge of the project, had written to Chadwick that he felt a first class British worker was needed in Halban's team, in which nearly all the senior scientists were refugees. Chadwick agreed and named Alan as suitable. Alan wrote: 'Of course I was not aware of this background at the time, but Chadwick dropped hints that Halban was something of a problem child, dictatorial with his staff, and having inflated ideas of his own importance. In our discussions the question of my politics never arose directly and explicitly, but he suddenly asked me "Did you know Nahum?" Nahum had been well known in Cavendish circles as the CP organiser of the science students. I said "Yes" and Chadwick went on: "We tried to get him for work on the project, but the security people made objections, on very silly grounds". And he looked at me with one of his quizzical stares, seeming to wait for me to get all the implications. The implications were very interesting. First, that Chadwick knew that like many of the nuclear physicists at the Cavendish I had been a party member, otherwise why raise the Nahum question at all? Second, that he personally regarded this as no bar to recruitment to the project, and so did the other scientists in charge. But the security people were liable to raise difficulties which made life awkward, so better not ask any embarrassing questions, and would I please play it cool. Incidentally one must add a word about Nahum, an exceptionally fine physicist and comrade. He did join the project, but was killed in an air raid on Cambridge.'

Alan continued: 'Chadwick's attitude may seem surprising, and will scandalise authorities on cold war security who regard my recruitment as proof that there must have been a mole in MI5. The truth is that Chadwick's attitude was at the time perfectly normal and unavoidable. This was a war against Fascism in which Russia was our ally, so a history of resisting Fascism and of support for Russia were no bar to recruitment, even a positive recommendation. In any case there were precious few good scientists available, and if Chadwick had followed the criteria of the cold warriors he would have been unable to find anyone for the job. I was reluctant to leave Bristol because the work there was congenial, whilst work under Halban could well be most uncongenial. Also I suspected that the project would turn out to be mainly of postwar interest. But Chadwick argued strongly that the heavy water project could well be the simplest and most direct path to the Bomb, by producing plutonium, and that the Germans were known to be working on heavy water. It was therefore essential to find out whether this method would work. The experimental evidence so far was distinctly promising, but far from definite. In particular one needed to know how much heavy water would be needed to make a reactor. Present estimates were too vague; altogether there was a lot of work to be done. In the end I succumbed to his arm-twisting, and agreed to join the project, thus sealing my fate to a far greater extent than either of us realised.'

Alan then went to see G. P. Thomson who also briefed him (Photo 44).
'Too many damned foreigners' was his verdict on the Halban team (which by
this time included Berti). 'It seemed that my mission was to keep an eye on
their nefarious activity, to act as Our Man in Halbania.' He then signed the
Official Secrets Act form. He had already consulted a very senior scientist,
whose political and scientific judgement were impeccable, and who was
already fully aware of all the implications of the nuclear fission project. His
verdict was immediate, that Alan must join the project, it was simply a
matter of getting the bomb before the Germans and nothing else counted.
So Alan was quite happy that he was doing the right thing. In the spring of
1942 he left Bristol to become a member of the Halban-Kowarski team, so
entering a somewhat strange environment of scientific politics and intrigue.

Joliot-Curie, Halban and Kowarski had been at the forefront of the spate
of publications following the discovery of fission. In early 1939 they had
been the first to establish the emission of secondary neutrons, and to estimate
how many such neutrons were emitted at each fission. Then they did large-

44. G. P. Thomson, 1946
© Godfrey Argent Studio. The Royal Society, with permission

110

scale experiments with mixtures of uranium oxide and water in which they achieved about two or three successive steps of a chain reaction, as shown by the increase in the number of neutrons present. But it became clear that systems in which the neutrons were slowed down by collisions with hydrogen could never become critical, and they turned to other 'moderators' to slow down the neutrons. The crucial decision was taken to go for deuterium oxide as the moderator because deuterium was known to absorb hardly any neutrons.

After France fell in June 1940 and the precious 185 kg of heavy water had arrived in Britain, Halban and Kowarski were provided with facilities to continue their experiments, in particular the crucial test of whether a chain reaction would be maintained with a mixture of uranium oxide and heavy water. As expected, their measurements showed that this system did indeed have the potential to start a chain reaction. It was a notable result, but there was still a long way to go before an actual chain reaction ('divergent system') could be achieved. Much more heavy water would be needed, and more uranium. To get a more accurate estimate further experiments were needed with perhaps half a ton of heavy water, and also detailed studies would be needed on the effect of using heterogeneous systems (with uranium rods for instance) instead of the homogeneous mixtures so far studied. There were also other issues to be studied such as methods of cooling and control.

The trouble was that the only possible source of further heavy water would be in the USA or controlled by the Americans. This led to complicated negotiations between the British and Americans, between Imperial Chemical Industries (ICI) and the British government, and between Halban and all the other parties. The Americans had the strongest hand and were the toughest negotiators. Halban had the weakest hand, but secured very favourable agreements with the British government and ICI at the cost of antagonising the Americans and many senior British scientists. His main bargaining counters were the patents which Joliot-Curie and other members of the French team had secured together with the French government. It was not at all clear that he had any authority to use the patent rights in this way, but both ICI and the British government appear to have accepted the ploy, and regarded the patents as very valuable. In the end the Americans disregarded them. Halban's other main bargaining strength was from the Cambridge experiment showing that uranium and heavy water could form a divergent system. Even at the beginning the Americans were very mistrustful of these results, and demanded that Chadwick should re-examine these data. His report was favourable, but this did not prevent Fermi from making his own detailed criticism and at a much later date writing a scathing report.

There had been another major difficulty for the Halban-Kowarski team when the British looked on isotope separation as the main problem and U235 as the most likely material for a bomb. This is clear from the MAUD report, where Halban and Kowarski's line of work was regarded as to do with nuclear power, and therefore only of post-war importance. But in 1940 E. Bretscher and Feather suggested that the new element Plutonium (formed by neutron absorption in U238) would be just as good as U235 for making a bomb. This idea had also occurred to Chadwick, to Turner in the USA and to Bothe in Germany, all at about the same time. But a firm decision on this point could only be reached by producing enough plutonium to be able to measure its nuclear properties, which meant quantities of the order of milligrams instead of the micrograms or less that were available. Again only the Americans could do this, so the British passed this problem to them and pressed hard for the experiments to be done as quickly as possible. In May 1941 Seaborg and Lawrence showed that plutonium was in fact better than U235 by a factor of 1.7, but this crucial information was not given to the British until the Halban-Peierls-Simon-Akers visit of 1942. So for a whole year the British mistakenly continued to regard the slow-chain problem studied by Halban and Kowarski as only of post-war interest.

Thus by 1942 the slow neutron work had become important, hence Chadwick's summons. Fermi was pressing ahead with the construction of uranium 'exponential piles', using graphite as the moderator, which were giving steadily improving reactivities as he used purer materials and better geometrical arrangements. Alan wrote: 'The reports on his work began to reach Cambridge, and it was clear that this work was far more systematic than the Halban-Kowarski measurements had been, and was guided by a deeper understanding and more thorough analysis. There was no mistaking the hand of The Pope (as Fermi was known by his associates). So by now the British were seriously behind in the slow-neutron work. They were trying to establish that the heavy water reactor would be a valuable parallel development to the Fermi graphite work. But there was the fundamental difficulty of the only source of heavy water being under US control. If Fermi's reactor did not reach the critical value, then the US would certainly take all the heavy water for themselves. On the other hand if Fermi's graphite piles did go critical, then the British might be allowed to follow on behind at a respectful distance with their heavy water, or rather, the heavy water provided by the US.'

Alan wrote that the rational way out of this impasse would have been a thorough unification of the British and American teams. This was later achieved for the fast-neutron work, but never for the slow-neutron work. There were several reasons for this; the most important was simply Halban. Not only did his personal aura of the rich playboy rub up the Americans the wrong way, but his close links with ICI, his exploitation of the French patents and his insistence in being foremost of the very important physicists all led to a general mistrust. In any collaboration with the Americans with slow-neutron work the leadership would be with Fermi, and Fermi made it clear that he had a rather low opinion of the work so far carried out by the Halban-Kowarski team, while Halban would not have accepted a position under Fermi's command.

Team members did their best to initiate Alan into the mysteries of Halbanian politics. Meanwhile he worked on the design of ionisation chambers, especially those containing boron trifluoride, which they were developing as a better measuring device than the detectors which the team had used until then. Alan was also trying to master the reports and other documents about the previous work of the team, including the patents. This involved discussions with Kowarski and, on the theoretical side, Nicholas Kemmer (Note 24). There was a largely autonomous chemistry group under Guéron and Alfred Maddock, while Kemmer provided the theoretical guidance which was essential for understanding the stream of papers arriving from Fermi's team in Chicago. Also in the Cavendish, but with only rather remote connections, was the Feather-Bretscher team, the parents of plutonium, and therefore of the possibility that slow-neutron reactors, producing it, might lead to a Bomb.

Getting to know this large team took Alan a little while, especially as he was also engaged in more directly political activities with a quite separate set of friends. He had found a comfortable set of rooms, and soon after he moved in he had an unexpected visit from some Party members he had known as a research student. They urged him to re-bind himself to the Party. After all, Churchill had declared that Russia was an ally. Alan objected that he was doing top secret government work, to which they replied that all other scientists in the group were equally top secret. He was told to report to the appropriate Party cell, one specially designed for such undercover mole types. The chairman of this group was a fervent activist, and would play a key role in Alan's future. Until he went to Canada Alan then attended their weekly meetings. The other members of the group were engaged in government work of various kinds. Alan's vague memory and natural discretion prevented him from saying more. They studied the Party literature and took part in political work, which at that time was totally non-subversive, being entirely devoted to winning the War.

Meanwhile the Germans were advancing in Russia, after being held before Moscow by a desperate Russian counter-offensive. The Nazis swept towards the Caucasus and by the summer they were approaching Stalingrad where they were finally held. The first retreat for the Germans came only with the capitulation there of von Paulus on 31 January 1943. On the other fronts 1942 was a series of disasters with the loss of Singapore, Burma taken, the dismal failure of the Dieppe raid and fighting back and forth in the North African desert, which only in November began to show better results. Throughout the year the greatest battles and the decisive actions were in Russia, and this continued to be the case throughout the War. The response of ordinary people in Britain was an immense admiration and enthusiasm for the Russians and the Red Army.

After the Americans and British decided that there would be no Second Front in 1942 someone had to break the news to the Russians. Churchill travelled to Moscow and saw Stalin, promising action in North Africa instead and possibly an attack on France in 1943. A by-product of the meeting was a secret agreement to exchange information in full on any new military weapons being developed on either side. The Russians had asked for more details of British radar, but the British were reluctant to give them anything about the latest air-borne equipment in case it fell into German hands. The Russians offered in return their latest rocket-propelled mortars. Churchill offered that all such exchanges should be covered by a formal agreement. Averell Harriman, who was present as an observer representing Roosevelt, thought it was a good idea, and was sure that a similar agreement between the US and the Russians would be welcome, so that there would be an exchange of information between all three allies. But those present either forgot about the Bomb or never knew about it, and when Roosevelt heard about the agreement he was just giving the go-ahead to a new US programme to make the Bomb before the end of the War. The last thing he wanted was such free exchange of information.

The main importance of the agreement was as evidence of the strong feeling that all assistance must be given to the Russians in their dire struggle against the Nazis. In Churchill's words the Soviets had a 'vast front flaming and bleeding along nearly 2000 miles, and the Germans but 50 miles from Moscow and advancing towards the Caspian Sea.' Although the terms of the agreement would certainly have included any British project to make an atomic bomb, almost from the moment it came into effect the project became an exclusively American affair, with the British playing a very subsidiary part supplying a few scientists as members of a team under exclusive American control. This agreement was a closely guarded secret until long after the War, and so could not influence public opinion, but it represented the way public opinion wanted things to go, at least in Britain.

Since Alan thought Hans Halban's personality became an important issue in the history of the Atomic Project, he set out his sceptical view of him: 'After a month or so during which I made preliminary contacts with the work, the Great Man himself (Halban, not Churchill) returned from his trip to the US, and I had my first encounter with him. Here one should pause to give some pale indication of this colourful personality. The official histories give tactful hints of some aspects of this. *The Times* obituary said that he "always moved easily from the laboratory, through the ministerial office, into the board room". In *Joliot-Curie* by Maurice Goldsmith he is described as "a rather self-willed and autocratic person" while Otto Frisch in *What Little I Remember* describes him as "Austrian by origin and a skilful organiser, who immediately took the leading role (over Kowarski) because he spoke English and knew how to impress people as a man of the world". Put crudely, he was a playboy, like a character out of some Viennese operetta, rich from his father, and from marrying a banker's daughter, always staying in the very best hotels, and moving with easy assurance in the company of ICI directors, ministers and the really rich and powerful. He had a weak heart, which he exploited to the utmost – critical meetings would be interrupted so that he could use his inhaler to recover his breath – so that anyone who opposed him would be scared of causing an attack. Really important sessions had to be held at his bedside, either in Brown's Hotel, or some equally impressive haven of the rich. This heart condition was also the reason for special arrangements on all journeys, from the Master Bedroom on sleeper expresses in the USA, to the special low-flying aircraft for Atlantic crossings. But his greatest ploy was the priority system – this was at a time when "priority" had to give way to "immediate priority", that in turn was overtaken by "top priority", and then by some even higher super priority. But Halban was always in the front with the highest and best kind of priority on the market. It was this kind of pushfulness that had produced the high level of equipment that I saw about me in Cambridge. It was easy to overlook in all this the fact that he was a really first-class physicist, with a series of important papers to his name, and experience of working in first-class laboratories – with Joliot-Curie, and in Copenhagen with Frisch in the Bohr institute. Indeed it was this work in Copenhagen which provided much of the basic data and techniques which were used in all the slow neutron experiments in France, Cambridge, and in the USA, not to mention Germany.'

Soon after Halban returned to Cambridge he returned from a Tube Alloys committee meeting with a special assignment for Alan. There was an American report on 'Radioactive Poisons' which suggested that the fission products from a working reactor could be used as poisons. Dropped in a bomb or otherwise dispersed, they would make a large area uninhabitable. There was the implied fear that the Germans might already have a reactor working and could be about to use this weapon. The Smyth report of 1945 (Note 25) quotes a report by Wigner and Smyth of December 1941: 'One day's run of a 40,000 KW reactor would produce enough fission products to make a large area uninhabitable.' They did not recommended it for use by the Americans, but that serious thought be given to the possibility of the Germans using it, and defensive measures planned. This episode was a result of a message to Leo Szilard that was vague but conveyed the idea that the Germans were actively working on the uranium problem, that Heisenberg was in charge, and that a reactor might be a better route to the bomb than the separation of isotopes. Szilard convinced Compton that there was an immediate danger of German bombardment with radioactive poisons. The information was considered by the Tube Alloys committee on 14 August

1942. This reported that there was a US report that the Germans already had a reactor working and that there was alarm about it being used for spreading radioactive poisons. Halban then undertook to ask Alan to make a report. At the following TA meeting on 9 September Halban said that Alan had made a preliminary report and had discussed it with G. P. Thomson.

Alan's seven page report (and an addendum) are in the National Archives (AB4/130). They include the following: 'Wigner and Smyth in a recent report discuss the possible offensive use of the radioactive fission products from a Uranium power machine. They show that the products from a machine developing 10^5 K.W. could be used to contaminate an area of 25 Km² so that a man could not remain in the area for a day without getting a dangerous dose of radiation. These calculations are very rough because they depend on estimates of the intensity of long lived gamma radiation in the fission products and of the single dose of radiation which a man can tolerate. ....

Summary: The possible offensive uses of the radioactive products from a 10^5 K.W. uranium power machine are considered. The decay of the products for a long activation period are computed. It is shown that the radioactive products could be used to make an area of 1 (Km)² uninhabitable. In this area a man would receive a fatal dose of 10,000 rontgens over the whole body in 10 hours. The contamination will decrease in a few days or so. If the contamination is not detected, then longer periods of exposure to the radiation must be considered and areas of 10 (Km)² could be contaminated so that a dangerous dose would be received in 200 hours, while over large areas of 10^4(Km)² a dosage rate could be maintained by successive attacks which would be dangerous to health in the long run. ....

The defensive measures consist primarily of detecting the radiation. For this a large number of portable Geiger counter sets of fool-proof construction would be best. Once radiation is detected, the dangerous area could be mapped out by trained staff using standard ionisation chamber technique. A N May Cavendish Lab., 29 August, 1942.'

Alan commented: 'It seemed to me that if the Germans did ever use this weapon they would be far more likely to use it against the Russians than against the West. This was where the really critical front was, and anyhow they regarded the Russian people as sub-human, and would have little hesitation in using such weapons against them.' He referred to Rhodes for his interesting view of the attitudes of some of the other participants of the Project: 'Richard Rhodes' *The Making of the Atomic Bomb* makes clear that the Americans were really scared of a German attack on the Chicago Metallurgical Laboratories or other US targets. Late in 1942 they appointed a committee consisting of Conant, Compton and Urey (Note 26) and it worked through 1943. Independently Fermi proposed to Oppenheimer at an April 1943 conference that fission products might be used to poison German food supplies. This proposal was to be kept secret between the two of them, even within the overall secrecy of the Manhattan project. But in May Oppenheimer saw Groves and learned about the other "poisonous" committee, and discussed it with Conant and with Teller. They agreed that it would be best to concentrate attention on strontium 90. Oppenheimer wanted to keep the plan as secret as possible within the project, and held that there was no point in it unless they could achieve enough poison to kill a half million men, though (regretfully) he conceded the number might be less because of non-uniform distribution. Rhodes notes the discrepancy between this attitude and the high-minded philosophical follower of Buddhist *Ahimsa*.'

Alan continued: 'Goudsmit in *ALSOS* (Note 27) tells much the same story – how the US scientists jumped to the conclusion that the Germans already had reactors working, and would use the fission products to poison water and food supplies in the USA. They were even sure of the actual date of the attack – Christmas Day 1942 was the favourite, Chicago the target. Many sent their families into the country for safety while Geiger counters were set up to warn of the expected assault. The panic seems to have diminished during 1943, although in the invasions in 1944 men with Geiger counters were supposed to scan the beaches for radioactive defensive poisoning. This was at a time when it was clear that reactors could be made to work, but not at all clear that the Bomb would work. So the "radioactive poison" weapon was seized on as a weapon that could be made. It would have been especially abhorrent to look back on as a bomb, especially now that we have experienced Chernobyl and other disasters. One cannot help feeling that there is something slightly comic about the panic in the Chicago Metallurgical Laboratories at a time when the cities of Europe, and especially in Russia, were suffering real and overwhelming attacks with conventional weapons. There is no indication that the civilian non-scientist population of

Chicago were offered any protection. By the time I visited the Metallurgical Laboratories in 1944 they had recovered their nerve, probably because they were reasonably sure by that time that the Bomb would work.'

Shortly after Halban's return it became clear to Alan that the team was not at all happy and united, especially with the idea of going to Canada. Kowarski was strongly opposed. He said he would be keen to go and work as part of Fermi's team, but not to continue under Halban in a separate unit, which he felt was 'off on a limb'. He was very resentful of Halban's climb to pre-eminence on the basis of their joint work, and especially of Halban's use of his influence with ICI. He also mistrusted the TA Directorate in London (all recruited from ICI), especially Michael Perrin (Note 28). Alan wrote that Kowarski often said that 'after you have caught Perrin out telling a lie, you can have quite a valuable conversation with him'. Kowarski had a considerable influence with the others in the team; he was witty and there was a good deal of truth in what he said. Halban, on the other hand, put pressure on people to go to Canada. Leading members of the team and their wives were entertained to dinner at Brown's Hotel and offered glittering prospects. In all this Alan found himself in a pivotal position; as the senior British physicist, he was expected to give a lead, whereas as a radical and trade unionist his instinct was to side with the revolt amongst the team members, but that would not have been politically correct in the circumstances. The primary political objective was to win the War, and in this all the usual claims for workers' rights had to be laid aside. Although he had a feeling that Kowarski's criticisms were to a large extent justified, and that the trip to Canada might not be all that productive, that was really for the Directorate of Tube Alloys to decide. It was not for him or the team to 'reason why'.

This led to Alan's first fateful step: 'In this dilemma I sought the advice of my political mentor, the chairman of the rather secretive party group to which I adhered. He already had a good idea of what the team was doing, as any Cambridge scientist would have unless he had been quite exceptionally stupid. It did not take much special knowledge to link the names of Halban and Kowarski with nuclear fission. So nothing very serious in the way of breaches of the Official Secrets Act was involved in this discussion, at least to start with. But then he asked whether any information on the project had been given to the Soviet Union. I replied that as far as I knew nothing had been disclosed officially but I could not know for sure. As regards unofficial information, in view of the left-wing views of many of the participants that was possible, but again I could not say for sure and I had not taken any steps in that direction. He then disclosed that he had met a young Russian diplomat at a reception in London who he was sure would be very interested. Perhaps he could arrange for us to meet.'

Alan continued: 'I had long considered that the Russians should be informed of what was being done. My recent contact with the "radioactive poisons" project had reinforced this. It must be remembered that at this time (October-November 1942) things were at their most critical on the Russian front. If there was any danger of a German bomb, or of a radioactive poison attack, this was clearly where it would be used, and it seemed criminal to let the Russians be unaware of this danger. So I agreed, and wrote a brief memorandum outlining the current status of the project and what was planned by the British and the Americans, so far as I knew. The interview took place in a rather seedy café after the usual ritual of a seemingly casual meeting in the street. I handed my memo over across the café table, which was next to a window. I had the impression that my contact glanced at the window just as this took place and as I followed his eye I saw a man in the street just turning away. This was rather off-putting, as I felt that this had been a witness, perhaps even making a photographic record. Even a naïve young man might have suspected the first steps towards blackmail.' It was this episode that Alan revealed for the first time just before he died. After his death I found among his papers a sealed envelope that I had previously kept securely for him for several years, before he asked for its return. It turned out to contain the account of this episode given above. It was not part of the memoir he had hoped to publish because he had feared that he would lay himself open to a second prosecution.

'Back in Cambridge my group leader told me a few days later that although my memo was interesting it was not all that important. The atomic project was regarded by the Russians as in principle a post-War problem, and part of the basic Anglo-American rivalry. I was rather relieved because that meant that I did not need to risk my neck by supplying information. Actually this lack of interest was probably due to the fact that adequate alternative channels of information were available, but of course that was not even hinted at. But, he added with great emphasis, it was most important that I should support the team in going to Canada, as a contribution to the war effort, despite the somewhat unenthusiastic evaluation he had heard from the Russians. There I should get myself an apartment where I could be secure from observation and prepare to act as a centre for gathering and processing information. I protested that this was not at all what I had in mind. I was willing to hand over some information which I thought important, but I did not want to become a professional spy and I pointed out that the team had been warned that we would be under the scrutiny of the British, Canadian and American security services, not just working together, but in deadly rivalry to catch the omissions and mistakes of the others.

'These objections met with rather short shrift. Was I not proud to be operating practically as a serving member of the Red Army? Did they flinch from a necessary task because of danger? Anyhow the centre of a top-secret project was just the perfect place for such an operation – no-one would expect such a bold manouevre etc. A little shame-faced I agreed to try my best to comply, but with a secret reservation that it would be a very cautious attempt. So the arrangements were concluded. When my centre was ready I would send an innocent postcard to a girl, an entirely and genuinely innocent participant. She would be sure to show it to her acquaintances. Then I would expect a visit from a stranger in Montreal, who would open the proceedings with the key phrase "greetings from Alex", that being my mentor's *nom-de-plume,* but not his real name of course.'

'Then followed a serious warning. There were rival channels working and I would probably be approached by some other and possibly more attractive agency for communications of this type. If so I was not only to refuse, I was to refuse on high moral grounds, be profoundly shocked, invoke the Official Secrets Act etc. On no account was I to suggest that I was already booked on another line. The wires must not get crossed. Moreover, enquiries indicated that the political left in Canada was in some turmoil. The switch from regarding the War as an imperialist one aimed at enlarging the grip of the capitalists, to one in defence of freedom and democracy, had been a painful affair and there were ill-digested fragments littering the political landscape. Such beasts as Trotskyites and other deviationists were at large, making Canada a very dangerous place for naïve British party members. To avoid getting ensnared he suggested that I should avoid all left-wing entanglements.

'Sure enough on a visit to London soon after, I was instructed to meet

Springhall, the CP secretary (Note 29). He gave me a piece of cloth which I was supposed to sew into the lapel of my jacket, certifying that I was a fully paid-up member of the Party. This was for use in the unlikely event that I would be in need of assistance from the Canadian Party. This transaction took place in (another) rather seedy cafe. Springy went on to enquire whether I had made arrangements for transmission of technical information to the Russians, and offered his services. As instructed I expressed shocked surprise and refused. Springy was not a little taken aback, but probably guessed what was happening. A year or so later Springhall was convicted under the Official Secrets Act, so I was lucky not to be recruited into his part of the system. We were to meet in prison, but that part of the story comes later.

'About the same time there was a crucial meeting in the headquarters of the Tube Alloys Directorate to which Kowarski and I were invited, he to represent himself, I to represent the team. We had thought that this was going to be a discussion in which we would have a chance to put forward the team's views. In fact we were left kicking our heels in a waiting room outside the committee meeting for some hours, and when the meeting broke up we were informed by Perrin that the team was to go to Canada without Kowarski, who would stay in Cambridge where he would be provided with research opportunities and some collaborators. Kowarski and I returned to Cambridge in a somewhat sombre mood to tell the team. At least the way this had been done relieved me of any guilty feeling I might have had if I had had to urge the team to go to Canada against my better judgement. In the event the whole basis of the plan to transfer to Canada turned sour.

'Meanwhile there were more visits to London to acquire warm clothing with our special issue of clothing coupons. I blew mine on a magnificent fur-lined overcoat from Aquascutum which later was inherited by my brother Ralph whilst I was unable to wear it. By 1953 it had become his by right of customary use, and I never wore it again. There were final visits to my family, with dark hints of important secret war work, and promises of food parcels from Canada.'

It is of interest to add what has become available from Russian sources (see Introduction). As set out in *Spies* (Note 5), in 1945 the chief of KGB foreign intelligence noted that Soviet sources in England were the first to provide Moscow with atomic intelligence, since the British project began in 1940, more than a year before the Manhattan Project: 'There is highly valuable info. coming in from the London station regarding scientific work on "En-s" ("Enormous"). The first materials on "En-s" were received at the end of 1941 from the source "Liszt". The materials included valuable and top secret documents, both on the substance of the problem of "E-s" and on measures taken by the Brit. gov't to organize and develop work on the problem of atomic energy. These materials served as a starting point for laying down the groundwork and organizing work on the problem of atomic energy in our country. Because Amer. and Canadian work on "En-s" is sent to E. as part of a tech. information exchange, the London station sends materials covering the state and progress of work on "En-s" in three countries: England, the USA and Canada.' "Liszt" was John Cairncross, the Fifth Man, working at the centre of Government, in the Foreign Office, the Treasury, and in MI6. In 1941 he was secretary to Lord Hankey, who was a cabinet member and head of a committee that reviewed Britain's atomic programme. According to Soviet archives he passed over an almost incredible 5823 documents between 1941 and 1945.

Thus before his departure for Canada Alan had joined two others who had given information to the Russians, Cairncross and Klaus Fuchs, who was enrolled by the GRU in August 1941. *Spies,* based on A. Vassiliev's notes from the KGB archives, also mentions three unnamed members of the team going to Canada as possible recruits, but does not mention whether steps were taken with them. As will be seen in Chapter 14, the same source reveals that shortly after Alan's departure for Canada Berti took active steps to make contact with the Russians.

12

ALAN IN CANADA 1943-44

The convoy with Alan and his colleagues on the banana boat SS *Bayano* took six weeks to get to Canada. Halban went on a special low-flying flight and more senior and fragile members of the team went by fast ocean liner. Alan's cabin had four or five young members of the team and most of his time was spent reading. The leisurely pace of transfer to Canada perhaps reflected a lack of urgency on the part of the authorities. Meanwhile the Fermi group in Chicago had attained their goal, an exponential pile which (nearly) attained the magic figure of $k = 1$, and they then proceeded to build the first ever divergent chain-reacting pile that went critical on 2 December 1942. There was then a nearly complete shut down on the flow of information to the British in general and to the Montreal team in particular. Furthermore, the materials for which they had come, uranium mined in Canada and also heavy water made in Canada, were commandeered by the US project, so the purpose of the journey seemed to have evaporated.

Alan met George Placzek who was to lead the theoretical team, Bruno Pontecorvo who had been recruited from the USA, and several Canadians (Note 30). Placzek, Pontecorvo and Alan had many discussions on the Halban-Kowarski papers, at which it fell to Alan to act as defending counsel, a job for which he was not very well qualified. First, they both knew far more about neutron physics than he did. Placzek had advised the Paris group and the Chicago team on theoretical problems, and Pontecorvo was one of the original Rome group and had worked directly under the Pope of neutrons, Fermi, and was a part-owner of the famous Rome patents on uranium fission. Secondly Alan himself was not fully persuaded that the Halban-Kowarski claims were valid, and during their discussions what little faith he had began to dissipate.

The situation was as Kowarski had predicted, only considerably worse. They had no equipment, no laboratory, and no prospect of obtaining any materials, and the Americans who had provided such encouraging reading in Cambridge were now cut off from them. Reading the Halban-Kowarski papers and arguing about their validity was a poor substitute for productive work. The team felt rather let down and the higher echelons were deeply disturbed by this development. While the high command alternated between desperate plans to go it alone in the UK and meek submission to the stringent conditions the Americans set for collaboration, in Montreal the best was made of a bad job. In March they started to equip a laboratory. The precious heavy water had come by air, sealed in jerry cans. On the advice of ICI the interior of the cans had been coated with a special paint to guard against corrosion. This was disastrous as the heavy water froze in the hold of the high-flying plane and on melting, the lumps of ice had scraped the paint off the insides of the cans, forming a suspension of paint. So the chemists had to re-distil all 185 kg.

Halban was Director and Alan was in the Experimental Physics section headed by Pierre Auger, a distinguished French physicist. Chemistry was under F. A. Paneth, a famous radiochemist, Engineering was under Newell from ICI, and Placzek headed Mathematics. However, little progress was possible as long as the Americans refused to cooperate. In February, Auger and Bertrand Goldschmidt paid a visit to Chicago and returned with a good deal of information they had obtained unofficially. Goldschmidt managed to persuade his friends to let him have a useful quantity of fission products and plutonium for chemical studies. But although this served to keep up morale, it would hardly be possible to maintain the team unless the Americans relented (Photo 45).

Alan wrote: 'A crucial issue was the validity of the claim by Halban to have "proved" the possibility of a chain reaction in heavy water and thus to have a claim over all future work. This was strongly contested by the Americans and especially by Fermi, who had now attained an actual chain-reacting system, not just a possible one. There was a feeling in the team that the real interests of the heavy water work were being sacrificed to bolster Halban's claim and the patent rights which he shared, in some complicated way, with ICI and the British Government. There was a crucial conference in New York between the British and the Americans when Halban was present. It was then that he phoned back to Montreal on a Saturday morning asking that Jackson, the administrative head, should be summoned to open the Top

45. At Montreal, c.1943. From left, Henry Seligman, Bruno Pontecorvo, Bertrand Goldschmidt, Jules Guéron, Hans Halban, Pierre Auger

Secret safe to secure some documents which he needed. Jackson was fetched from home, and urgent arrangements were made for a courier to fly to New York with the documents and deliver them under diplomatic seal to Halban. Halban was then rung again to ask him which papers he needed. The reply was "Oh, any documents, it doesn't matter which ones." The whole thing was a charade to impress the Americans.

'Many of the Montreal team felt that they were pawns in a game between the British and the Americans, and there was some truth in this. There was a bitter dispute between Sir John Anderson on the British side and (Vannevar) Bush and Conant on the American side. Each side was determined to secure their national interests, first in the control of the bomb, and second in having a major share in the development of nuclear power, which was seen by all concerned as the ultimate answer to the world's power needs. For some of the team the move to Montreal had at first seemed a good idea, but even they had soon to admit that it had turned sour. But they did not get into recriminations, but set about an active programme of experiments and theoretical studies. The Americans were insisting that they should restrict our work to the design of a heavy water power plant, but many of the items on the programme ranged considerably wider.'

In the War the Eastern Front had been transformed. The great struggle for Stalingrad which had raged from October 1942 had resulted in the first and very heavy defeat of the Germans, and the Russians then re-took Kharkov. From then on there was a prolonged German retreat, reflected on a smaller scale in the West with the Germans retreating from near Cairo. Then the joint American-British landings in North Africa led to the first landing in Europe, in Sicily.

Alan continued: 'As regards the atom bomb project it now began to look as though it would be hardly possible to produce it in time before victory by conventional means. Reports which filtered through revealed the colossal scale of the American project and made the time needed to produce the bomb seem to be a matter of years rather than months. The very scale of the project also made it seem very unlikely that the Germans could mount anything similar. I have discussed the urge I felt to warn the Russians of the danger of the German atomic project, which was then thought to be a serious danger to the British and Americans. The response I received did not then show any great sense of alarm. My urge to pursue the matter was now considerably weakened, because the Russians were no longer in such military danger, the Germans were now thought to be rather far from completing their atomic project, and anyhow owing to the closing down of communications with the Americans even if I had been prepared to run the risk involved there was little I could have done about it. A truly dedicated apparatchik would have barged ahead regardless, but that was not my style at all. Some accounts of my case following the Canadian Royal Commission report suggest that it was at this stage that the Russians first contacted me, but I am afraid that like many other statements in the case this is inaccurate.

'Downtown in central Montreal there was a cosmopolitan atmosphere. French, Chinese and Jewish restaurants jostled one another and it was there that we usually migrated for our evening meals. Weekends were spent ski-ing in winter, and bathing in the St Lawrence in the summer. There was a ski hut which we rented and a house on the banks of the river, both easily accessible by rail. So leisure was spent in an idyllic fashion, which had little relation to the war-time hardships being endured by our families and friends in England. Alan Moorehead (*The Traitors*) has some comments about this special aspect of the team. He says that the wives of other scientists asked me to dinner, not out of any special friendship, but because they thought I was so much alone and they were sorry for me. I could have done very well without their pity, or their formal dinner dates, which were regarded throughout the team as one of the bores one had to endure, so as not to offend the high and mighty. Moorehead never got very far in pumping my real friends for malicious gossip. This is shown by his having to resort to heavily faked photographs, instead of the many which were available from my friends. Rather, my friendships were with junior staff and undergraduate assistants.'

Despite the frustrations of the political dispute they made what progress they could in clarifying the basic principles of the nuclear reactor programme, hoping that before long it would be possible to go forward from principles to actual design. The Halban team's first task arose from the incredulity of the Americans, especially Fermi, about the Halban-Kowarski heavy water-uranium experiment in Cambridge. As soon as possible a repeat was carried out using great care to deal with all the many sources of error. There was some relief when the Cambridge result was confirmed.

But there was another Cambridge result which was even more difficult for the Americans to swallow. This was the so-called n-2n effect. The atoms of deuterium in heavy water consist of a combination of a proton and neutron, bound together by nuclear forces. It was known that they could be torn apart by energetic gamma rays, producing free neutrons, and that it was likely that a fast neutron colliding with a deuteron nucleus could also liberate a free extra neutron, so adding to the number of neutrons present, and helping to make the system more reactive. In their Cambridge experiments Halban and Kowarski had found a large n-2n effect, an increase of 18% in the number of neutrons. Such a large effect would have a major influence on the design calculations for a heavy water reactor, and so it was important to make sure it was genuine. A later experiment gave an effect of approximately zero indicating that there were serious errors in the original result. Alan's group then did an exhaustive third experiment that confirmed that the effect was very nearly zero. This work was mostly after the Chicago conference, described later, and was largely academic since by then the Americans had set up working reactors both with uranium-graphite and uranium-heavy water. Also by the time these results were confirmed, Halban had ceased to be Director, and had been succeeded by Cockcroft. While doing this work Alan looked out for reports of other experiments or theoretical calculations on this n-2n effect. It was very intriguing to him that there were German papers published in 1942 indicating that the Germans were also working on the possible use of heavy water in a reactor, though the fact that they openly published their results suggested that they were not seen as important military secrets.

The idea for another experiment arose while Alan was checking on the possible unforeseen nuclear reactions which might occur in a heavy water reactor. For this purpose he kept a list of nuclear properties according to the latest available data. It was well known that certain light nuclei, namely lithium, boron and nitrogen, absorbed slow neutrons and so had to be avoided in materials used in the construction of the pile. In checking on other possible dangerous nuclei he found that a rare isotope of oxygen O17 was a very likely candidate, and since the other isotopes of oxygen had a very small probability of absorbing neutrons, this would be measureable. He was able to procure samples of oxygen enriched and depleted in O17. He also had an ionisation chamber capable of detecting particles in a gas at high pressure that he had designed for quite different purposes, measurements on fast neutrons. Because his neutron source was weak they needed to avoid any spurious pulses due to electrical disturbances or acoustic noise. They set up an electrical screening for the whole room consisting of copper-coated wall paper, giving the room a somewhat exotic, oriental, opulent appearance. Visitors were most impressed, but then wrote reports stressing the disregard for traditional sealing wax and string methods in this spendthrift team. However, the experiment worked and a rough estimate was made of the degree of absorption by O17. So when it became possible to use the much more powerful neutron beams from the Chicago reactor this was an early candidate for a joint Montreal-Chicago experiment. As we shall see, this gave Alan early access to the American reactor scene, and played a major part in the subsequent history.

As mentioned above, during all this period the British and Americans were engaged in a struggle over the control of the whole of the Atomic Project. The British assumption that they should be treated as equal partners was rather roughly dealt with by the Americans, who tended to assume that as they were doing all the work and paying for it, they should have sole control. The Montreal team was subject to a slow decline in morale that became a matter of concern in the British Establishment. They had visits from leading figures such as Chadwick, Oliphant and the High Commissioner in Ottawa who all tried to reassure them and begged them to hang on. Then in August 1943 came the Quebec Conference, and there began to be some lightening of the gloom, but the team was of course quite unaware of what had been agreed between Churchill and Roosevelt, and especially that Churchill had given the Americans a virtual veto over post-war British nuclear developments.

There was now some prospect of being able to start meaningful work, and the team looked forward to the re-opening of channels of cooperation with the Americans, to getting the heavy water and uranium needed for experiments connected with reactor design, and of eventually getting enough of these materials to build the reactor itself. But the decisions at Quebec took a long time to diffuse down through the American chain of command and it was only in December that the team was told that they needed to prepare for detailed discussions with the Americans in Chicago. These were to review the reactor programme and the relevant experimental programme. The strict compartmentalisation of information insisted upon by General Groves meant that the physicists were only present during the discussion on the physics programme. Three items on the programme concerned Alan, and in these he had to join the discussion. This was quite testing, since Fermi himself was present and inclined to be very critical of their proposals. However, all these projects were approved and became the basis of the collaboration between Chicago and Montreal that had a decisive influence on the rest of Alan's story.

One of the three projects with which Alan was concerned was on the n-2n effect, which was ongoing and confirmed as important. The second was the O17 absorption question, and this was to be continued using the Chicago pile as an enormously powerful source of neutrons. This involved a visit to Chicago to actually operate a reactor, and a big lift to Alan's standing in the nuclear physics world. The third line of research also involved working in Chicago, using materials made available only recently by the American project. It was to investigate the properties of uranium U233, which does not occur naturally along with the other two isotopes, U238 and U235. Bretscher and Feather had suggested that it could be produced by irradiating thorium with slow neutrons. Like U235 it would undergo fission with neutrons, and was a candidate for making atom bombs and nuclear reactors, rivalling U235 and plutonium. It was also thought that it might be easier to separate chemically than plutonium. Moreover, since it was thought that there might be a world shortage of uranium, a great advantage from the British point of view was that thorium minerals were plentiful in India. The Americans had made enough U233 by irradiation of thorium in their reactor for a comparison to be made of how it performed relative to U235. This involved only milligram quantities, enough for laboratory measurements. There was also academic interest in the new series of decay products derived from U233.

The chemists also agreed on a programme, and, most important, the engineers agreed on the lines of development to be followed in designing the new reactor. But there were also some negative aspects to the conference. Thus the green light was given for designing a heavy water reactor to be established in Canada, but not for other forms of reactor such as the uranium-graphite reactors that were to form the basis of the future nuclear programmes in Britain. Nor indeed was there a green light for any developments not directly linked to the Canadian project. Naturally the British found this an unreasonable restriction on their freedom of thought and frequently indulged in illicit speculation on 'future systems' and other euphemisms for forbidden topics, and even did their best to twig from the Americans some hints on how such 'future systems' might be brought about.

The result was a great upsurge in activity on all fronts. With his Canadian collaborator E. Hincks, Alan prepared the equipment for shipment and all was ready and working by March 1944 for the first Montreal-Chicago collaboration. The experiment in Chicago was highly successful; they obtained a more definite result for the O17 absorption, and the result showed that the absorption could be ignored as far as the design of the pile was concerned. So everyone was satisfied, including Fermi, whose *Collected Works* included a note on their result, a distinction of which Alan was very proud. However, the engineers in Montreal and the physicists helping them in the design of the new reactor were finding themselves increasingly hampered by the difficulties in getting information from the Americans. Even those items that were officially allowed took a long time to filter through the official channels, and there were many items on the periphery which they really needed, but could not get. So before Alan left for Chicago they gave him a shopping list of urgently needed information and asked him to use his powers of persuasion to winkle some of this out.

When Alan arrived in Chicago he explained to Herbert Anderson, who was in charge of experiments on the pile, the concern about information and showed him the shopping list (Note 31; Photo 46). Anderson agreed that the rules established by Groves and the other top people were too restrictive and being interpreted too literally. He agreed to produce many reports that had not so far been available in Montreal, and allowed Alan to read them and take notes. Thus when Alan was not actually carrying out the measurements on the top of the reactor he was engaged in a reading and note-taking marathon. On subsequent visits to Chicago the same thing happened. Alan had a shopping list and took the results back for the use of his grateful colleagues. This activity did not escape the notice of the Americans, but for Alan it was a pleasant antidote to what happened later that Cockcroft noted in his diary that Alan had brought back a great deal of useful information.

46. E. Fermi (front left), L. Szilard (with raincoat), H. L. Anderson (front right) and others, taken in 1946 on the fourth anniversary of the first critical pile chain reaction.
© University of Chicago, with permission

Early in 1944, Halban stepped down from the directorship to head Physics, while Cockcroft took over as Director. This was partly the result of the improved prospects of victory in Europe, due to the Red Army pushing the Germans back. Because of this, research on radar, which Cockcroft was heading at Malvern in the UK, became less important since any fundamental changes would not have practical applications by the end of the War. On the other hand nuclear physics was seen as vital. The Bomb might well be needed to finish off the War with Japan and would be of basic importance in the post-War world, whilst nuclear power, although not relevant to the War, was seen as immensely important for industrial development after the War. So it made sense to move Cockcroft to Montreal. As he took over, decisions were taken on the design of the reactor, but it became clear that the Canadian reactor could not be completed before the end of the War. Thus the Canadian parliament would be presented with an account of vast expenditure on an incomplete project that many might regard as pointless.

Alan saw a way out. He had been worrying about the method used to calculate the best arrangement of uranium rods in the tank of heavy water. He was struck that there was no method of checking these calculations short of building the full-scale reactor, when it would be too late to alter anything. It was a short step from this to propose making a small-scale working model which could be modified. It would be big enough to be a reactor, but would not be allowed to run at anything above a negligible power level. Thus it would not need concrete shielding or cooling plant, and the contents would not become highly radioactive, so that it could be tested in different configurations. He discussed this idea with his colleagues and then it was presented to Cockcroft. Alan's memorandum dated 10 March 1944 has survived as PR 97 AB 2/653 in the National Archive:

'Proposed use of a polymer pile at very small powers for the investigation of critical dimensions (polymer was the code-name of heavy water) ...'

Final paragraph (page 2): 'For the experiments discussed above shielding is not necessary except to guard against the danger of accidentally running the pile at a considerable power. After the completion of these experiments it would be very useful to run the pile as a source of neutrons. Even at a power which would not necessitate any form of cooling the neutron flux would very probably be as great as that from the Argonne graphite pile. For this purpose the pile would have to be provided with a concrete shield and the same type of central rods as used for the pilot plant at full power. This would provide a very valuable opportunity of testing the effectiveness and speed of operation of these controls before they were installed in the main plant. A N May, Montreal, June 10th, 1944.'

Cockcroft had secured from Groves a grant of heavy water and when Kowarski arrived from the UK some months later Cockcroft put him in charge of the project. Kowarski gave it the name ZEEP (Zero Energy Experimental Pile) and always took great pride in its success. ZEEP just managed to become active by the end of the war whereas the main reactor did not become functional until 1947. Alan is not mentioned in the histories of ZEEP and commented: 'I am probably partly to blame for this. It will be recounted later that at a rather crucial meeting in London Cockcroft asked me to list all the experimental results which should be published in scientific journals, and to which I had contributed. Maybe I should have listed my contribution to the origin of ZEEP amongst these. It simply did not occur to me. The one who gained plenty of well-deserved credit from the success of ZEEP was of course Kowarski. He seems to have thought that my contribution was best left in discreet silence. The Americans had an already functioning heavy water reactor in Chicago and naturally Kowarski went there to see it and get some advice. I accompanied him on this occasion, and we sent a postcard to colleagues in Cambridge to celebrate this event, dated 30th September 1944, just fifty years ago as I write this. This lapse of time has somewhat mollified my feelings. After all it now seems rather pointless to have assisted Canada to enter the Nuclear Age a little ahead of most others.' Alan's note in his memoir attached to this card reads: 'This postcard sent by H. L. Anderson, K. F. Freundlich, L. Kowarski, and ANM to Bertie Broda in Cambridge was intended to inform him that the collaboration with the Americans was on track. We were in Chicago to discuss equipment for the ZEEP heavy water pile.' (Photos 47, 47A)

Alan's last visit to Chicago was for the experiments on the nuclear properties of U233 and comparisons with U235, and were carried out with Anderson. Alan had no record of this work since it was reported in an American secret paper, and he was unable to trace any open publication. The result seemed quite favourable to U233, but later work showed that it had a high level of spontaneous fission that made it unsuitable as a bomb material, but quite interesting as a component of power reactors. These experiments

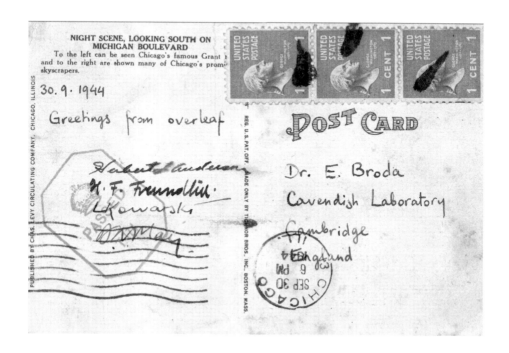

This postcard sent by H. L. Anderson, K.F. Freundlich, L. Kowarski, and AHWM to Berta Broda in Cambridge was intended to inform him that the collaboration with the Americans was on track.

We were in Chicago to discuss equipment for the ZEEP heavy water pile

47. Postcard to Berti from Alan, Lew Kowarski, K. F. Freundlich and Herbert L. Anderson in Chicago, 1944, addressed by Kowarski, and 47A. Alan's note on this postcard

were interrupted by an urgent demand for the use of the reactor for other, super-secret, experiments: 'I gathered from casual observation that these experiments involved careful monitoring of the reactivity of the pile, and switching off the pumps which normally circulated air through the reactor. At first I was mystified by these goings-on, but soon recollected that we had had discussions in Montreal about the possibility that some of the fission products from the uranium in the reactor might have a large cross-section for capturing the neutrons, and so act as a poison, an effect which would only appear when the reactor was run at full power. The big reactors at Hanford had just started up, and so it was possible that this was the reason for this sudden near-panic.

'After a few days I was admitted back for the U233 experiments. After a further interval of a few days Anderson told me that it had been decided that the recent secret experiments could now be revealed to me, because they were relevant to the work of the Montreal team. Very foolishly I said "was it to do with poisoning with fission products – probably Xenon?" He looked hard at me and said "Yes, that was just what it was". It was foolish of me to show off in this way, because I was now labelled as a dangerous man to have around if you wanted to keep things secret. In fact Groves in his memoirs *Now It Can Be Revealed* complains that the matter of the xenon poisoning was known in Montreal within 24 hours. This is a pardonable exaggeration, since it took at least 48 hours before I got back from Chicago and was able to give my colleagues there the full details. It was a matter of some importance to us because the reactor had somehow to be designed to have extra reactivity to overcome the poisoning. At the end of the experiments Anderson took the samples of Uranium 235 and 233 and divided each in half (they were only a few milligrams each). Then he gave one half of each to me, and kept one half of each for himself, saying that if any repetition of the measurements should give a different result it was important that the samples on which their measurements were based should be available to either of us for reference. My sample was, I am afraid, destined for other uses.

'Meanwhile through Chicago visits and other grapevines we heard rumours of the progress towards making the Bomb, and the arguments about its use. My Chicago friends were quite explicit that General Groves and all the senior establishment scientists had decided that the Bomb must be used, and that it must become a means of enforcing American domination over the world. This was to be the American Century, and any resistance could be easily "nuked". Above all no information on nuclear matters was to be given to anyone likely to take an independent line – this included the French, and of course the Russians.'

13

ALAN IN CANADA 1945

The War in Europe was drawing to a close, with the Russians driving relentlessly towards Berlin. In the West, the battle of the Ardennes was the last German counter-offensive. At Yalta the Western powers had to acknowledge the predominant role of the Russian forces in the War in Europe. In Montreal Alan's experimental programme was going quite well. His academic future also seemed more secure because he had been invited to apply for the Readership at King's College London. As Charles Ellis intended to stay at his post as Scientific Adviser to the War Office the new Reader would be Acting Head of Department. If Alan got the job he would have to be in London well before the new academic year in October, so he drafted his application giving Blackett and Cockcroft as referees and in due course was informed that he had been appointed.

The main reason why many of the British team had joined the nuclear project was the danger of a German atomic bomb. It began to be clear during 1944 that this danger had been overestimated. A special secret mission, code-named ALSOS (Note 27), had been set up in November 1943 to track down the German project. When Paris was liberated in August 1944, they failed to find any trace of it. With the recovery of Strasbourg in November they came to a provisional conclusion that there was no German bomb, but it was not until April 1945 that this was finally confirmed. This was of course highly secret but the Montreal team did get an inkling of the new state of affairs. It began to appear that Hitler's 'secret weapons' were the V1 and the V2 missiles, which would not change the War's outcome.

Discussion then raged in the American team about the use of the Bomb, long before it had been tested and shown to work. The cause for unease was the disappearance of the German threat, and the expectation that the Bomb would not be ready before the end of the War against Germany. If so, it might still be used to end the War against Japan. There was a strong feeling in Montreal that the Americans would see the Bomb as a vital component of a post-war play for world dominance. Then Niels Bohr made a radical and rational proposal. He had been brought secretly to Los Alamos to advise on the physics of the Bomb, but started to worry far more about its politics. He felt strongly that the whole project should be disclosed to the Russians so as to avoid any post-war rivalry in nuclear weapons. Indeed he predicted just the state of affairs which made the Cold War so dangerous. But when Bohr was in London in 1944 a meeting arranged for him to put the case to Churchill proved to be a disaster. Indeed Churchill was so disturbed by these ideas that he had a special session with Roosevelt in September at which they agreed that there should be no relaxation on strict secrecy, and that Bohr was a dangerous character who should be watched.

Nevertheless similar ideas began to appear amongst the American team, especially in Chicago, and there were many memoranda and counter-memoranda. A final decision was only taken near the completion of the Bomb. The last word from the scientists involved was given in June 1945 by a panel of four, Compton, Fermi, Lawrence and Oppenheimer, who said that the Bomb should be used at the first opportunity without warning and against a war plant surrounded by houses. Alan wrote: 'When the switch to Japan became more or less official the only member of the British team who resigned was Joseph Rotblat, to his eternal credit.'

Alan continued: 'In early 1945 the Montreal team received several senior recruits from the UK who had worked with Cockcroft on radar, and were now being given their nuclear baptism. Clearly the plan was to lay down the foundations for a British project for post-war nuclear power and (in hushed voice) our own Bomb. Both these were well outside the agreement with the Americans so discussions on these matters were very discreet. I was in favour of these developments. After all I was British and hoped to play a part in all this, but also because it might provide some check on American dominance in the nuclear field.'

Meanwhile, quite unknown to Alan, events were unfolding at the Russian Embassy in Ottawa which would devastate his career and have a serious effect on relations between the Western Allies and the Russians. The Military Attache, Colonel Zabotin, had activated a group of sympathisers within the Canadian National Research Council headquarters staff in Ottawa who gave him information about a number of topics. Through these contacts he heard of a new and important project involving uranium, under very special security. He found the security too difficult to penetrate, and then his Director in Moscow sent a message that a certain Dr May might be a valuable source on this topic, but should be approached with caution. He was known to have been a Party member, and would respond to the special introductory code 'Greetings from Alek (*sic*)'. Only Zabotin and his immediate staff knew about this and of course the messages to and from Moscow were in code. The coding and decoding was carried out by Igor Gouzenko, who then defected taking with him copies of the more important messages he had dealt with. These messages have provided the basis for accounts of the affair. Alan's side of the story, he wrote, suffered in comparison from a certain vagueness due to lack of documentation. However even after more than fifty years some things remained quite clear in Alan's memory, and he could refer to notes he made as soon as it was feasible, eight years later. So what follows is Alan's version of these events, somewhat vague, but probably as reliable as the versions available in the literature.

'One evening in early 1945 it may be supposed that I was minding my own business after a hard day's work in the laboratory, probably playing a Beethoven sonata on my piano, when the telephone rang. A man with a rather marked foreign accent first made sure that I was Dr Alan Nunn May. He said he had a message from some friends of mine and could he come and see me? Intrigued by this I said yes and gave him directions how to get to me. When he turned up he used the phrase "Greetings from Alex". This was rather a surprise to me, but not completely unexpected. So this was how I first met my contact, who according to literature cited later was a Mr Angelov with the code name Grant, operating from the Russian Embassy in Ottawa. But this was not disclosed to me at the time. In fact he told me that he had come from New York, probably because he felt correctly that I would have more confidence in the discretion and competence of the New York outfit than in the local one at Ottawa. But my confidence turned to alarm when he started to discuss his mission. It appeared that he thought that the giant plant being built near Chalk River was a conventional factory for making explosives and he had no inkling of any nuclear project.

'It is difficult at this distance of fifty-odd years to recall exactly what went through my mind in the few seconds before I replied. I was very much influenced by loyalty to my socialist faith, by the sense of obligation to the

Russian forces which had nearly completed the destruction of the Nazi menace, and to some extent by the fact that I had in fact made some sort of compact (as explained earlier) which was now bearing fruit. Anyhow I replied by welcoming my visitor.

'I had been worrying for some time whether the British and Americans had informed the Russians about the atomic bomb project. All the signs were that they had not. My American colleagues had made it clear to me that General Groves and other leaders of the Manhattan District Project were determined to use the bomb as a means of ensuring American domination of the post-war period. Also in the Montreal team we had had enough experience of the American attitude even towards we British with our Special Relationship and Close Links of Common Language etc. to guess what their attitude would be to the Bolsheviks now advancing towards the West. All very well to give them all possible aid when they were about to be completely over-run, but now things were different. It seemed to me, then, in the highest degree unlikely that the Americans would voluntarily share their atomic weapon with anyone, and certainly not with the Russians. I had devoted a large part of my time to securing as much information as possible from Chicago on behalf of the British. I decided that the time had come, now I had the opportunity, to extend the same help to the Russians. This was not only because of my loyalty as a socialist to what was then the only socialist country in the world, but also because as a bulwark against American domination, Russia seemed to me a more reliable force than Britain, as certainly proved to be the case.

'Fortunately I was well equipped for the job. I had a broad knowledge of the Chicago part of the project and some whiff of the rest. I had also been responsible for the induction of the new staff arriving from the UK. So I knew which were the key data and the essential reports to be read by anyone coming fresh into the field. Nothing much could be done at this first meeting, but we fixed up subsequent meetings at which I undertook to hand over typewritten reports of my own summarising the projects and some laboratory reports to be copied.

'The official reports presented some difficulty since they were not supposed to leave the laboratory, but in fact many of the senior staff did take them home for week-end reading. The way we worked it was that I borrowed a report from the library on a Friday, and gave it to Angelov that evening. He returned it on the Sunday so that I could bring it in with me to the laboratory on Monday morning. I kept away from the laboratory on the Saturday so that anyone asking for this report would simply be told it was out in my name, and that they should ask for it on the Monday. This way we worked through most of the basic material available on the chemistry and metallurgy of uranium and plutonium, the design of the American graphite piles, the basic nuclear data, and the various special effects which had caused difficulties, such as the xenon poisoning and the Wigner effect. In fact, everything that an aspiring nuclear designer would want to know.

'In this way things went swimmingly, until Angelov asked me to accept a small gift of money or possibly some drink. Surely I must have some expenses to be re-imbursed, or needed to entertain my friends? When I refused the offer he was offended. Surely I would not object to taking a gift from someone who was simply grateful? He returned to the attack on another occasion, and this time implied that I must somehow be ashamed of helping the Red Army. Having failed at persuasion he used a trick. On the next occasion when I had to pick up a parcel of returned reports from him at a street corner I found myself with a package which seemed much larger than the one I had given him. I was suspicious, but could not run after him without the danger of attracting the attention of passers-by. On returning to my flat I found that the parcel contained a bottle of Red Label whiskey and wrapped round it under a newspaper, that day's issue of an Ottawa paper, two hundred Canadian dollar notes, new notes with consecutive numbers.

'This really scared me. For a time I thought the whole thing had been a police plant, and expected the RCMP to come to my door. The money was especially dangerous, as it was far too easily traced for comfort. I burned the notes, and put the ashes down the toilet. The whiskey I could cope with by more conventional means – the bottle seemed to have no identifying marks. But there was still the annoying fact that my contact seemed to come from Ottawa. This was bad, but it was far worse that having told me he came from New York he was then so careless as to give me evidence that he did not. There was the further worry that the Russians should be so persistent about the money. It seemed that they could not tolerate my amateur status, and had to have me on their pay-roll.

'My immediate panic subsided when a week passed without anything untoward happening. But it spoiled my relationship with Angelov, and I became rather mistrustful. It began to worry me that I had no real proof that my information was getting through to someone who would understand it. After much thought I came to the conclusion that one way of making sure of this would be to send samples of some isotope of uranium which could only be produced in the project. This would be proof that I was really in contact with a functioning atomic set-up, and at the other end, in Russia, the sample would have to be sent to competent scientists to check it. Fortunately I had in my possession the minute samples of U235 and U233 which I had worked with in Chicago. I had meant to take them as personal trophies with me to England, but it would be much better to send them to Russia.

'This still left the possibility that my information might not be brought to the attention of military authorities. Perhaps there was some set-up concentrating on nuclear power, and regarding the bomb as not their business, or as something to be kept quiet. I decided that the only way of overcoming that possibility was to send some information of obvious military but non-nuclear interest. As it happened several scientists who had worked at Malvern on radar had been transferred to us, and had been regaling us with stories of the newest devices, especially those which the Americans had refused to disclose to the British. These concerned defence against Japanese suicide bombers. They would certainly not have been disclosed to the Russians who were not then at war with the Japanese, although it was obvious that they soon would be, and would then need just such defences. So I thought it justified to send some hints of these devices, although this was a second-hand and therefore garbled account.

'With the successful nuclear test in New Mexico in July and the forthcoming Potsdam Conference there was hot news to be transmitted and Moscow was now eager. So I swallowed my scruples about money and whiskey and set to work with renewed enthusiasm. The laboratory was seething with more or less authentic rumours about the tests, the views of various factions in the USA on how the bomb might be used, and how all this would bear on British postwar developments. At this time some of the British and European scientists who had worked at Los Alamos and elsewhere in the American project began to return to Europe. They mostly flew via Montreal and Newfoundland and called on us, giving rise to a fresh flow of unofficial information releases. One such was Aage Bohr, son of Niels Bohr and himself a leading nuclear physicist. Cockcroft arranged an informal debriefing for young Bohr, consisting of sessions with individual members of our team, who were told to pump him dry. For physics Cockcroft chose Pontecorvo and myself as the (separate) inquisitors. Most of what he told us later appeared in the Smyth report, but not all. My notes were of course transcribed into my official laboratory notebook (after checking with Pontecorvo for any points I had missed) and were transmitted with my other notes on American reports to London. Another copy went to Moscow.

'When the bombs were dropped on Japan on 6 and 9 August my first feeling was one of relief that at last this war was finished. Only later did the full horror of what had been done become clear. Meanwhile I had my work to complete before returning to London. First of all a little extra information on the bombs needed to be sent, together with the samples which I had intended to take to London in my pocket. Then my official job had reached its climax with the start up of ZEEP, the first reactor outside the USA to go critical. I went to Chalk River for a week to check over the instrumentation and discuss the start-up procedure with Kowarski and Watson-Munro, and then returned for the actual start-up on 5 September, the entry of Canada into the Nuclear Age. Of course I was completely unaware of the defection by Gouzenko and its disastrous consequences. But I had become increasingly uneasy about the prospect that seemed to have been forced upon me of being a permanent apparatchik in the Russian espionage set-up. My real ambition was to be a physicist, not a spy, and my contacts with Angelov and his somewhat objectionable behaviour and resort to trickery had done nothing to reconcile me to such a career in espionage.

'In addition, there were a number of false alarms during my last few months in Montreal. Once Mr Manning, the technician in charge of the photographic dark room, came to me in my capacity as the physics representative on the security committee. He reported that there were signs that someone was making unauthorised use of the dark room. Stocks of photographic material were being used up, and not returned to their proper places etc. I was able to reassure him that there was nothing serious and that our colleagues belonging to the Free French might be equipping themselves with copies of some material for post-war use in France, which both Manning and I considered well-justified and indeed commendable. However, I asked him to put a notice in the dark room warning against unofficial use, and I heard no more. It may be mentioned that in fact on the occasion of a visit by

General De Gaulle to Quebec one or two of the same colleagues took the opportunity to convey to him some inkling of what was going on, an action which had no penal consequences.' It is now known that Guéron was delegated by the other Free French to do this, because he had not signed the Official Secrets Act.

'Two of the English members of the team got married. I knew them both well and it was a great occasion for the English members of the team. Unfortunately it was fixed for the day on which I was due to meet my contact for the last time before leaving for London. As the wedding was at mid-day and the contact time was in the evening I thought I could manage both, but fate supervened. The bride's transatlantic call home was heavily delayed and so the guests drank and danced until the call came through late at night. It would have been impossible to leave without making myself conspicuous. By the time the party broke up I was in no condition to carry out such a task calling for complete discretion and self-control, and anyhow it was much too late. So I never received the final revised instruction for the assignment in London on which MI5 was later to base their strategy.

'I had to hand in my personal notebooks and copies of reports, which I could not take with me. I was assured that they would be issued to me in London when I was appointed as a consultant to the British project. I was naturally anxious to check on whether this arrangement was proceeding smoothly, because any stickiness in the proceedings would indicate some falling off in my security status. I was on my way to the travel section of the Administration to collect my documents for the flight when I saw walking down the corridor ahead of me two unmistakeably English civil servants complete with bowler hats, umbrellas and standard issue brief cases. They were welcomed by Jackson, the administrative head of the British part of the team. As they shook hands and started their conversation Jackson saw me approaching from behind them, and said: "Why, here *is* Dr Nunn May", making it clear that I was the main topic they had just started to discuss. The two visitors spun round, with expressions of shocked surprise which one might have expected if Jackson had said " Why, here *is* Josef Stalin". They quickly recovered their composure, we shook hands, and exchanged pleasantries about their flight and the weather in London, and I went on my way deeply disturbed. Although not over-modest, I knew that my name was not so famous that a senior civil servant would spin round on hearing it.

Perhaps something had gone seriously wrong, and my name was indeed a matter of urgent top-level concern. I had no means of checking on this until I got back to London.

'Before I left Montreal there was a very emotional farewell ceremony at which I was presented with a magnificent slide-rule and a briefcase embossed with my initials. The slide-rule I still have, but the briefcase has disappeared. The ceremony was photographed by Mr Manning, and shows the whole team (with some significant exceptions) with myself centre-stage. Curiously this official photograph, readily available, one would think, was never used in the many newspaper comments or books which were to appear later. They preferred a very smudgy and faked picture from my student days. Mr Manning then took another photograph of me alone, an excellent likeness, though a little over-confident and cheerful considering later history (Photo 48). The ceremony was a little marred by the absence of Cockcroft and some other senior team members. Cockcroft had just returned from a hurried visit to Ottawa where he had been summoned on 9 September by the High Commissioner to come in the utmost secrecy to hear the grisly details of the Gouzenko defection, including an account of my misdeeds. At that time the authorities had not decided whether to arrest me then or to let me return to London, where it was hoped I would act as a decoy to enable them to catch some bigger fish. All this was under urgent discussion between Ottawa, Washington and London in circles far above Cockcroft's head. Doubtless he felt that it would not be appropriate to appear at the farewell festivities to wish me a happy journey and prosperous future career.

'On 11 September the decision was to arrest me straight away, and two MI5 men were sent over. These were Roger Hollis and Peter Dwyer (Note 32). Possibly these were the two characters I met, but that seems difficult to fit with the dates. All this will become clear only when the archives are finally opened. Anyhow the decision for immediate arrest was reversed and I was allowed to depart as arranged on 16 September but last minute arrangements were made for me to be accompanied by a man from the RCMP (Royal Canadian Mounted Police) in mufti, presumably to make sure that I did not hijack the plane and take it straight to Moscow. This probably accounts for what seemed to me at the time a rather curious feature of my flight. I was issued with a form which carried a receipt for a parachute that would be under my seat, but I found none. The attendant said it was of no consequence

48. Alan on departure from Montreal, September 1945
© Canadian Library and Archives C-138883, with permission

as there was little point in using a parachute to land in mid-ocean in the North Atlantic, or indeed in the Arctic snows. But it was a little disturbing. The simple explanation is now clear. The flight had to carry an extra passenger at very short notice – my RCMP companion. This led to a shortfall in parachutes, and the obvious non-parachutist was me.

'There was another curious feature when we arrived in the UK. Our flight was supposed to go to London but instead we landed at Prestwick because of adverse weather conditions. The weather seemed perfect, but nevertheless we spent most of the day in Prestwick. I made a number of phone calls to my expectant family and friends, and on behalf of colleagues who had asked me to contact their families on arrival. When the time came to fly on to London we were informed that the plane used in the transatlantic flight was no longer available and we would have to go by separate planes to London. Moreover our luggage would go separately, and we would collect it the next day. Even then I thought what a wonderful arrangement this provided for an examination of my personal luggage. Later I had a rather similar difficulty with my heavy luggage coming by sea. I was told that the ship carrying these had suffered a collision and there was delay so I could not have my luggage immediately. It probably provided cover for someone to make a detailed check of this.'

14

BERTI IN CAMBRIDGE AND EDINBURGH
DECEMBER 1942-MAY 1947

The reports that Berti produced and the respect in which his colleagues later held him show that he was an effective member of the Tube Alloys team. His co-authors on the sixteen reports included Guéron, Kowarski, Denys Wilkinson and Feather, and the six papers he published include four letters to *Nature*, three as sole author. Berti also made visits to Chadwick's department in Liverpool starting in November 1943, and later spent time at Thorium Ltd. The MI5 files say little about Berti in 1942, when both Alan and he were at the Cavendish. Berti stayed behind when most of the TA team went to Montreal at the end of 1942. It might be that he was not asked to go, but Hilde said that he could have gone and also taken me, but that she had refused this unless we went as a family. He rejected this and much later wrote to me that I was the reason that he stayed. But another letter from him indicated that he made a positive choice not to go. Other reasons to stay in Europe might have been to do with the Party, the Austrian Centre, his friendship with Edith Tudor Hart and the prospects of an earlier return to Austria.

MI5 became increasingly anxious about Berti during 1943. In May Hollis wrote: 'As we cannot be told the nature of the work for which Broda is required we can only state that we know of Broda's connection with the Communists, and mention the definite risk that any information which he gets will be given to the Communists', and in July he noted: 'He now knows a considerable amount of the more secret aspect of the work. DSIR is very anxious about Broda'. A few days later Hollis wrote: 'I agreed that we should keep a careful watch for any references to Broda's work during our investigations upon the Communist Party's espionage activities'. When Kowarski did eventually go to Canada in 1944, the authorities were determined that Berti did not go too: '...while the Directorate have decided that at all costs they will not send Broda overseas, they have given the latter a sufficient excuse for not doing so.'

MI5 remained concerned, because in April 1945 Berti's old boss Charles Goodeve was asked directly for his view by Wallace Akers, head of Tube Alloys, on behalf of MI5: 'Goodeve confirmed that Broda is a very able scientist and that he is also a man who can be left to work by himself and, at the same time, he will maintain his keenness and industry. Goodeve went on to say that he expected that I knew that Broda was suspected of "red" tendencies. He told me that he had given a fair amount of attention to this side of Broda and that he, personally, felt that Broda's political views were no more than those of a great many people of his age and he, Goodeve, would have felt no anxiety in entrusting Broda with highly confidential Admiralty work, if the possibility had ever arisen. I think therefore that you can accept it that, so far as Goodeve is able to express an opinion, he does feel happy about Broda.' Hollis commented: 'The letter is an extremely useful addition to our records, though I do not feel that Goodeve's opinion about Broda can override the other evidence on our file. I see that Akers himself hints at this in his final paragraph.'

These concerns were well-founded. *The Haunted Wood* (1999) (Note 5) refers to an agent Eric, and in 2009 Vassiliev's new book *Spies* with Haynes and Klehr identified Berti as being Eric. It states that Berti gave information to the Russians from the end of 1942, and according to the KGB files gave much more significant information than DSIR and MI5 thought would be possible. Comparison of this claim with what the MI5 files narrate suggest that the British were naive on what could be happening, and equally that Berti was lucky to have escaped detection and a lengthy prison sentence. Here is an extended quotation from *Spies* that includes Vassiliev's transcripts (double quotation marks); I have omitted quotation marks from names and "Enormous", the code name for the Atom Project:

'In December 1942, KGB's London station reported: "Edith (Hart) sent us a detailed report through Mary (unidentified) on the results and status of work on enormous, both in England and in the USA. Eric had given her this report on his own initiative to pass to the fraternal (Communist Party). The materials will be sent out in the near future. According to additional information that has been gathered, Eric – who since Jan. 1942 has been

Professor Halban's assistant in a special division (devoted to enormous) of the central laboratory on explosives in Cambridge – is completely informed about all the work done on Enormous, both in England and in the USA, b/c he has access to Amer. materials on enormous that the English had received as part of an information exchange ... Eric is a long-time fellowcountryman (Communist) who understands the need for such work."

'Impressed with the report and Broda's volunteering it, the KGB London station, with Moscow Center's agreement, arranged for Hart to press Broda for more. London reported: "We instructed Edith to conduct a preliminary conversation with him to get him to agree to meet with our comrade. During the conversation between Edith and Eric, the latter was initially hesitant and said that he had to think about it and that he does not see any need to meet with someone, b/c he has already written down everything he knows about Enormous. Later in the conversation, Eric's attitude changed, and he said that he hopes the person he meets will not be an Englishman, b/c English comrades are generally very indiscreet. And, in the end, once Edith had told him that everything had been properly arranged, Eric said that he would be happy to meet with our comrade."

'In January 1943 Broda met with a KGB officer, and the London station told Moscow: "Eric met Glan (unidentified KGB officer) cordially and carried himself with great ease and friendliness, although it was obvious that he was nervous. He carefully verified all of the rendezvous terms. At the outset of the meeting, Eric said he had only been notified of the meeting the day before and therefore was unprepared for a serious discussion about Enormous. Because Glan's primary objective was to strengthen ties with Eric, obtain his direct consent to work with us, and determine the course of this work, Glan did not press him for information right away and instead set about achieving the aforementioned objectives. The first conversation with Eric lasted over an hour and a half. As a result of the conversation, Eric gave his full consent to work with us. During the conversation, nothing was called by its proper name, but Eric knows who it is he agreed to work for .... Eric reports that in their field of work, the Americans were significantly ahead. As part of a tech. information exchange, their laboratory receives bulletins from the Americans on the progress of work on Enormous in America. Owing to the nature of his work, Eric has access to these bulletins, and the info. he gives us reflects Amer. achievements in this field as well as English ones."

'Broda agreed to meet a KGB courier every two or three weeks to provide reports and technical information on the atomic project. The KGB relationship with Broda went well, and in August 1943 Moscow referred to Broda as "at pres., the main source of info. on work being done on E.. both in England and in the USA." In 1944 the London station reported that Broda's access to British and American technical data had further increased, explaining: "One of Eric's colleagues went to Canada for a while and gave him his personal key to the library containing reports on En-s ... We made Eric a copy of the key and arranged contact terms that allowed us to contact him in London three times a week without any prior arrangement. In accordance with these terms, on arriving in London on one of the agreed upon days, Eric was supposed to mark a page of a phone book inside a designated phone booth. After entering this phone booth at a fixed time and finding the mark he had made, we would go out to meet him at the appointed place and time ... As a result, we were able to receive from Eric all available Amer. reports of the second batch, as well as oth. interesting maters on En-s ... Eric continues to work willingly with us, but he still balks at even the slightest hint about mater. assistance. We once gave him more than he asked to cover his expenses. He was displeased by this and said that he suspects we want to give him a certain kind of help. He asked us to give up any such thoughts once and for all. In such circumstances, we fear that any gift from us as a token of appreciation for his work will make a negative impression. Eric is completely selfless in his work with us and extremely scrupulous when it comes to anything that could be seen as 'payment' for his work." '

'Among the specific information Broda was credited with delivering were Miles Leverett and Tom Moore's plans for one of the Manhattan Project's early reactors. (Leverett and Moore, lead engineers at the Metallurgical Laboratory at the University of Chicago, designed larger and more practical reactors to replace the first experimental reactor built by Enrico Fermi). The plans he delivered were described as including "all the necessary information to build a plant, and (it) is exceptionally valuable." '

The allegations in this quotation ring true. My opinion is that Berti was as dedicated and zealous a communist at the end of 1942 after four and a half years in England as when he had arrived. He saw the desperate situation on the Eastern Front and would have felt a personal responsibility to help the Russians if he could, and the opportunity arose. Self-interest was not a part of Berti's thinking, and he would have weighed the odds of being able to pass information without being detected. He would have known that he would be in serious trouble if caught. I find it difficult to see how he was not detected, but he had self-discipline, and probably confided in no-one other than Edith Tudor Hart, who was involved at the start. He had already been incarcerated in Germany, Austria and Britain, but the idea of him in prison for ten or more years is hard for me to take in. In passing, I believe that Hilde never knew that Berti became a spy, in part because it happened after their separation.

Berti had opportunities because of the informal regime in the laboratory and the trust placed in him, exemplified by him being lent a key (not by Alan, who had already departed for Canada). He also had cover stories for his frequent visits to London, to see me and to be at the Austrian Centre. It is striking that even in 1947 the British authorities placed so much less value on what he could have known than what the Russians claimed to have got. One question that could be answered without recourse to a proper scientific audit of what is in the Russian archives is how much information was coming from Chicago and Los Alamos, for instance, to Cambridge, and when. Another question is how Berti transferred information to the Russians, when at any moment he might have been stopped and searched.

At the start of 1944 Berti moved to live with the Shoenberg family on the outskirts of Cambridge. David Shoenberg was an eminent low-temperature physicist who was the contact for the Cavendish with Kapitsa both before and after the War. I remember him and his wife Kate with fondness, as I stayed with them for periods and also saw them after the War. Nearby were the Bretschers, whose son Mark was my playmate. In the summer of 1943 Berti and I spent a holiday with the Kowarski family and Guéron in Devon (Photo 49). Tess was also in Cambridge until October 1944 and took a close interest in me. No doubt she also helped Berti with his networking on behalf of Austrian refugees.

The idealism that gave Berti his lifelong adherence to the dream of Socialism also made him deeply attached to the concept of an independent Austria. It was not obvious that the Allies intended the restoration of an

49. Berti and Paul with Lew and Dora Kowarski and family in Salcombe, Devon, 1943

independent Austria after the war, rather than recognise the forced annexation of 1938 as a pragmatic solution for a rump successor country to the defunct Habsburg empire with poor economic prospects. The decision to have a post-war Austria only became an Allied objective in 1943, and the Austrians had the status of victims, even though many were enthusiastic supporters of the Anschluss and of Hitler.

Berti's particular concern was to emphasise Austria's cultural importance, including philosophy and science. His devotion to the physicist Ludwig Boltzmann started when he studied Austrian science in the Cambridge University Library. Possibly the activities of such as Berti in making the case for Austria had a significant effect. He also led an Austrian Movement group in Cambridge, and later collected donations for Austrian university libraries. The authorities were sceptical about taking such activities at face value, rather than as communist-led conspiracies. They would have been confirmed in this view when in November 1944 MI5 intercepted a note from the Austrian Centre requiring Berti to leave Cambridge for London. It 'requires (him) to be freed from another function and he will talk with him on the subject as the need for him is so great.' However, an MI5 theory that a friend at the Austrian Centre was the paymaster of a secret cell was discarded when it was realised that the payments to him they were noting were in fact for his work as their dentist.

Hilde and I lived in Scotland from the autumn of 1944 until the spring of 1945 (see later). In this time Berti received the postcard from Chicago

50. Berti and Paul, c.1946

51. Berti, c.1946

described earlier, and passed it on to me. But in the spring of 1945 Hilde took a job in Cambridge and for the next eighteen months all three of us were in Cambridge, with Hilde and Berti living apart. An intercepted letter from Hilde to Ala Löw-Beer in October 1945 says that 'with Berti everything is unchanged – a stranger who often visits us' (Photos 50, 51).

After the War, contact between Berti and his family was surprisingly slow and sparse. The first letter I have from Viola to him is dated 21 December 1945 from Fünfturm. She reproached him that she doesn't hear from him, and in another letter five days later acknowledged a photo of me, which she said compensated a bit for the meagre news from him. She did not understand why there was so little of it. Ferdy Marek had disappeared, and much later it was established that he had been abducted by the Russians and died in the Lubianka prison in Moscow. Willi Pabst and his family had survived, and so miraculously had Christian, although many of his communist friends had been killed. Egon Schönhof had been murdered by the Nazis at Auschwitz.

Emmi Obst, Ernst's sister and Berti's aunt, had been protected by her neighbours in Graz until 1945, when she was denounced as a Jew by the mother of a later classmate of her granddaughter Marietheres (Maresi) and died of a heart attack. At the start of the War Emmi's daughter Erika and Maresi had been in Latvia, which was invaded by the Soviet Union and then the Germans. In the German retreat they went to Poland where Erika survived as an interpreter in prisoner-of-war camps and was involved in anti-Hitler activities. At the end of the War they were in a displaced persons' camp in Austria, and Maresi, still with Soviet citizenship, was in danger of deportation to Russia until she acquired Austrian nationality.

Kaspar reported to MI5 in 1945: 'On 3rd November a Conference of Scientists for the promotion of Austrian Science took place at Burlington House under the auspices of the Association of Austrian Engineers, Chemists and Scientific Workers. The whole conference was stage-managed by Dr E. Broda, and it is said in Austrian Communist circles that the object of this meeting was to establish contact with scientists engaged on atomic energy research. Although I have no definite proof, I have always suspected Broda of being engaged in scientific espionage, and according to Edith Tudor-Hart he has for some time occupied himself with secret scientific research at Cambridge connected with atomic energy. She stressed Broda's importance to the party in view of his qualifications and connections. In view of the intimate relations existing between Edith Tudor-Hart and Broda, it must be presumed that she is well-informed of her lover's activities. As Chairman of the Association of Austrian Engineers, Dr Broda maintains close contacts with Austrian and foreign engineers and scientists and with Austrian students in the provinces, through whom he links up with British Communist student circles. Although outwardly the above conference appeared above board and non-political, I learned that secret meetings took place afterwards at which Dr Broda presided. At the official Conference Professor (Sir D'Arcy)

Thompson took the chair, and speeches were made by Professors Blackett, Donnan, Hogben and Karl Przibram'.

Alan was arrested on 4 March 1946 and Kaspar reported shortly after to MI5: 'On 8th, at about 7 p.m., in the presence of (deleted) Edith Tudor-Hart answered the door bell, and had a conversation with the caller which lasted for about ten minutes. She then returned rather irritated and told (deleted) that a man had just called, introducing himself as Mr Francis, and enquired about Alexander Tudor-Hart who he thought was living at her place. When she told him that Tudor-Hart was not staying with her, and that she did not know his whereabouts either, as it was none of her business, the man pretended to be surprised, and tried in a very clumsy way to start a conversation with her, asking her if she was Alexander's sister. She stopped him by saying that she was not his sister, but his ex-wife, as she had realised that the caller was nothing more than a snooper, not an ordinary one, but a special one, judging by his Oxford accent. Edith seemed rather worried, and said the incident must be in some way connected with Broda, or with one of his friends who might have got into trouble with the police. She then wondered whether she would be forced to give evidence against Broda, and accused him of being too careless. "When a man is involved in such a business as he is," she added, "he ought to be careful and not endanger his friends by writing to or visiting them." The following Wednesday, the 13th, early in the morning, Broda came up from Cambridge by the first train, and told her that a man had been caught by his landlord in the act of trying to get into his (Broda's) room. Broda suggested that this might have been a general check-up, but he added: "all of our people are all right, don't get alarmed, don't write and don't phone."' A note was added: 'Any discussion about intelligence work or even the mention of anything of the sort is now strictly prohibited.'

Then on 10 April Kaspar reported : 'Broda is still very careful, refrains from meeting people and using the telephone. He is in contact with Ilona Suschitzky, wife of Wolfgang Suschitzky, Edith Tudor-Hart's brother whom he knows from Moscow. She is active at the Austrian Centre.' The implication that Berti was in Moscow appears here for the first time in the MI5 file.

Berti's wish to return to Austria at the end of the war was frustrated. His own explanation was that he had militarily-important knowledge that the British were unwilling to let out of the country. That was indeed in the minds of the security services, who continued their surveillance. The first note in the

MI5 file on whether Berti should be allowed to return to Austria was on 20 March 1946: 'While (Sir Wallace Akers) has not heard anything definite about Broda leaving the UK, the latter has always told everybody that he intends returning to Austria "as soon as things settle down". In the opinion of Sir Wallace, Broda can no longer be looked upon as a key man, in fact when Dr Feather, who has now gone to Edinburgh, asked Akers if Broda could be spared for ordinary academic research, Akers agreed to give Broda up, but this led to nothing. Akers would not mind very much if Broda did return to Austria, and while he would not be seriously concerned if Broda found himself, willingly or unwillingly, in Russia, General Groves would be alarmed in the extreme.' A later note in the file stated that Perrin thought that Akers had not intended his remark about Groves to be taken too literally.

Gouzenko's defection raised the question of whether Berti was implicated in Alan's activities. Alan had returned from Canada on 20 September 1945, and on 1 October in an intercepted letter Berti wrote: 'Dear May, I am glad to hear you are back safely. Will you come to Cambridge some day, or may I look you up in London? I shall love to see you. Yours, E.Broda.' In this way, he made himself a prime suspect as Alan's supposed accomplice. They were known by MI5 to have met twice, with others including Kowarski, in October 1945 and January 1946. Hollis forwarded a list of Alan's friends to the Americans in February 1946, before Alan's arrest: 'I forward as requested some notes for the F.B.I. regarding the contacts and friends of Dr Alan Nunn May. You will appreciate that much of the information I am now sending you is of particular delicacy, and I should be grateful if you would see that it is specially safeguarded and that no security action is taken against any of the characters mentioned in the report without prior reference to us.' After Alan's conviction on 1 May 1946, the Chief Constable in Cambridge reported: 'Discreet enquiries have been made, also observations on the man Broda, as to his reaction in this case. He does not appear to have mentioned the fact, other than express surprise at May's appearance in Court on this particular charge.' That he did not mention it should perhaps have seemed odd to the authorities.

In May 1946 the Directorate of Atomic Energy wrote to MI5: 'Engelbert Broda has asked us to help him to get a Military Government permit to visit Austria at the end of August. As he is also resigning from that work about that time we believe that he may, if he gets to Austria, decide whether to stay there permanently or not. I do not think we can actively support an application for a permit and I shall tell him so; but you will remember that we have always been extremely careful about Broda and it may be that you will want to decide whether active steps should be taken to prevent Broda going to Austria. He has, of course, had access only to a limited section of the work at Cambridge and that section was devoted to fundamental investigations. On the other hand he will have picked up in the course of conversation quite a lot about other aspects of the work. I should think that unless you have evidence that he has been going out of his way to make undesirable contacts here, it would be hardly advisable to stop him.' Hollis noted: 'The letter seems to me most unsatisfactory. It is not for us to decide whether active steps should be taken to prevent Broda from going to Austria. It is a matter for the Directorate who know what information Broda possesses. We can say that Broda is in touch with Communists and is clearly is sympathy with them and that therefore there is a considerable risk that he will tell them what he knows about atomic research. The only safe assumption must be that he will communicate this information to the Communists if he goes to Austria. Does the Directorate mind taking this risk? If so, it should be prepared to take the responsibility of preventing Broda going to Austria. Another point for consideration is whether Broda can be given a "no return" visa so that we should be finally rid of him if he once decided to leave this country.' The reply from the Directorate was then definite in not objecting to Berti going to Austria.

In September 1946, while waiting to be allowed to leave, Berti did go to Edinburgh to work with Feather. Shortly before this he underwent the removal of 2 gms for bone to test whether he had taken up radioactivity in his work. I remember him in Cambridge with a walking stick. Much later he referred to having been young and foolish in Liverpool in 1943 with radium D. It seems that he was given the all-clear. In Edinburgh Berti started to negotiate an invitation to work in the University in Vienna. He treasured a document given to him by his Edinburgh department, Natural Philosophy (whose head was Max Born) (Note 33), which read: 'This is to certify that Dr E Broda, long famed for his bluntness, rudeness and dislike of discussion on the topic(s) of weather, has qualified with high honours for the title, given only after due deliberation, of the rudest man in the Department.' It was also in Edinburgh that this man of inexhaustible energy started to write a book that was published as *Advances in Radiochemistry* in 1950.

A report from Kaspar suggests that the basic idea of the Hydrogen bomb was being discussed, though I don't know how Berti would have been privy to this inaccurate information: 'Before leaving for Edinburgh, Dr Broda had several confidential talks with Edith Tudor Hart about the Russian experiments in atomic bombs. According to Broda, the Russians have already solved the problem or are near the solution. Broda states that, contrary to the Anglo/American methods, the Russian scientists have found a way of releasing atomic energy through the combination of "four hydrogen atoms to helium" which proves to be much cheaper and more efficient.' (Note 34) Edith Tudor Hart confessed to MI5 in February 1947 that she had been working for the Russians. She would certainly have been asked about Berti, but I don't know how much she told MI5 about him or indeed her other contacts, who had included Philby.

Political concerns were then raised about American reactions to Berti being allowed to leave Britain. MI5 noted on 12 October 1946: 'Mr Perrin was satisfied that Dr Broda was not in possession of highly secret information and from the security point of view he saw no objection to his return to Austria. The case was, however, complicated by American proposals to evacuate large numbers of scientists from Austria and Germany not so much with a view to making use of their services as to denying their services to the USSR. He had no doubt that if the Americans were consulted they would certainly take the view that Dr Broda should not be sent back to Austria, and if they sent him back without consultation there would be the danger of subsequent protest by the USA. This was further complicated by the fact that Dr Broda was a Communist who had been active in the Free Austrian Movement in the UK. Mr Perrin was therefore anxious to have the considered views of the Security Service on the case. The Security Service would reconsider the case in consultation with MI6 and forward their recommendations to the Ministry of Supply.'

A week later this reconsideration took place: 'D/C & D, A.D.C., Colonel Collard and I (Hollis) discussed the Broda case. We agreed that in the light of the opinion of the Directorate of Atomic Energy, we could not prevent Broda returning to Austria on the grounds that he was the possessor of secret information which he might betray and that, therefore, if he were refused permission to leave this country, it could only be done with the intention of depriving the Russians of his services as a scientist. Broda had expressed the wish to return to Austria and such action would therefore have to be taken against his will. We did not believe that the Home Office would be prepared to sanction such action and it would be manifestly impossible to take it without reference to the Home Office. We agreed that we should advise the

Directorate to discuss the case openly with their American contacts in order to find out firstly, whether the Americans would be worried if Broda were to return to Austria and secondly, whether there was any likelihood that the Americans might offer Broda alternative employment in the United States. D/C & D said that he thought the Directorate wished to have a short up-to-date note on the case of Broda, possibly for communication to the Americans.'

Berti's relationship with Ina Jun, who became his second wife, is mysterious. I have no letters between them. An MI5 note of February 1947 refers to letters intercepted from Ina and states: 'She would clearly not object to marrying Broda.' Ina was born Ina Ehrlich in 1900 in Zagreb (then in Austria-Hungary) and so was ten years older than Berti. She was a translator and a poet of distinction. She had been married with a teenage son, but both husband and son were murdered by the Ustachi, the pro-Nazi forces, and Ina joined Tito's partisans as a nurse. Berti seems to have met her before the War through Party circles. After the War Ina was in Rome with her sister, and Berti learned this in September 1946 (Photo 52). In spite of Security Service reluctance to let him travel and then to re-enter the UK (see below), Berti flew to Rome to meet her on 3 March and returned eight days later, firm in the intention of marrying her. He finally left Britain on 22 April 1947 for Rome and marriage, and from there they went to Austria (Chapter 20).

Tess had a role in this. Her version was recorded in about 1988 (Note 14). 'Engelbert Broda was a refugee from Austria who dearly loved his country and was determined to go back there at the earliest possible time. After the war he learned that a woman he admired very much was alive and living in Rome. ... Broda was corresponding with her, and now was most anxious to see her. However, in the circumstances of the time, and holding only an Austrian passport, it was very difficult for him to get a visa for Italy. We knew all the European science attaches and I was able to ask the one from Italy to see Broda. As a result Broda was enabled to go to Italy, and meet his friend. They subsequently married.' Letters between Tess and Berti are the only source I have on Berti's second marriage, and I return to it later.

After Berti left, Hollis played a straight bat: 'We should merely say that the Directorate of Atomic Energy, after consultation with their American contacts, said that Broda did not have access to anything of really major secrecy, and raised no objection to his return to Austria.' At the same time Kaspar reported: 'According to Mrs Tudor-Hart, Broda has just returned

52. Ina Jun Broda, c.1947

from a visit to Rome. He flew to Rome about 3 weeks ago where he contacted a certain woman called Ada Drakovitch, Jugoslav, employed by UNRRA (United Nations Relief and Rehabilitation Administration). Broda was in touch with this woman about 10 years ago in Belgrade when he visited Jugoslavia on orders from the Party. From what Tudor-Hart said it would seem that Ada Drakovitch is employed by the Russian Intelligence.' I don't know what the links are between Ina, her sister Vera (who worked for UNRRA), and the mysterious Ada Drakovitch, nor about Berti's pre-war visit(s) to Jugoslavia.

15

HILDE AND PAUL IN LONDON, INVERNESS AND CAMBRIDGE DECEMBER 1942-47

From late in 1942 until mid-1944 I went between Hilde in London and Berti in Cambridge. Berti came to the Austrian Centre at weekends, when he also saw me. I was in the nursery at the Centre, which was also Hilde's registered address from November 1942 until July 1943. We then lived nearby, and I remember looking out of my bedroom window at night and seeing many lights, which would have been caused by the V1 rockets. From September 1942 until July 1944 Hilde worked for Middlesex County Council. Kaspar stated inaccurately that 'for 6 months prior to April 1943 she was employed full-time at the Austrian Day Nursery'. Kaspar also reported in July to Miss Bagot (described in Peter Wright's *Spycatcher*) that 'she is on the best of terms with Broda, who spends almost every weekend with her in London.' He stated that it was 'impossible to ascertain whether she is a member of the Austrian CP but her views are undoubtedly communist. She may be regarded as a member of the inner ring and an observer of Party discipline.' This last sentence is also untrue. A feature for her of the Austrian Centre was the malevolent attitude of some towards her. She was for instance criticised for her poor grasp of Marxist-Leninist theory and her inability to parrot the necessary phrases in study groups. She was also taunted because of her separation from Berti. Hilde saw the Austrian Centre as a focus of strife as to who would get what important position in Austria after liberation. She did have Austrian friends but she certainly also had enemies.

Hilde kept her independence of mind and her determination to pursue her medical career. She then decided to move away with me to have a more self-sufficient life. The V1 onslaught that started in June 1944 may have been what made Berti accept this move. She got the job of Medical Officer in charge of a Fever and TB hospital (and Poor Law M.O.) at Culduthel, near Inverness, far from London. I also had negative feelings about the Austrian Centre, because when told about this move, I asked if it had an Austrian Centre and when told that it did not, I said 'Oh Good!' I'm rather proud of that as a first political remark. The move to Culduthel was brave and exciting, and although it only lasted from August 1944 until March 1945, for each of us it began a life-long love of Scotland. Hilde was fully engaged, including going in the ambulance to remote places to assess possible cases of notifiable diseases. Most patients at the hospital had TB; some of these had gone from the Highlands and Islands to Glasgow tenements, to war-work and TB. They lay in their glass pavilions with cold fresh air, having the treatments that my mother herself knew well including lung-puncturing, and many eventually died, because antibiotics were not yet available.

Culduthel Primary was my first school, with three classes in three rows in Miss Moir's schoolroom, all scratching away on our slates. I loved it. I also remember going to the Isle of Skye. Hilde was touched by the loan ('give it back after the war ends') of a radio by a fellow guest in Portree, a cattle dealer who kept it there for his visits. She enjoyed her status as an attractive woman (though still with a wedding ring), socialising in the officers' mess of an RAF station nearby. Berti visited us in October and over Christmas.

The TB patients would throw things at the cook if she passed by. This was because of the appalling food, a diet of swedes and little else. This bad behaviour (and the bad food) worried Hilde. Until Hilde arrived, the hospital was run by Matron, a pillar of the community. When Hilde first met her, Matron offered to continue the dispensing, and Hilde gratefully agreed. One day as they were in discussion, a sunbeam fell on Matron and Hilde saw that her uniform was stained with food and remembered from a textbook that morphine addicts are careless with their dress. She checked the dispensary, found a large shortfall in the morphine stocks, and took her allegation that Matron was an addict to her superior in Inverness, who naturally doubted the young alien woman doctor. He summoned Matron and said: 'Dr Broda alleges that you are a morphine addict. Do you wish to sue her or will you resign?' She resigned.

With this climactic event, everything fell into place; Matron had been blackmailed by Cook, who was selling the patients' food on the black market, and both were being blackmailed by the Night Sister, who was having an affair with a patient. Many staff had to go, and Hilde was seen as being somewhere between a heroine and a trouble-maker. She was offered a job at the main hospital, and also one as doctor on an island, with payment partly in kind as meat, fish and vegetables; I regret that I don't know which island was on offer. She was tempted, and taking the other fork in the road (Austria and Florence were later ones) would have given us both quite different lives. However, as described later she then gave in to pressure from Berti to return south.

For me this time represented peace, security, playmates, time with my mother and not being shuttled between two very different parents. Hilde was fulfilled in her work and gained confidence in a community that respected her. Much later Hilde and Alan, on leave from Ghana, bought a ruined Highland croft to rebuild for retirement. This was Alan's touching acquiescence to Hilde's dream of returning to her beloved Highlands. But money, its remoteness and Alan's need for a library all told against it. The realisation that a deer fence was essential for any garden also reminded Alan too strongly of incarceration.

In late October Hilde wrote to Berti, after the first visit, that we were both sad after his departure. A few days later she thanked him for some Beatrice Webb books, with which she was very pleased. The MI5 summary continues: 'Today, says the writer, a victory for her, when the patients were asked if they had any complaints about the food, there were none at all. Life presents one with some comic tasks, but she enjoys the fight, and hopes that generations of patients and nurses will reckon the food from "Dr B's days". She is again, as often before, in love with medicine. And books. She thinks she has never read so much before. Talking about a relative who brought her up (Frau Lesmeister), she says that for long she (Hilde) had judged her unfairly. "For a long time I have unfairly blamed her for my lonely and unhappy childhood. Certainly she was middle-class and narrowly Catholic, but does not think now that that matters very much. For too long she proudly thought that political views alone constitute a personal morality, but the development in personal life and in relation to surroundings, in the conduct of life as Beatrice Webb calls it, has nothing to do with politics and very little with intellect." ' The reference to a lonely and unhappy childhood is one that she never made to me, and her tape-recording in 1987 suggests that she changed her mind.

He replied: 'Did I write to you that Guéron was here? He's in France now, looking for missing relatives. I was very pleased to see him and he brought with him lots of welcome wishes and also a particularly fine slide rule. The Kowarskis are fine. He has an appropriate project. I've been asked if I would write a popular book on vision and I have prepared a synopsis. I'm curious whether this time something will come of a book that I start. Congratulations that the patients are happier about the food. Any practical effects? A word about Fr Lesmeister. Her friendly and kind manner were worth more than the ice-cold … theory of some intellectuals, and if you don't see her again, you will have a loving memory. That such goodness is not enough is shown by the fate of her family, who indeed all actively or passively went along with the devil of Naziism. But I don't say that to denigrate her, quite the contrary, I know how bad a place the world would be without people like Fr Lesmeister. If I had the choice between being the child of Fr Lesmeister or Viola Broda, the choice would not be difficult. Unfortunately it is only too likely that Egon Schönhof, if he did not escape, was murdered at Buchenwald. After the war I will see to it that in Austria he is not forgotten.'

An MI5 reader reported on a later intercepted letter, in March: 'Affectionate letter from wife. She and the child are thinking of coming to Cambridge. She thinks it would be better if they could see one another and talk things over and so come to a decision. From the general tone of the letter it would seem that she is not too keen on the divorce and hopes they will decide to stay together.' Divorce had first been mentioned by Berti in February 1943, and in further letters to Hilde in March he insisted on it. He stated that desertion as the grounds for divorce meant 3 years from November 1940, just after we were bombed out. He returned to the question in May 1944 and finally in September 1944 from Scotland, Hilde gave in and filed for divorce. She obtained a decree nisi in July 1946, and an absolute divorce in September 1946. Berti's letters to her show that this all caused Hilde much distress, as did her required appearance in the High Court.

Berti's letters also touched on whether he might go to Canada, and his view on his own life thus far: 'Like with you, it is so difficult for me to write about the things that so preoccupy me. When we were in our twenties we decided quickly to live together and then to marry. How little we considered the pros and cons for a whole lifetime, whether in ones marriage one is in the right place. I now think that people should do something about it if things are not right. As I see it now, it is not so much being in love, it is our own love that enriches our lives and gives us more strength. It allows us to look back from time to time and to say "I've done what I could". What I hate when I look back at my own past is the complacency with which I lived for many years, enjoying the milieu, and allowed myself not to have a real plan of action. In hindsight, at the basest level was Fünfturm, where I spent months eating, sleeping and making trips. In my twenties, although I often, indeed mostly, felt uneasy about the wrongness of that life, I didn't have the insight to express things or to confront them. I know that things were similar for you, that is, I know *now*. Equally we did not have the insight, the strength, or the inspiration to help each other in this basic problem of finding ourselves a better way, and thus to support each other and so achieve a purpose in life that was not in eating fried chicken and making trips, even though one should eat chicken when there is the opportunity. Where were my achievements before I was thirty?'

He had been most reluctant for Hilde to move to Scotland and when she was there he put strong pressure on her to bring me south. But he was adamant about not getting together again, whereas the implication from what he wrote was that she did want to. But then when they are together at Christmas 1944 at Culduthel the same patterns of behaviour between them re-surfaced. When against his expectation she decided in February 1945 to stay in Inverness, he put forward a proposal for split custody of me. He admitted as he wrote that it was unsatisfactory and I think it put his wants before my needs (as he had done in taking me away from the Sparks family) and also Hilde's. It forced her to move south so that he could resume access to me. So in August 1945 Hilde joined a general practice in a rather poor part of Cambridge. Again, she loved the work and we became quite settled. Although Berti was also there for over a year before he went to Edinburgh, I have little memory of him then.

In December 1945 Hilde received a letter from Felix Meyer from Brussels. He told her of the survival of his immediate family and also of Arthur Eichengrün, while the son of his sister Dora, Hilde's cousin, died in Belsen with his wife. But Felix did not mention the fate of his own twin sisters who had been institutionalised since 1910 and were murdered in 1942. There was then a long gap, and in December 1947 he castigated Hilde for her lack of contact with them. In a third letter, in May 1948 he wrote: 'My dear

Hildchen. I thank you for your sweet letter. It had already crossed my mind that to you we were serious Nazis, and that you would for that reason make a long pause.' She then received nineteen more letters from Felix before his death in 1950, and we visited the Meyers in Brussels (Photo 53).

What happened to Felix Meyer was indeed complex, and was eventually (in 1998) documented in a memoir by a cousin, Amelis von Mettenheim. As a loyal German and a wealthy industrialist he had much to lose from leaving Germany before the War. He had been an 'economically important Jew' who saw himself as far from the Nazi image of the Jew, and as being valued as an inventor, businessman and human being. Having grown up in the German classical tradition, he wouldn't at first believe that anything serious could happen to him and his family. Moreover he was supporting many other members of the family. But his company was aryanised in July 1938 and the staff accepted the new SS management. He then started to negotiate his exit with the Gestapo, always taking with him suicide pills and razor blades.

53. Felix Meyer, c.1948

After Kristallnacht in November 1938 he was arrested but released, whereas 268 other Jewish men went from Aachen to Buchenwald and Sachsenhausen. After three months he and his wife (who had Belgian nationality) got Belgian visas and passports 'against the will of the (Nazi) Party' and they left Germany in early February 1939 for supposedly neutral Belgium. After the German invasion Felix was arrested as a German citizen and then released. He and his wife tried unsuccessfully to reach Paris, and then returned to Brussels for the rest of the War. Their older daughter Claire, who had married the Protestant-turned-Catholic John Hennig in 1933, left Germany in 1939 for Ireland using her sister's Swiss passport. Her sister Margot had a child with her Swiss husband in Berlin in March 1939, but being Jewish she was denied medical facilities. The sisters then spent the War in Ireland and Switzerland.

In France, Jewish refugees from occupied Belgium were mostly interned in the Pyrenees in very bad conditions and Felix became involved in an aid committee, using his pharmaceutical contacts in France. He also started to help internees at a camp in Belgium itself. For this, he went to the German military authorities for authorisation to send materials. A requirement for Jews to register was introduced, and they were excluded from jobs and schools. Felix then went to the head of the Jewish Section to discuss those already in the camp. This was the start of his dealings with the Gestapo, and in his regular and frequent visits he again took his poison capsule. The family memoir states that he was fearless, and that his approach was always to stick to legalities. He was able to play on some differences within the German administration and became an accepted intermediary between the authorities and Jewish groups, and was later given official documentation. In 1941 conditions for Jews were made worse still, with a curfew and telephones being forbidden, and he did a lot of advising of Jews and others on how best to avoid trouble. A man behaving thus was going to be accused of collaboration after Liberation and this did happen. However, by 1947 he had been fully exonerated.

Hilde also renewed contact with the Lesmeisters but was unwilling to become too involved with them despite her love for Frau Lesmeister. This was because Toni, a favourite sister, had married a Nazi and Hilde felt she could not pick and choose within this tight-knit family. Dr Walter Dürrfeld was a principal defendant at a trial in a US military court at Nuremberg. He had been a director of I.G.Farben, a large chemical company with a subsidiary that made Zyklon B, a poison used at the extermination camps. They also developed processes for synthesising petrol and rubber from coal. The charges centred on preparing to wage an aggressive war, but also on plundering and slave labour. Dürrfeld was Head of Construction at their Auschwitz plant, and at Auschwitz III.

In March 1947, before the trial, Dürrfeld himself wrote to Hilde and until 1949 Toni wrote a succession of letters to her. Dürrfeld's lawyer also sent a request to Hilde for help in his defence, pointing out that the facility was fully seven kilometres from the extermination camp. He asked her to obtain affadavits from twenty listed English ex-prisoners, and provided a pro-forma with twenty-two questions about their treatment. I don't know if or how Hilde responded. Dürrfeld was convicted on one charge, 'war crimes and crimes against humanity through participation in the enslavement and deportation to slave labour on a gigantic scale of concentration camp inmates and civilians in occupied countries, and of prisoners of war, and the mistreatment, terrorization, torture, and murder of enslaved persons.' The judgement stated that in the case of Auschwitz, where I.G.Farben had constructed their plant next to the concentration camp with the clear intent to utilise inmates as slave inmates, the evidence was sufficient to prove that I.G.Farben had acted on their own initiative. Dürrfeld was sentenced to eight years imprisonment.

PART 4

POST-WAR LIVES

16

ALAN'S ARREST

Charles Ellis at the War Office gave Alan full powers to act in his stead as Head of Department. Alan's next contact was with Blackett. Colleagues in Montreal had asked Alan to contact him about the rumours that the future atomic project in the UK would be dominated by ICI. Their meeting at The Royal Society on 20 September started well but things took a bad turn when G. P. Thomson entered the coffee room and saw Blackett talking to Alan. Thomson knew Alan very well but he did not greet him or congratulate him on his Readership. Instead he beckoned to Blackett, and they had a whispered conversation. Then Blackett returned appearing rather embarrassed. He made some non-committal remarks, pleaded an urgent engagement and saw Alan off in a markedly cooler manner than his welcome.

Alan also began to worry about the supposed first contact with his Russian partner in espionage, on 7 October. Well before this he visited Cambridge thinking that besides meeting his old friends he might have a confidential word with the apparatchik there who had originated the whole affair in 1942. He proved very friendly, and indeed effusive in his good wishes for Alan's scientific career, but was reluctant to talk to him privately. Alan felt that he knew something but did not have clearance from the apparatus to discuss it with him, which left him distinctly uneasy. Alan received (and MI5 saw) the note from Berti, mentioned earlier and dated 1 October. This suggests that the apparatchik and Berti were different people.

At King's College preparation for the new teaching year involved meetings with colleagues from other colleges of London University. At one meeting a well-respected colleague said to him during a coffee break: 'I think you will find this an interesting topic', or words to that effect. Thinking he was suggesting an examination question, Alan glanced at the piece of paper he was handed. He read 'Do not keep your appointment' and replied with a smile that he agreed entirely. A little later the same colleague took another opportunity to remark that there had been a very encouraging development in international relations in that the old ways of doing things were being discarded. Alan took this as an explanation of why his rendezvous was now no longer necessary. He was greatly relieved at this, but not altogether reassured that nothing had gone wrong.

He then received a negative message from the DSIR head office on the reactor project. He had been told in Montreal that he would be appointed as a consultant to the project, and so would be allowed to have the experimental notebooks and other data he had handed in for transmission by diplomatic bag. These included his notes on the American reactor project and so were rather sensitive. He enquired how soon he might expect the notebooks to be released and when the appointment would be made. The reply was non-committal – the notebooks had to be studied – the consultancy was still under discussion, etc. etc. Worse was to follow. A few days later he met a colleague who had been in the Halban team in Cambridge and in Montreal and was now back with the British team. He greeted Alan, and then said: 'What have you been up to? We have all been told not to talk to you.' Alan replied with a vague indication of disagreement about the notebooks. It was all very friendly but it was the first firm sign Alan had that he was under suspicion.

Alan thought that he was probably being followed and his phone bugged and so he tested this. His aborted appointments at Great Russell Street were for 7 October, or failing that 17 October, or 27 October. October 27 was a Saturday, and Alan knew that in the City of London on Saturdays the streets were deserted, so it was good territory for a test of whether he was being followed. Sure enough he found that he was being shadowed, but this test was interrupted by an unexpected meeting with an old friend from Cavendish days whom he had not seen since 1939. They stopped and chatted, and went into a nearby tearoom where they were soon joined by two men, one of them his shadow, who sat at the next table, despite the rest of the cafe being empty. Alan tried to avoid implicating his friend, and later felt he had succeeded. This episode was followed by another sign that things had gone wrong. A colleague asked him: 'You were in the atomic project during the war were you not?' and then said: 'Have MI5 questioned you yet, because they have been interviewing A and B (two colleagues who had worked in the American team). MI5 seem to think someone has been telling the Russians about it –

that would be a rather good thing wouldn't it?' Alan replied that he had not been approached by MI5 and knew nothing about the suggested leakage, but was less confident than he tried to appear.

The back story from the point of view of the authorities is recorded in Alan's file. A top level meeting was held on 18 September at the Cabinet Office to discuss his case. Akers was brought in. 'Akers was told the story in outline and in a certain amount of detail where it affected May. He was clearly deeply shocked. He said that if he had been asked to draw up a list of those employed on atomic research in Canada on the basis of their integrity he would have placed May at the top. May is an extremely able physicist. He has worked very hard and is considered extremely good in the lab. He has also earned praise for his handling of the younger students.' Alan's involvement in the atomic power project was discussed, and also how to restrict his access to new material. It was decided to exclude Alan as much as possible from any atomic research. Makins from the Foreign Office saw this as very important, since if the Americans thought that he was still going to be able to get information they might cease collaboration on the whole project. He also thought that all precautions ought to be taken to prevent Alan from getting out of the country and worse still going to Russia. The others responded that it was difficult to have it both ways. Alan had been brought back in order to identify Soviet contacts in this country. He was clearly somewhat suspicious and if he was followed closely until 7 October he might discover that he was under observation. Other decisions were to monitor the departure of any Russian aircraft and not to search Alan's luggage at the docks. It was being assumed that there was not yet sufficient evidence to justify arresting Alan, but comparisons were to be made on his handwriting with material provided by Gouzenko. Akers was to be taken wholly into their confidence, as he could help a great deal.

On 1 October there was a discussion involving Akers, Cockcroft, Hollis, J. Marriott and Lord Rothschild. In spite of instructions that documents returning from Canada were to be inspected by DSIR, it was thought that it could be arranged for something to be passed to Alan which he might transmit to the Russian agent on 7 October. During this discussion it was stated that in the documents which were on their way to this country 'there were 3 copies of a diagram relating to development in America that Primrose (Alan) was certainly not entitled to keep. They should have been handed in in Montreal. First it is difficult to understand why he should want 3 copies and secondly there was the rather sinister fact that these particular documents were not in the list submitted by Primrose to Cockcroft before his departure.'

On 3 October Akers reported that he had offered two documents to Alan but that Alan had shown no interest in either of them and said he did not want to receive them. It was thus extremely unlikely that Alan would have any planted documents before the rendezvous. Later Akers went through all the notebooks and documents brought back by Alan from Canada, including the drawing referred to above, and said that there was nothing in the whole collection including the drawing which it was in the least surprising or particularly improper for Alan to possess. Akers had however explained to Alan that to keep some check on too-wide dissemination of information about the Tube Alloy Project, a rule had been made that no information should be kept by TA employees returning from Canada unless they continued to be employed on the project. This meant that other than half a dozen or so papers, Alan could not keep the documents, or even his own notebooks. Alan took this very well and said that he thought it was a very sensible rule. He then asked Akers to keep for him even those notebooks which could be released to him.

After Alan did not keep the rendezvous on 7 October, observation was continued. A telegram on 31 October to Hollis set out the position: 1. No decision yet by Prime Minister on action and decision would probably be postponed until after the meeting between Prime Minister (Attlee) and President (Truman). 2. They inclined to the view that whatever type of action was then decided, in Britain they ought not act at the same time against Alan but leave him alone. 3. The reasons were that they did not yet have enough evidence, that they thought he had already been warned of possible compromise, and that 'an abortive interrogation of Primrose serves no useful purpose and indeed may induce him to do the thing we most fear, namely to escape to Russia. 4. We doubt if even a successful interrogation of Primrose would produce material of use to the interrogation of the other suspects, whereas general interrogation in Canada might possibly produce useful material for dealing with Primrose.' A copy of this was handed to Philby. Meanwhile Alan's bank records had been scrutinised and it was decided that he could quite properly have saved £900, as he had done.

Later in the year Alan's mother fell ill, and he spent several weekends at home to see her. She died on Christmas Day and was buried on 28 January after a service conducted by the vicar who had taught Alan and prepared him for confirmation. It was a consolation for Alan that she never knew what was to come. By then Alan was convinced that things had gone seriously wrong. Then came a call that Cockcroft was back in London, and wanted to discuss his consultancy with the Atomic Agency project. He saw Alan on 7 February. As Alan climbed the stairs he met Chadwick coming down. He was extremely cold and distant, not even saying 'hello', but pointing to the next landing he said 'Your meeting is in there', and turned his back. The small office had a table with two chairs set opposite one another, and under the table was a box large enough to house a tape recorder.

Cockcroft came in and seated himself with a minimal degree of courtesy. He explained that the consultancy needed careful consideration. He had only just returned to the UK to take up his job in charge of the project, which was in a very early stage. Then Cockcroft changed the subject; he asked what pieces of research Alan had done in Montreal that would merit publication. So Alan told him of his work on the 4n+1 series, the O17 capture of slow neutrons, and the n-2n reaction in deuterium. He thought that the work on U233 would probably be published by the Americans, though he later doubted whether it ever was. Alan failed to mention his original suggestion on the ZEEP project, an internal memorandum rather than a piece of research. This part of the interview was very fruitful because eventually all these papers were published, but the cold atmosphere of the talk and of the meeting with Chadwick, and also the suspected presence of the tape recorder, confirmed Alan's feeling that he was under suspicion.

Shortly after this Akers invited Alan for dinner at his club. The conversation carefully avoided touchy issues such as politics or nuclear weapons. Only at the end, as he saw Alan off, did Akers broach the topic that was uppermost in both their minds, putting his arm on Alan's shoulder and assuring him that it would come out all right. He went on to say that Alan should not worry about the consultancy; Cockcroft would look after that. Alan left not greatly reassured and considerably puzzled. He later felt that Akers genuinely wanted to make contact and offer some sympathy, since his later actions suggested a very real understanding of Alan's predicament, possibly prompted by his own experience of struggling against American domination in the early days of the Project.

Then on 15 February Michael Perrin asked Alan to come to his office nearby. Alan thought this would be for a discussion of his future role in the UK Atomic Project, but when he arrived Perrin introduced him to two uniformed Army officers from MI5, Burt and Spooner. 'This interview has been described several times in the relevant literature. My own recollection is of course a little blurred by time, but it is still quite strong. Burt opened the proceedings by greeting me using the ultra-secret password which had been assigned to me (Greetings from Mikel) while looking me straight in the eyes for my reaction. It flashed through my mind that this could be a sign that MI6 had been penetrated (as indeed it had by Philby among others) but the style of the interview made this seem highly unlikely. The alternative explanation was that something had gone seriously adrift. However, I managed to maintain an air of calm indifference. Burt does not include this episode in his account of the interview, but my recollection is sharp and clear. According to Burt he first told me that there had been a serious leak in Canada of information about atomic energy, and several people had been detained. I replied that this was news to me. (I might have told him that I had heard rumours, as a result of his having interviewed other scientists in London, but that would only have caused trouble.) He then told me that he had reason to believe that I had been in contact with Colonel Zabotin, the Russian military attache in Ottawa, and that I had given secret information to an agent named Baxter or Angelov. This I firmly denied. He then went on to ask if I had had contact with anyone else at the Russian Embassy. This I also denied. I also denied giving any information to any unauthorised person. Then came an awkward question: "Are you prepared to give us any information in connection with this matter?" This was an invitation to become a participant in MI5. I avoided this by saying "Not if it is going to be used for counter-espionage". Burt regarded this as equivalent to an admission of guilt. He felt he had got his man.

'After this Burt and Spooner produced a search warrant and proceeded to carry out a detailed search of my clothes and the contents of my pockets. The lapels of my jacket were carefully examined – apparently a favoured place for hiding small titbits of information. They were then joined by my friend Akers and the whole group adjourned to the professorial office of the Physics department at King's. Here the search presented difficulties as the office still contained books and documents dating back to the days of Wheatstone and

Clerk Maxwell. They let me point out the material which belonged to my period in the office. Akers inspected each item carefully but found nothing incriminating. Nevertheless they took my passport, my diary and other personal documents. Finally we all went to my flat where a similar search was carried out, with equally poor results. This was not surprising because I had had good reason to think I might have to undergo something of this sort, and had carried out a careful clean-up.'

After the search of his flat they returned to Perrin's office. Alan was told that they would probably need to interview him again in a few days, and he then returned to King's. He then saw the posters for the evening papers: 'Spy ring in Canada – Many Arrests'. That was alarming enough, but then he saw that he was being followed, not in the previously hardly detectable way, but quite blatantly with the obvious intention of disturbing him. 'At King's things got even worse. As I went past the entrance desk a clerk pressed a red button which had been installed at his desk. Startled by this I turned around and made for the entrance again. He then pressed a green button next to the red one, and when I changed tracks again and went towards the stairs, he pressed the red button again. So the watch was extended into the college and organised with their cooperation. When I got to the Physics Department I found the technician still on duty although it was well past his normal working hours, and he remained in his room until I left. As soon as I left I was followed again and when I called in at my eating place for supper I noticed that someone was talking to the waiter and waitress, which they found so interesting that they continued to comment on it even within hearing distance. So I gathered that they did not have any idea what I "had been up to" but found it quite intriguing.

'When I reached home I sat thinking about the catastrophic situation that I found myself in, and what to do about it. Suicide? I decided against that as a cowardly way out. My problem was pretty desperate. MI5 clearly had evidence that could send me to prison. The complication was that all this evidence was in Canada. If I persisted in my denials they could either bring the evidence to London, or they could arrange to have me extradited to Canada with the additional risk of further extradition to the USA – who after all were the main victims of my misdeeds – and this brought further risks – capital punishment, etc. Since the evidence was mainly from the tapes of radio messages to Moscow it probably did not cover in detail the actual information in the form of reports and technical data I had supplied, mainly from the laboratory library, but also from my notes of American reports picked up on my visits to Chicago (mainly in response to requests from the UK team) which were now held by the London office. It would probably be better to keep quiet about this as it would only serve to make my offence seem more serious. These dangers led to the conclusion that it would be best to provide the UK authorities with just enough data to enable them to prosecute me here, taking care not to incriminate anyone else. But it would be a tricky procedure, especially as I did not know how much evidence they already had. With that conclusion I retired for the night, under the watchful eyes of MI5.

'One of the main issues would be the two hundred Canadian dollars which the Russians had tricked me into receiving by wrapping it around returned documents as the defence against the accusation of "treason for money" that I had burned the wretched bank notes was not proveable. One further complication was the origin of the famous (or rather infamous) password, "greetings from Alex" which of course implied other previous contacts. Fortunately MI5 did not raise this issue in my interview with them – they probably thought they had enough material from this event without going into previous history. Only after I was in prison, when they interviewed me at Camp Hill, did they try to raise this question. Then I did not feel under any obligation to provide any more incrimination, either for myself or for others. All this is the memory, after fifty odd years, of my turbulent mental stresses before the decisive MI5 interview. It did not go quite according to plan, and indeed has been widely criticised as completely incompetent as a piece of legal defence. Perhaps I would have done better to have called in a lawyer, perhaps from the Association of Scientific Workers (AScW). But I was afraid that this would simply lead to trial in Canada where I had few friends to support me – or that was how I felt, possibly wrongly.'

The MI5 file records this first interrogation thus: 'Primrose was interviewed by two experienced interrogators. ... Immediately on the introduction being made and before the purpose of the meeting had been disclosed, Primrose turned very pale and was clearly greatly distressed. He frequently paused as long as two or three minutes before answering questions and almost always limited his replies to "yes" or "no". The impression given was that the interrogation came as a very great shock to him, but once having pulled himself together and overcome this, he was following the programme of admitting nothing which he may well have decided was the right one. Both the interrogators who have very wide experience were convinced that he was guilty and that his behaviour throughout the interrogation and during the subsequent search was not that of an innocent man. ... It will be seen from the statement that Primrose made a blank denial of all connection with the Corby case. ... The final sentence of paragraph 5 of the statement needs some explanation. The meaning of that sentence is that Primrose was asked whether, as a British subject, he was not prepared to give all the help he could and he answered, rather oddly; "Not if it is counter-espionage". He was asked to explain this and said he only meant that he would not wish to give information which would implicate his friends.'

His actual statement on 15 February contains this extract: 'During the whole of the time I was in Canada I was not approached in any way by any unauthorised person for any information in connection with my work, namely, atomic energy. Nor have I ever been approached by any Russian official or any person acting in the interests of the Russian Intelligence. In fact, I have no knowledge of anyone working in the Russian interest. The only person I met in Canada who could be said to be anything approximating Russian was a man named Davidson who was on the laboratory staff. There was also another named Kowarski who was also on the laboratory staff. The names of Angelov and Baxter convey nothing to me – I have never heard of them. But I do know a man named Norman Veal who was on the Laboratory staff. I have never been approached by any unauthorised person in connection with him. I heard for the first time this afternoon that there has been a leakage of information in connection with atomic energy. If it means getting any of my late colleagues in Canada into trouble over this, I should feel some reluctance. This statement has been read over by me and is true.'

Alan then made a partial confession at a second interview, on 20 February (see later). A telegram on 22 February shows that Alan's fear that there was a proveable offence against the Americans was justified: 'Cockcroft told me in September that there is no repeat no enriched U235 available in Canada although he could have obtained 233 isotope in Montreal. If this proves correct it is not impossible Primrose may have obtained U235 on one of his visits to Chicago pile. We draw your attention to this possibility since it might mean that British scientist working in Canada had stolen and passed to USSR atomic material belonging to USA.' Then Hollis cabled the Canadian police: 'In the view of the Attorney General, Primrose is liable under UK Official Secrets Act and, subject to assent of the Canadian Legal Authorities, under Canadian Act. He considers there is a prima facie case against Primrose, though this is based almost entirely upon his confession. The Attorney General concurs in view of Director of Public Prosecutions that the statement by Primrose which was taken without caution, should be admitted ... The Attorney General has addressed a note to the Prime Minister stating that in his opinion, proceedings should certainly be taken against Primrose, either in Canada or in the UK ... Please consult your legal authorities and let us know if they wish to prosecute Primrose in Canada.' As before, Philby was kept informed at all stages.

Alan's arrest followed twelve days later. It later seemed very odd to him that during this interval he made no attempt to contact friends or muster support. He was charged with having, on a day in 1945, for a purpose prejudicial to the safety of the state, communicated to some person unknown certain information which was calculated to be, or might be, directly or indirectly useful to an enemy contrary to the Official Secrets Act, 1911 Section 1(1)(e). He was remanded in custody. Coincidentally Churchill's 'Iron Curtain' speech at Fulton, Missouri, was fully reported in the same issue of *The Times*.

17

ALAN'S REMAND AND TRIAL

Alan provided a concise statement of what happened next, and his thoughts on how to cope with his fate: 'On 1 May 1946 I appeared at the Old Bailey on the charge that contrary to the Official Secrets Act I had communicated to an unauthorised person information about the atomic project on which I was engaged in Canada. I pleaded Guilty, and my counsel, Gerald Gardiner (Note 35), pleaded in mitigation that the Russians were at the relevant time our allies, and that they had been promised by the British government all possible assistance in prosecuting the war. He might have reinforced this plea by reference to the Agreement of 29 September 1942 between the Governments of the UK and the USSR binding each party to give freely to the other party full information on all types of new weapons being developed, including any necessary plans, specifications etc. Unfortunately this agreement had been kept secret, and no-one in court including myself knew of its existence. The judge, Mr Justice Oliver, did not accept Mr Gardiner's plea; in fact he expressed some surprise that such ideas could be put forward. He sentenced me to ten years penal servitude. As the maximum under that section of this Act is fifteen years, and the minimum five, I felt he had struck a middle course, despite the severity of his remarks, and I had no hard feelings about that. The case excited a great deal of comment, much of which was fairly sympathetic. But soon a hard line began to be taken by some writers who clearly had official encouragement. The most bitter of these was Miss Rebecca West, who published comments in *The New Statesman* and *The Evening Standard* …

'The following sections on my prison life are based on notes which I typed out immediately after my release and my letters to my family, which they kept and returned to me on my release. So this material is not so subject to the fallibility of memory as the interval of forty years might lead one to expect. I should add that the prisons of those days were much less crowded than those of today. I always had a cell to myself except in the "open" prisons where we had dormitories. Nevertheless, the conditions were quite tough enough. I must pay tribute to one book which was a great help to me: Macartney's *Walls Have Mouths* which as a foundation member of the Left Book Club I had read many years before, and had the foresight to retain when the rest of my LBC books had been given away. I re-read it when it became increasingly clear that I was due for a lagging, and found it in the event an admirable guide.

'At the start I decided that I would try to make my lagging as quiet and bearable as possible. My main aim was to come out with the minimum mental and spiritual damage possible. So I never attempted to fight the system, to promote mutiny and insurrection or even mild ridicule of authority. Reform of the prison system is an admirable cause, but not one to which I had ever given my first priority, and I hoped to give my hand to more urgent causes if I retained my strength till my release. So I had no hesitation in accepting what help the prison afforded to make my stay bearable, rather than beating my head against the prison walls. Nevertheless I could not help reflecting on the almost total lack of rational basis in the prison as a cure for crime.'

After the magistrate had remanded Alan he was placed in the prison hospital at Brixton. There was a hospital bed, a commode, a chair and a locker. It was an observation cell and at night the light was only dimmed. It was his home for the next two months, and he spent most of his time reading physics and most of Conrad. The food was plain but better for him than the restaurant food he had been eating, so the digestive troubles which had troubled him eased and never returned. Alan had no watch, since his valuables were taken into safe keeping, so he kept track of time by drawing a sundial on the wall of the cell. His commode had to be emptied in the morning. This was his first introduction to slopping-out and the disgustingly primitive level of sanitation tolerated in prisons, even in the hospital.

There was exercise in the yard twice a day for half an hour, the only time that Alan saw much of his fellow prisoners. The capital cases on remand were in another ward; there were about a dozen, including two young men who were tried at the same assizes as Alan. They were both reprieved and he saw much of them later. He was visited daily by the doctor and by the Governor, and his only other entertainment was when the hospital Prison Officer (PO) or another officer came for a chat. This was part of the 'observation' under which his mental state was being assessed, and would form part of the Medical Officer's evidence if Alan decided to plead insanity.

Visits were generally held in the Solicitor's visiting room with an officer in attendance, listening to everything that was said. Once he was taken to the ordinary visiting room, where each prisoner sat opposite a glass window through which he could see his visitor, and if he could shout hard enough he might even have been able to talk a little. But with thirty prisoners and their friends shouting at one another it was an approximation to pandemonium. Although Alan had decided to plead guilty he had much material to prepare for his solicitor. He wrote his life history and his connection with the Atomic Project, together with the basis of his fears for the future exploitation of the bomb by the Americans and the need for deterring them. This helped his defence counsel, but Alan considered that Gardiner's speech in his defence was much more telling than his own material. Alan had several interviews with the solicitor, but just one with Gardiner before the trial, when he was told that he had been very foolish to have made any statement to the police.

Alan wrote: 'These interviews with solicitors and counsel are the hardest part of a remand prisoner's life. He is completely in their hands, and usually does not trust them at all. Most convicts feel that they have been let down badly. Indeed the solicitor often makes some arrangement with the prosecution for a guilty plea on certain counts to secure withdrawal of a more serious charge, or he may decide that evidence that the prisoner regards as most important won't help, or will tell against him. The result is a strong feeling that the solicitor is in league with the prosecution. Even if the prisoner does not feel this at first, he will be persuaded by the other prisoners, and even by the POs, that he is being delivered over to the prosecution bound hand and foot. A few days before my trial I was called into the office of the Chief Medical Officer. He asked me if I planned to plead insanity. This took me rather by surprise. When I said "No" he explained that he would have to come and give evidence about my state of mental health if I did so plead, but he added that he had not detected any sign of insanity, which pleased me. He added "You are pleading guilty, aren't you?" I agreed, but was rather put out at finding that what I had imagined to be a confidential decision between me and my solicitor was known to the prison officials. He explained: "They have put you down as the first case in Number

1 Court. That is always a guilty plea, because the Sheriff and the Lord Lieutenant have to be present at the opening of the Assizes, and they don't want to have to sit through a long case." But he did not warn me that these worthies would enter the courtroom to a rousing fanfare of trumpets, and be clothed in all their ceremonial glory of ermine, scarlet and gold chains. It is a pity that all the characters in the court room drama are given fancy dress, except the prisoner. Surely he should be permitted a ceremonial suit of sackcloth and ashes, or something diabolical with a forked tail, and enter with appropriate music and the smell of hellfire.

'I asked Gardiner what my chances were. He said "Well, there are no liberal or progressive judges, who might let you off lightly. The maximum sentence under the Act is fifteen years and the minimum five but they don't usually give the maximum because they like to keep something in reserve to discourage appeals. Think of a number between five and fifteen – your guess is as good as mine." So I said it looked like ten was a likely bet, and he agreed. He said, not quite seriously, that it was a pity that I couldn't establish that the whole thing was a put-up job, and that I had been a double agent instructed by MI5. Apart from that he couldn't see any possibility of getting me off.

'Ralph (Alan's brother; Photo 54) gave me the impression that Gardiner was his first choice, and I certainly agreed with it. I was not quite so happy with the solicitor, Kenwright, who was recommended to Ralph as a tough and experienced man. He was certainly tough, but never displayed any sympathy for, or indeed consciousness of, the implications of the case. Maybe it is better to have such a man as legal advisor, with a mind tuned to respond to the "right-minded" establishment views which certainly predominate in the legal world.'

During his remand there was a most peculiar burglary at the professor's office at King's College. The thief took Alan's briefcase and some papers. Ralph wrote to ask if he had insurance against theft, and in his reply, doubtless copied to MI5, Alan gave as much detail as he could of where his papers were, so that any future 'thief' would know where to look and would not need to disturb the accumulated dust of professors since Clerk Maxwell. He was confident that there was nothing in the office or anywhere else that MI5 would find useful. Alan received newspapers and magazines and was most disturbed that the anti-Russian propaganda which had been laid to rest during the War, while the Russians were gallant allies, was being vigorously

54. Ralph Nunn May c.1946. With thanks to Diana MacDonell

revived. The Labour government, elected on a manifesto which had emphasised the close understanding that they would maintain with fellow Socialists, was proving hardly less adept at this line than the Conservatives. As the political climate got colder, he felt that every degree drop in temperature meant another year on his sentence.

The MI5 file has a copy of a letter sent to Alan just after his arrest by his Chicago colleague Herbert L. Anderson, which sets out clearly the political issues being debated in the US, for which Alan's arrest and trial had implications: 'Dear May, The American newspapers are covered with large headlines dealing with your recent arrest in connection with the atomic bomb secrets. The whole thing has come as a great shock to us here, particularly since it strikes so close to home. The story breaks at a highly inopportune time for those of us who are anxious to see some sensible legislation passed through Congress. As you are probably aware, there is a great battle in progress between the nuclear scientists on one hand and General Groves on the other to determine what form the domestic control of atomic energy shall have in this country. General Groves is anxious to have Congress pass the May-Johnson Bill which would permit the military to maintain a strict control over atomic energy work in much the same way as they have enjoyed during the war and up to the present. On the other hand the nuclear scientists are supporting the McMahon Bill which puts th control in the hands of a civilian body; specifically excludes from th dominate (*sic*) role the stipulations of secrecy in basic physics.

'Needless to say the recent "spy scare" in Canada and now your arrest both coming at a time when the Atomic Energy Committee is sitting in executive session to determine which point of view should prevail, seemed to be timed in a way which strengthens the hand of General Groves who i making an effective point of these events to persuade the Committee to grant him the strict rule which he wants. On our part, it seems more difficul than ever to convince the Committee that just such strict control will strik at the very core of any progress which might be made in this field. More than this, many of us firmly feel, if General Groves has his way, the army will hav gained far more power over the people of the United States than the founder of the American Constitution could have dreamed.

'Your arrest comes as a shock because we physicists like to believe that w are members of a small and uniquely intimate family which knows and trust its members. Certainly, because of our past associations I find it very difficul to believe that you could have intentionally given away any real secrets to . foreign nation at a time when there could be no sympathy for such a mov from our fellow scientists. We would be sincerely interested in learning som facts about your case. First, because, if we can, we would like to help to try to get you out of your mess and, second, because we badly need an answer to the charge that our friends among the nuclear scientists are not trustworthy Sincerely yours, Herbert L Anderson'

Alan's senior colleague F. A. Paneth also wrote to confirm that th preparation of the new edition of the *Manual of Radioactivity* involving Alan had become something of a headache. After Alan's name had appeared in th papers he had received a letter from the Oxford University Press urging him to revise the arrangements, to which he had replied that in his opinion it wa not yet necessary. He wrote that he would be extremely sorry if finally the should have to do without Alan. Moreover he had tried to find out from Alan's solicitor whether he could be of any help.

At the committal proceedings on 19 March Akers, now Sir Wallace and appearing as a witness, was asked by Gardiner: 'Is there a strong feeling among scientists rightly or wrongly that contributions to knowledge made by them with regard to the benefits of atomic research ought not be the secrets of any one country?' He answered that there was. When Gardiner then asked if Russia was not our gallant ally, the prosecution objected that they did not know why Russia was brought in.

At the trial itself Alan pleaded guilty and the Attorney General, Sir Hartley Shawcross, otherwise active at the Nuremberg Trials, led for the prosecution (Note 36). In his speech he introduced the phrases 'somewhat squalid case' and 'apparently for reward', and then referred to Alan as having 'so far set himself above the laws of the country and the policy of the country as to communicate information which his Government in agreement with the other Governments concerned had felt must for the present be maintained as a secret.' An historical account followed and Shawcross then focused on Alan's access to information and to actual uranium samples, and continued with an account of Alan's two meetings with Burt, including highlighting Alan's remark in the first 'Not if it be counter-espionage'.

He then read out, as the prosecution case, the statement that Alan made in the second meeting: 'About a year ago whilst in Canada I was contacted by an individual whose identity I decline to divulge ... He apparently knew that I was employed by the Montreal laboratory and he sought information from me concerning atomic research. (2) I gave and had given very careful consideration to the correctness of making sure that the development of atomic energy was not confined to the U.S.A. I took the very painful decision that it was necessary to convey general information on atomic energy and make sure it was taken seriously. For this reason I decided to entertain the proposition made to me by the individual who called on me. (3) After this preliminary meeting I met the individual on several subsequent occasions whilst in Canada. ... He did request samples of uranium from me and information generally on atomic energy. (4) At one meeting I gave the man microscopic amounts (of material) and I also gave the man a written report on atomic research as known to me. This information was mostly of a character which has since been published or is about to be published.' Shawcross then made the point that not all the information was published, and that such information would have enabled scientists of other countries not already in possession of it to shorten their researches.

The statement went on: 'The man gave me some dollars ... in a bottle of whisky and I accepted these against my will. Before I left Canada it was arranged that on my return to London I was to keep an appointment with somebody I did not know. I was given precise details as to making contact but I forget them now. I did not keep the appointment because I had decided that this clandestine procedure was no longer appropriate in view of the official release of information and the possibility of satisfactory international control of atomic energy. The whole affair was extremely painful to me and I only embarked on it because I felt this was a contribution I could make to the safety of mankind. I certainly did not do it for gain.' Shawcross then repeated that Alan had accepted money. He concluded: 'That is the whole case. As I have told your Lordship, he is a scientist of standing against whom nothing whatever is known and a person, apart from these matters or the motives which have led up to them, of excellent character.'

A much abridged version of Gardiner's speech is as follows: 'Dr May tells me that the person to whom he gave this information was a Russian. He does not desire that there should be any mystery about the matter. ... What are the circumstances in which a man of high principle comes to do what Dr May did? First, he did not do this for money. There was apparently a bottle of whisky left for him at an apartment. He says he accepted it against his will. This statement is the case for the prosecution and I ask your Lordship to accept ... his statement in it that he only embarked upon this because he felt it was a contribution to the safety of mankind, "I certainly did not do it for gain".

'He was asked to concern himself with this ... subject matter because it was represented to him that he would thereby be making a ... contribution to the British war effort which he was most anxious to do. He was working on atomic research and not on atomic bombs. There was work going on on atomic bombs but he was not concerned with it. I suggest that the information that he gave, whilst I do not minimise its importance, was not information of substantial importance. The highest the scientist who has given evidence (Akers) puts it is that if everything Dr May knew up to September 1945 had been known, that would have saved the scientists a certain amount of time.

'Doctors take the view, rightly or wrongly, that if they have discovered something of benefit to mankind, they are obliged to see that it is used for mankind and not kept for any particular group of people, and there are scientists who take substantially the same view. What Sir Wallace Akers was saying in the Court below was that there was a strong feeling among scientists, rightly or wrongly, that the result of atomic research might not be kept as the secret of one country. That was a view which rightly or wrongly Dr May strongly held. Dr May tells me that in doing what he did and in the view which he took he was not acting in concert with any other British scientist. He came to this decision entirely on his own responsibility and without reference to anyone else.

'It is not possible to do justice to a man on the question of sentence without considering what was in his mind at the time and the circumstances which existed at the time. February 1945 was a time when the then Prime Minister had not made statements which he is since reported to have made. At that time the British Army was mostly in Holland ... and the Russians were in the course of their drive to Berlin. It was customary to refer to them as Allies who were doing at least their fair share in the war. It is perhaps an ironical expression if anyone at that date referred to them as enemies or potential enemies.'

The Attorney General interjected: 'My Lord, I think I ought to make it abundantly clear that there is no kind of suggestion that the Russians are enemies or potential enemies. ... There is no suggestion that this prosecution contemplates the Russians as possible enemies ... What is hit at by this section is the fact that once information passes out of the control of His Majesty's Government, although in the first instance it may be to persons whose attitude to this country is entirely friendly, there no longer remains control over it and it may get into the hands of enemies.'

Gardiner continued: '... If one has to consider what was in Dr May's mind one has to see the relevant circumstances. It is right to bear in mind as he did the statement which had been made by the then Prime Minister, that we had offered to the Government of Russia any technical or economic knowledge in our power which is likely to be of assistance to them. Dr May was also aware that Russian scientists with the scientists of other countries as well had themselves made contributions to this subject and were in a position to make further contributions, and he had in mind the terms of the alliance under which the parties had mutually undertaken to afford one another military and other assistance and support of all kinds in the war against Germany, and rightly or wrongly he felt full of indignation that the promises of the communication of technical assistance which had been given to one ally, as it appeared to him, should be made the monopoly of another. ... He considered this discovery was one of great consequence to humanity. As soon as he learned that the Government ... were themselves about to publish information he at once decided to have nothing further to do with it. I appreciate that it will be said, as he himself now recognises, that this was not a matter in which an individual ought to take a decision of that kind.

'As I have said, this is in no sense an attempted justification, it is mitigation. He had nothing to gain, except what we all have to gain by doing what we believe to be right, and he had everything to lose. What this scientist has in fact done, and for which your Lordship now has to sentence him is this. Contrary to law and to the orders of his government and in breach of an undertaking which he had given some years before at a time when he would say he could not reasonably contemplate that the government which had said that it was giving all technical knowledge to an ally would not carry out that statement, he was giving a limited amount of information before the date when the Government subsequently decided to publish most of it of a scientific discovery of great value to humanity in which he had participated to a representative of a country which was then an ally.'

Mr Justice Oliver: 'Alan Nunn May, I have listened with some slight surprise to some of the things which your Counsel has said he is entitled to put before me: the picture of you as a man of honour who had only done what you believed to be right. I do not take that view of you at all. How any man in your position could have had the crass conceit, let alone the wickedness, to arrogate to himself the decision of a matter of this sort, when you yourself had given your written undertaking not to do it, and knew it was one of the country's most precious secrets, when you yourself had drawn and were drawing pay for years to keep your own bargain with your country – that you could have done this is a dreadful thing. I think that you acted not as an honourable but a dishonourable man. I think you acted with degradation. Whether money was the object of what you did, in fact you did get money for what you did. It is a very bad case indeed. The sentence upon you is one of ten years' penal servitude.'

Shortly after the trial Ralph approached the Labour academic Harold Laski, who had voiced concerns about the US and sympathy for the USSR. He shared a widespread view at the time that Alan's sentence was much too severe. A similar view was expressed by Alan's union, the AScW, and already in May 1946 its Council passed the following resolution: 'That this Council strongly supports the action of the Executive Committee in protesting against the harsh sentence of ten years penal servitude passed on Dr Alan Nunn May, and instructs the Executive Committee to take all possible steps, including a nation-wide publicity campaign to secure mitigation of his sentence.' On 1 August 1947 a deputation led by Laski saw the Home Secretary to ask for a reduction in Alan's sentence, but were rebuffed. The files show that civil servants held strongly to the view that Alan's offence was graver than that of Springhall, who had received seven years (Note 29). The intended deputation of fourteen included P. M. S. Blackett, the philosopher C. E. M. Joad; N. Kemmer; N. Lawson (National Council for Civil Liberties); W. Lawther (President, National Union of Mineworkers); Professor R. E. Peierls; J. B. Priestley; Jack Tanner (President, Amalgamated Engineering Union) and Sir Robert Watson-Watt, the pioneer of radar, although Lawther, Priestley and Tanner were unable to be present.

The deputation presented three documents. One was a letter on Alan's behalf signed by fifty of his colleagues in the Canada team. The second was a petition with thirty-three signatures that also argued that the ten years sentence was too severe. It focused on rejecting the idea that Alan acted for other than principled reasons. Nine of the names are of MPs, and among those whose names are still recognised are (again) Laski, Joad, and Priestley, and also Gerald Brenan, Julian Huxley, William Empson, Graham Sutherland, Olaf Stapledon, Sibyl Thorndike, V. S. Pritchett, Herbert Read, Joseph Needham, Ethel Mannin and George Orwell.

The third document was Nicholas Kemmer's assessment of what Alan could have passed to the Russians, in the context of the publication after Hiroshima and Nagasaki of the detailed description of the Manhattan Project in the Smyth Report (Note 25). One of Kemmer's conclusions was that the prosecution's statement that 'The disclosures could shorten the effort of a major power by several years' was factually incorrect. He also stated: 'The real significance of his action was to inform of the *existence* of the vast atomic energy programme. The disclosures were made before the bomb was dropped on Hiroshima and it was not known at the time in what military or political circumstances the weapon might be used; it was known however that the whole development was being kept secret from the Russians.

Assuming the secret had previously been well kept, May's disclosures could have had the effect of inducing a commencement of activities in the fields of research, mining, technical planning etc. In this sense May's report may have speeded the Russians' effort by as many months as its arrival in Russia preceded the dropping of the bomb. Quite evidently the samples were sent with the same purpose. A report unsupported by other evidence is not with certainty going to be credited, even less is it likely to be acted upon immediately. A sample of a substance hitherto non-existent in nature, and, as any physicist would realise, produced at enormous cost, is evidence of much greater weight, evidence too which might more easily reach those specialists capable of understanding its implications.' This seems fair on Alan's own thinking, though we now know that the assumption that the secret had been kept was false, as the Russians had other sources that included Cairncross, Fuchs, Hall and Berti.

The person who Alan might have felt that he let down personally was Chadwick, but I never heard Alan comment on this. Chadwick wrote from the US to H. S. W. Massey, who was chairman of a committee that set up an Association of Atomic Scientists: ' ... There is a ... danger ... of taking too partial a view of the May case. I suggest that you should be very cautious indeed how you approach this matter. I am not suggesting that you should not act as an adviser on scientific matters to his counsel, if you are asked to do so, but I think it would not be wise to espouse his cause too warmly or to jump spontaneously to his defense without some knowledge of the circumstances. He is entitled to the best defense that can be provided for him, but I am afraid that some of our friends and colleagues may take up May's cause without reflection and from political prejudice. I have already heard the words 'scientific witch hunt' and similar phrases. This is pure nonsense. I am quite certain that proceedings would have been taken against May only after very thorough investigation and out of a deep conviction that he had committed a serious offense. I was a little uneasy to read that you had *volunteered* to act as an adviser for the defense. I may be unduly cautious but to me this is a very different matter from consenting to act as adviser on the request of his counsel. I expect you know that the Canadian affair in general and the case of May in particular, have produced a very strong effect on this side. Whatever the result of May's trial may be, there will remain a deep feeling of uneasiness. In every way this is a most unfortunate affair.' Margaret

Gowing quoted Cockcroft as viewing the sentence as twice the length that it should have been.

An alternative view came from the noted geneticist J. B. S. Haldane. As part of a lengthy article in *The Daily Worker,* the Communist Party newspaper, in May 1946 he wrote: 'Now on June 22, 1941, Dr May probably heard Mr Churchill's broadcast statement offering the Soviet Government "any technical or economic assistance which is in our power". If not, he read it in the papers next day. And until that offer was withdrawn as publicly as it was made, Dr Nunn May had every right to assume that it still held.

'As a matter of fact the British Government did not give the Soviet Union all the technical assistance in its power, though of course it gave a lot. I can speak from personal experience. I was engaged in research on underwater operations. The work in progress was shown to naval officers of several navies, including American and Dutch, but not to Soviet naval representatives, although it would probably have saved the lives of Soviet sailors. Many scientists who were engaged in secret work could give similar examples.

'Mr Churchill may have been foolish to make the pledge which he did. But he made it, and it was not kept. A failure to keep British pledges to foreign countries led to the complete isolation of Britain in 1940, and similar failures are likely to have a like effect in future. Dr May presumably took the view that pledges made on behalf of his country should be honoured, even if his superiors took the opposite view. He was also, of course, influenced by the great tradition of internationalism in science.'

After his conviction Alan wrote to Ralph explaining why he told his interrogators about his having been given money: 'My reason for mentioning this was simply that the police knew. Even if they couldn't prove it, they would have found an opportunity to use it, perhaps at this stage in the proceedings, with just as damaging effect. In short I decided to draw the enemy's trumps early. Maybe a mistake, but at any rate people who support me now can't complain that I've led them up the garden path on that score. In general I was afraid that a not guilty plea with no information on my side would completely mislead public opinion – and if anything was proved *then*, I couldn't have expected much support. My friends would have been saying that such an excellent fellow couldn't possibly do such things. There are obvious disadvantages in this policy including the fact that I am here – but I'm not sure that an alternative would have been better in the long run.'

Alan, by making an economical statement and by pleading guilty, thus avoiding the calling of witnesses and cross-examination, did limit what could be held against him and the identification of his contacts, as he had intended. Naturally MI5 continued to worry about his contacts.

He also commented on an American nuclear test: 'I see that the American navy can withstand atomic bombs, at least when manned by guinea pigs and goats. I'm not sure if this is a good thing. They will probably feel a bit panicky at not having a bomb which will completely wipe out all resistance – or a navy which will stand up to *any* bomb. I hope people don't begin to think that it's quite an ordinary weapon, and that special arrangements for its control are unnecessary.'

Within the family Ralph continued to be active on Alan's behalf and his father and sister Mary visited him in prison, as did two aunts, but his eldest brother Ted cut him off completely. Much later Ted's widow and daughter re-established contact, to Alan's great pleasure. Alan's father wrote to E. W. Barnes, a noted mathematician as well as being the Bishop of Birmingham who had confirmed Alan. He replied that he shared the opinion that the sentence of ten years penal servitude was excessive, and thought that Alan had already been sufficiently punished. He wrote that the difficulty of those who sought to have the sentence reduced was that Alan had received payment for his information. But the amount of money received and the bottle of whisky were almost ludicrously inadequate. He extended to the family his deep sympathy, the more so as he was convinced that it was only as they showed willingness to share with Russia the secret of the atomic bomb that they could build up such a friendly understanding as was necessary for permanent peace.

Two of the books published in the years that Alan was in prison deserve brief mention. One was Rebecca West's *The Meaning of Treason* (1949). The other, *The Traitors* by Alan Moorehead (1952), concerned Alan, Klaus Fuchs and Bruno Pontecorvo, and was written with government help: 'Please see a draft paper written at DB's request and it is intended that it should be shown to Alan Moorehead. I am passing it to you in draft form …' 'Traitor' applied to Alan was libellous, but these authors used it with impunity.

West had attended the trials of British collaborators with the Germans, and then Alan's trial. The main character of her book was William Joyce (Lord Haw-Haw) who was hanged for treason in January, 1946. West's book had a section where she characterised Alan and Joyce as the Communist-Fascist and the Nazi-Fascist. She then expounded her view on the threats each posed to democracy, and linked these to their physical appearance and demeanour in the dock, with much respect for Joyce and much contempt for Alan. Her book and the flights of rhetoric and invective contained in it were admired by many. But they were viewed with anger by Alan for her inaccurate and contemptuous words on him ('he was poorly-built though he had a very large head bulging in a conformation often found in men of exceptional talent'), the use she made of this to bolster her wider argument, and her refusal to give a fair account of Alan and other unnamed left-wing scientists, his trial and the issues involved. She insisted that Alan took payment and did not mention Gardiner's speech for the defence. There was comment at the time at West's personal animosity to Alan, which was initially seen in letters to *The New Statesman* just after his trial. Alan later commented on her litigiousness and that he was not the only one she hated, instancing H.G. Wells and their son, Anthony West.

Alan's views on West, and also on his own solicitor, are seen from a letter he wrote to Ralph in 1948, replying to Ralph's suggestion of libel action against West (extracts of the forthcoming book had appeared in a newspaper at the end of 1947). He would have needed Home Office permission and thought the whole idea inadvisable, at least from prison: 'I haven't seen the articles complained of, so I can only imagine the kind of thing Miss West would write. As you say the title alone is a quite clear libel, and it certainly hurts to be put in the same company with Joyce, etc. However it is another question whether it is advisable to bring an action now. Bear in mind the state of "public opinion" as expressed in the newspapers and the speeches of our statesmen; add to that the possibility that Miss W and her backers may enjoy support from official quarters; then add all the other people interested e.g. Hollywood wanting to engage in similar libels: I think it all mounts up to a very formidable outfit – not to be tackled without corresponding resources.' He continued: 'I have already experienced, in Brixton, the pleasures of legal affairs in prison. I can assure you that it is one of the most severe punishments I have had. One is completely at the mercy of the lawyers – being delivered to them – if not bound hand and foot, at least very effectively under control. If I ever go to law I mean it to be when I am in a position to attend to every step myself, to take advice certainly but not to be completely dependent on my advisers ... It is essential to replace Kenwright. I never met anyone so obtuse on the points involved in this, or better at prolonged inaction. I have only known him act quickly twice, and both times it was in response to a request from MI5 ...' In the event, even after his release Alan never went to court, but on several occasions he sent letters to authors and publishers through his later solicitors, and he once retained Gerald Gardiner again when a newspaper became too intrusive for him.

18

ALAN IN PRISON 1946-48

Wormwood Scrubs (May and June 1946). The baths were under the charge of a cheerful prisoner who filled Alan's bath, joking that he was sorry there was no heavy water, throwing him a bundle of clothes and saying, 'These will make you look just like one of us.' The trousers and jacket were of coarse grey cloth and the sizes were quite random, so exchanges were needed between the receptions to achieve optimum satisfaction. Alan's card showed his number as 2625, name May, sentence ten years, and FLL (Fit for Light Labour). He was taken to his cell, told to collect water in a jug from the 'recess', and locked in. The bed was three boards nailed to two cross pieces, about three inches from the floor. It had a very thin and much-used mattress of kapok. The *Regulations for the Guidance of Prisoners (Men)* on the wall laid down in detail the number of visits, letters, etc to which they were entitled, how to get them, and (most important) how the amount of remission for good conduct was calculated. Alan discovered later that all this information was completely out of date, and that on all such matters the only safe course was to get information from an experienced prisoner.

In the morning the doors were unlocked to the shout 'Slop Out!' Alan went to the recess with his chamber pot to find a scene of utter squalor. There was a queue waiting to empty slops, and when he got near the sink he found that quite a few had not used the sink at all, but just thrown the contents of their chamber pots on the floor. He did not blame them too strongly for this, for the sink was as usual blocked and the flushing device out of order. Anything put in the sink would overflow onto the floor anyhow, so why not put it there straight away? After slopping out as best one could, the next task was to visit the recess to draw fresh water, and then they were locked up again to wait for breakfast. After a long wait after breakfast they were opened up again to go along to the recess again to wash their plates and mugs. The recess was still in the post-slopping-out condition so this was not very effective as a hygienic washing up.

Then they were ordered to 'Stand to your doors!' whilst the screws went through the preparations for taking them out on exercise. During this wait a PO came to look at the cells of the last night's new receptions. This was 'Piss-Pot Charlie', a tall, distinguished looking officer with a severe manner and a sharp eye for detail. His nickname arose from the importance he attached to the cleanliness and precise positioning of the chamber pot, which had to be tilted against the wall opposite the door so that the screw, on opening the cell, could immediately see into it and admire its gleaming white interior. He took a long and apparently dissatisfied look at Alan's cell, sniffed and passed on to the next. Then he returned and barked 'Go next door and tell that fellow how to put his gear out.' This sudden promotion to instructor on cell arrangement was a trifle embarrassing for Alan, but fortunately the man next door was smaller than Alan, and even more nervous.

The Reception Board was supposed to decide on the work suitable for each reception. When asked his religion Alan replied C of E since he had been confirmed and it was broad enough to include any shade of belief or disbelief, and a new doctor friend had told him that atheists or agnostics were liable to be locked up on Sundays, whilst their believing colleagues had a good time singing hymns and listening to a rousing sermon from the chaplain. He was assigned to the cleaners and became adept in the various techniques of scrubbing floors, from the thorough scrub to be used when an inspection was threatened to the lick-over more suitable for everyday use. But his heart was not really in the job, nor was C Hall a very rewarding wing for a cleaner. The inhabitants were generally only there for a few days, on transfer from one prison to another, and so they could not be induced to take any pride in the cleanliness of the wing.

During these first weeks the chaplain visited Alan several times. He was one of the best chaplains Alan met. His services were popular, because his sermons were so entertaining. His style was that of a Hyde Park orator and his subject matter was drawn from politics, football or prison life. He was often interrupted by applause and claimed to be unpopular with the prison authorities. He was also a great help to Alan because he lent him books from the chaplain's library, which was much better than the general prison library. But the most useful things he did for Alan were to get him his sugar ration, and get him off the cleaning party. There had been no sugar so far in the breakfast issued on C Wing, but Alan had found out that D Wing had an issue not only at breakfast but at tea as well. Alan told him this, and the next day they got their full ration. When Alan said the cleaning party was rather boring, the chaplain had him shifted to the tailors' shop. After a day sewing on buttons, Alan was promoted to a treadle sewing machine making small canvas bags for the Royal Mint.

Alan then had his first encounter as a convict with a visiting magistrate, who shuffled over to where he was sitting, impatiently waiting to get on with the bags. He asked Alan how he was getting on and said: 'You are a Cambridge man, aren't you? I was at Oxford.' He pronounced his verdict: 'What you did was really perjury – just perjury!' Then he gave Alan a hard glare and shuffled out again. Alan did not get a chance to reply that on the contrary his main trouble was that he had been excessively truthful, and that his legal advisers bitterly regretted his having spilled so many beans. The instructor told Alan that many magistrates and official visitors seem to be actuated by this kind of morbid curiosity, getting their *News of the World* in the flesh.

After his apprenticeship on the treadle machine Alan was put on a power machine, a frightening experience at first. He graduated by stages from doing fly-pieces for Borstal boys' shorts to trousers for Post Office overalls, and eventually to the complete overalls. Such complicated problems as putting the sleeves in correctly caused him considerable difficulty, and he never attained the speed necessary to fulfil the minimum rate above which the prisoner was rewarded with a wage.

At the Scrubs the weekly bath was taken during working hours so the utmost efforts were made to persuade the men to bathe quickly. Half an hour was the official time from leaving the shop to returning again, and one had to loosen all essential buttons and take off one's tie on the way to the bath house for it to be possible to get into the bath and at least get wet all over before the cry of 'Plugs Out'. To get properly soaped and washed meant a serious risk of being late and a severe reprimand.

Alan had become eligible for transfer to D Wing after six weeks, but this depended on vacancies being available. He began to wonder when his time would come and approached the wing PO and was told that he was just an ordinary prisoner, and would have to wait his turn like everyone else, that he could not expect any sort of favoured treatment etc. So he consulted his doctor friend, who suggested that two Woodbines offered in the proper quarter might help and kindly carried through the negotiations with the wing red band who prepared the lists. The next day he was transferred to D Wing, where the cells were much cleaner since the men on this wing were more permanent, and could lose their privileges if their cells were not up to the exacting standards set by Piss-Pot Charlie. The floors were wooden and scrubbed until they were quite white. One always took off one's boots before entering a cell.

Alan then attained the further privilege of eating in 'association' instead of in his cell. The Association hut had two sections, one a small theatre for concerts and films and the other for meals. The hut was under the control of the Association Leader, the chief red band whose position Alan described as somewhat similar to that of a Regimental Sergeant Major or Chief Eunuch. He assigned newcomers to mess tables, arranged the mess duties, and dealt with the authorities. The chief clerk of the tailors' shop was in charge of one of the tables, which he prided himself on keeping for the most exclusive and intellectual company. Alan wrote that he was pleased and honoured to accept his invitation to join his mess. The matter was arranged with the Association Leader, whether with the help of tobacco Alan did not know. Probably this would have been beneath the dignity of such exalted figures and instead there might have been some reciprocal favour in the way of pressing clothes, or new shirts from the tailors' shop.

Besides having meals in company with real knives and forks, instead of the 'pushers' provided for those in cells, they had the privilege of evening association after tea. One could opt either to stay inside the hut to read or to play board games, or go outside onto the parade ground where the more active would play cricket while the others sat around and talked. This was pleasant in the summer, but cut down on Alan's time for reading and study, and he often opted for the hut despite the noise level inside. Soon after Alan joined his table the tailors' clerk suggested that he might take part in a projected concert. They needed a pianist who could read music, and he offered to help. He was asked to put on a solo act at the piano as well as accompanying the singers, but the difficulty was music, as Alan had never been able to play from memory. They found scores of Beethoven and of Schubert's *Moments Musicaux* and he started practicing and found his fingers unbelievably stiff, as he hadn't played for nearly a year. The main problem then was to persuade the compère not to announce him as a pianist of world fame. The concert was a great success and Alan was told that well-informed opinion, that is the opinion of the red bands and leaders, was that he was clearly a good pianist who was just a little out of practice.

Alan was then transferred to Camp Hill on the Isle of Wight (July to October 1946). The transformation from convicts into well-dressed city gentlemen for the journey was somewhat marred by their being handcuffed together in pairs. Camp Hill prison overlooked Parkhurst. The walls are not high or grim, and the buildings had more the air of a public school than a prison. The workshops and the theatre were outside the inner walls, and the chapel was outside the walls altogether and was used by the villagers as well. In their small House there was a wireless set in the main room but it was rarely used, except for the news; Knox men disliked the sound of background music, and whistling or other noisy behaviour was discouraged. For Alan this was a welcome change from the Scrubs and a contrast to the rest of the Houses at Camp Hill. Alan's table was led by a lifer who had just had his discharge date and the others included three more lifers, a fifteen yearer, and two tenners, so he was well below the average in length of sentence.

He started in the mailbag shop, his first and nearly his only time sewing mailbags. Then his leader, who ran the stores in the tin shop, secured Alan a good job there making the stencils which were used for marking mailbags with insignia such as royal crowns. It also produced all the tins for the prison system, such as mess tins for food, baking tins, funnels and bottles. There were also orders from government departments. As well as the stencils he had the job of cutting out the pieces of tin plate for such special jobs as small tin funnels according to set patterns, of which there was a large and rather confusing stock. It was very noisy as about fifty men were all hammering tin plate into shape.

The Camp Hill band centred on the cello player, a lifer who had learned music in prison, did all the music copying and arranging, and smoothed over the considerable emotional and artistic disputes that arose. The flute player, Tootie Flootie, had been an orchestral player and was still extremely competent, but was inclined to patronise the others as mere amateurs. The pianist was Lofty, a rather heavy-fisted ex-guardsman with whom he had a running quarrel. Tootie Flootie regarded Alan's arrival as a chance to secure final victory over Lofty. He affected to find Alan's playing an enormous improvement and dilated on his artistic feeling and expression. Alan did not wish to start life at Camp Hill with Lofty as a sworn enemy, and saw that his position in the band was important to him, whereas Alan wanted to spend most of his spare time reading. So they arranged that Alan only came in as the second pianist for public performances, which still allowed him to practice.

A friend was a highly skilled mechanic who had made surgical instruments but had then used these instruments to secure abortions, for which he was serving a long sentence. He had turned his skill to watch repairing. It happened that the chaplain was an enthusiastic horologist and he allowed Alan's friend to establish a small workshop in a room behind the chapel, where there was also a piano. Now the watch repairing, carried out in evenings and weekends, could be made more interesting by an accompaniment of classical music, of which Alan's friend was very fond. They met again at Leyhill in Gloucestershire where they resumed this collaboration.

Dave Springhall was an important inhabitant of Camp Hill, being in charge of education and other social activities. As mentioned earlier, he had been an even more important member of the Central Committee of the CPGB (Note 29). Indeed he was the emissary from Moscow who had arrived with the fateful message that the war against Hitler was an 'imperialist war'. As also told earlier, Alan had narrowly avoided being recruited by him as a supplier of information to Moscow. It turned out that MI5 had been keeping a close watch on him and in June 1943 he was arrested, tried *in camera*, and given seven years. He was promptly expelled from the CPGB, of course. The secret trial was presumably considered appropriate because Russia was then regarded as a valuable ally in the struggle against Hitler, whereas when Alan was tried the Cold War had started and so maximum publicity was arranged.

Springhall was on excellent terms with the Governor, and ran a wall newspaper with information about classes, concerts, lectures etc., doing his best to make the place a lively educational experience. Naturally Alan had quite a lot of contact with him, and found him very entertaining, especially when reminiscing on his time in the Navy or when demonstrating the correct way to make mulled ale with a red-hot poker. But they were both extremely guarded against any discussion of their respective offences against the Official Secrets Act. 'Finding ourselves in the same nick seemed too much like a trick to encourage this, and there was no way of being sure there was no bugging equipment. So we kept mum. I was to meet him again at Leyhill. ... At the opposite end of the social spectrum was a neighbour in Knox House. He enjoyed a very well-furnished breakfast – coffee, cream, toast, butter, marmalade, and generally seemed well looked-after. I enquired the reason for this and was told he was a VIP – very important prisoner, "The Man Who Sold Burma", a tale that was told with relish to all newcomers to the Knox mess.

'The evening classes were well-run, with a play-reading class doing Sean O'Casey, and a current affairs class which led to fierce political discussions. In all these activities the IRA terrorists who had by then served four or five years were the most active element. The Etymology class was very popular and had a long waiting list. I was intrigued to find that it included all the wide boys and barons and that the members were very secretive about the deep questions of etymology they discussed. Long after I was told that this was a disguised gambling hell.'

Even before Alan arrived at Camp Hill it was known that it was to be closed down and the prisoners shifted to the new open prison at Leyhill in Gloucestershire. As often happened full details of the transfer, including the dates of the various drafts, were known to the prisoners long before the governors had any official knowledge. Drafts were at monthly intervals, and all were going except for the Young Criminals (YCs) and a few considered unsuitable for an open prison, who would go to Wakefield. As the successive bus loads went away Alan became more and more convinced that he would be going to Wakefield. 'The Wakefield draft was the last to go, and for the last month the remnants of the prison lived in a strange world. The full number of screws were still on duty as they had to prepare for the Borstal boys who were coming in the day after we departed. By the time we arrived at Wakefield we were in a subdued mood, and the first sight of that gloomy pile in the dusk convinced us that the happy days of Camp Hill had passed.'

Wakefield Prison (October 1946-March 1947) was old, cold, dark and grimy. The thermometer in the reception block stood well below 50 F and according to the record chart nearby it had been no higher for the last three weeks. Alan's first impressions were confirmed during his later years in Wakefield. It seemed that there had once been a progressive Governor who had pioneered new approaches, but by 1946 Wakefield system was living on its reputation. The advances made earlier were gradually disappearing or becoming meaningless routine, and Wakefield had become the home of 'bullshit', securing the appearance of progress without the reality. Thus a special cell was always shown to visitors. It had linoleum on the floor, special painted furniture, a vase of flowers, and a set of leather-bound books on a bookshelf. No other cell had these accessories; this was the Bullshit Cell for display only. At all prisons the Governor had the responsibility of inspecting and tasting the food before it was issued to prisoners. At most other prisons he was given a sample dinner at random. But at Wakefield a special table was laid out in the kitchen, with a white table cloth and brightly coloured crockery. In the front of the prison where visitors came in there were flowers, and great care was taken to have a good display. On the exercise ground where the prisoners daily walked round and round for an hour they had to be content with some rather tired cabbages.

To the arrivals from Camp Hill all this was very disappointing. They had been at a prison where flower beds decorated the exercise ground, where every cell was as well-appointed as the special display cell and they had enjoyed a degree of freedom and trust undreamt of at Wakefield. The YCs were particularly hard-hit as their wing was still gaslit and without a hot water supply. They expressed their opinions of Wakefield in the strongest terms and were in a state of near-mutiny.

Alan struck lucky as there was a vacancy in the education office. The main job was running the logistics of the evening classes but there were other duties for prison staff and for the Imperial Training College (the 'School for Screws') across the road from the prison. There was enough work to keep the office busy and enough variety to prevent boredom, and after he had mastered the routine Alan found that he had some spare time for study. Alan's immediate boss was Mr Holland. Dutchy was then within a few years of retirement, having already earned pensions in the army and the police. He was a large florid man whose chief virtue was the complete freedom with which the lags could address him in their own language and be answered in the same style. He had a refreshing contempt for prison regulations and routines and in this respect, Alan thought, he was a frequent cause for alarm to the Governor. Dutchy would stand by his men through thick and thin, but he was very quick to detect the smallest hint of crookedness in a man's personal attitude to him, with explosive consequences.

The education system at Wakefield was complicated by the fact that as a 'cell task' each man was expected to sew about half a dozen mailbags a week in the evenings, in addition to the work he did during the day. Men attending evening classes were excused some of this task, and those who were taking correspondence courses or had evening work, such as Alan, were excused altogether. This made the classes popular, and led many men to take up studies for which they were ill-equipped.

The extremely severe winter of 1946-47 strained the inefficient heating arrangements of Wakefield to the limit. The prisoners had several ways of keeping warm. Those with cell tasks found the bags useful, as one bag over the legs and another over the head formed a passable sleeping bag. Many filled their chamber pots with hot water from the tap and used them to warm their beds. But despite these resources, and the wearing of two shirts and similarly doubling up on clothes during the day, the problem of warmth was their main concern. The pay office near Alan's office had a small radiator and he would visit the pay clerks to warm himself. He resolved that if ever he should have to spend another winter in Wakefield he would use every effort to get a job in that office.

Another warm spot was the central library. He helped the librarians with their correspondence, and in return unofficially had free run of the library. It was at one end of his wing, and when, as always during the winter, they were undergoing 'inside exercise' he would often manage to dodge out of the slow procession shuffling round and round the wing in semi-darkness, and creep into the library. Amongst the books he discovered were several on prison systems, really intended for the use of officers. 'One in particular by Leo Page was a constant source of amusement. His account of prison as it should be, officially, was clearly never intended to be read by those suffering the reality. By contrast Bernard Shaw's preface to the Webbs' *Prisons Under Local Government* shows such a complete imaginative understanding of prison life that it was difficult to believe that he had never suffered imprisonment.'

Alan was very unwilling to be interviewed by the Security Services when in prison. Even so, two MI5 officers, Cussen and Marriott, saw him without warning at Wakefield in November 1946. They recorded in the file that 'May listened to the foregoing address without comment, but at the end he made a statement recapitulating accurately the history of our original approach and of his eventual decision that he did not wish to see us. He said that in making any statement to us he considered that he was running the risk of forfeiting the support of his friends ... We both got the strong impression that if and when he ever does talk, the person or persons he will implicate are close personal friends. Thus, before leaving the room he expressed apprehension that if he were to be released in the near future people might attribute his release to the fact of our interview with him.' Marriott reported to Hollis: 'May's resentment against the Intelligence Service is, in my view, very strong indeed. This fact, coupled with the fact that both Cussen and I consider him to be not the disinterested internationally minded scientist which his colleagues represent him to be, but rather a fundamentally wicked, not to say criminal, man, decided us to run no risks in our relations with him. ...' He also wrote to Philby: 'I have just interviewed Alan Nunn May in prison, with the object of trying to obtain from him full details of the way in which he was recruited into the Soviet service, with particular reference to his contacts in this country. The interview was, I am afraid, unsuccessful ... that the person or persons who will eventually be implicated by any confession he makes are his close personal friends ...' Philby replied: 'I am sorry to see that your first attempt at May ended in failure. But I note that you are moderately optimistic about the prospects of getting more out of him in future. We will naturally be very interested in anything you may obtain.'

Alan wrote to his brother Ralph about the same interview, knowing that the authorities would read his letter: 'Yesterday I was called into the Governor's office and left with two (anonymous) gentlemen, one of whom was the one who had called on Kenwright, and seems to be an old friend of his. He held forth at some length, to much the same effect as he did to K, ending by saying that he could *not* say that saying anything would not lead to a remission, and a positive assurance that refusing to say anything would not count against me. Nevertheless anyone asked to report on the case must feel that as it stands it is incomplete – certain aspects weren't clear, there were gaps, etc. After listening to all this I pointed out that I had been asked through the Governor of Camp Hill whether I would talk to them. I had said "not without legal representatives present" and after receiving a letter from K and considering its implications I had decided not to see them and had told the Governor so. I read out bits of K's letter to them to drive home the point. I also pointed out that whereas K had written that I "should not be asked to give evidence" they had not at *this* talk said anything about anything involving evidence, at all. He replied that he quite saw my point, but had felt so strongly that the public interest etc… that he had been authorised to approach me in this way. They then asked had I seen the Canadian Blue Paper? Yes, the Deputy Gov. at Camp Hill had lent me a copy apparently at their suggestion. I pointed out a few trivial errors in it, like the mis-spelling of my name, but refused to agree that on the whole it was a sound piece of work. The whole thing was then gone over with some variations *da capo*. The other man asked what I felt about the other Canadian cases, were they justified? I refused to discuss this, and K's friend agreed that it was an improper question. After repeated assurances and a statement that I might communicate the whole thing to you and K. they went. They said that they would not come again unless I asked to see them. I assured them that that was *most* unlikely. I don't know how the idea has got round that I am a natural born squealer or copper's nark or even that I have anything particular worth listening to, to squeal about. Their main argument, of saving innocent youths from "corruption" of the same sort is quite inappropriate. In short I don't want to have anything to do with these gentry. They are bad company.'

Shortly after this, MI5 compiled a list of possible contacts of Alan who might have had a role in his espionage activities. The list of seven names included those of Berti, Kowarski, Powell, Gabriel Knight (a distinguished microbiologist) and Donald Sproule (an inventor). None seems to match the leader of Alan's cell in Cambridge whom he said he saw on his return from Canada. Dick White commented: 'I think the overriding consideration must be how we can compete against the Russian Secret Service, and one way is obviously the closest collaboration with the F.B.I. For that reason alone I think we should give them any and all relevant information in the hope, which I personally think it will, that it will be fully reciprocated."

After his first Christmas in prison Alan wrote to Cecil Powell: 'Very many thanks for the Christmas cards especially Jane's and Anne's (the Powell daughters). I had about 170 in all, far too many to thank individually. Quite a few were from Bristol, including ones from Occhialini and Mott. There were a lot from AScW branches and other Trade Unions and Trades Councils which was specially encouraging. I saw my brother last week and he told me that you had mentioned our paper. I think the best thing is to send it straight in. I saw the typescript when I was in Bristol and discussed the proposed changes ... It will be difficult to get the MS to me, and especially back again, so it is best for me to take the revisions on trust. If you are hesitant about shouldering me with your views put a footnote saying I haven't seen the final revision as if it were a posthumous work. My brother also mentioned the possibility of your sending me a microscope and some plates to work on. I don't know how feasible this would be from your end, I *think* it could be arranged here but it would probably need an application to HM Prison Commissioners and I won't broach it with them until I get confirmation from you. It would be a great thing for me to keep my hand in as an experimenter: one gets fed up with too much reading. I haven't any idea what work you have in hand, or what it would be best for me to undertake. It had better be something with a fairly long time scale, in view of the difficulties of communication. If you are willing to do this let me have a fairly full list of equipment, value, etc and the work to be done so I can lay the whole thing before the authorities. Don't expect anything to happen in a hurry. I have had an application in since August 1st for permission to carry on with the new Hevesy and Paneth and send the MS out and still haven't heard anything. I have managed to see the *Phys. Rev.* and get *Nature* and *Science Abstract*, so I am able to keep fairly up to date. I see that the new plates are a great success. I only saw the triple fission result in the *News Chronicle* – I should be glad of any reprints if you have any to spare.

'I have been fortunate in getting a good job here, in the education office, looking after evening classes, issue of periodicals. It is mostly secretarial work ... I am kept pretty busy and this is a good thing. It helps to keep prison rot at bay. The classes range from illiterates to matriculation standard. ... I am going to try and start a class in elementary science in the new year and try my hand at leading. These classes are a good feature of this place. On the other hand the buildings are the standard 19th century type – which is a cross between the basements at King's, and one of the older stations on the Metropolitan Line. The situation, in the middle of the collieries, does not make it more cheerful. However, millions live in worse conditions ... I have come to like the privacy of my cell, one sees quite enough of one's fellows at work and at meals without sleeping with them too.

'I have now done 1/10th of my sentence, which, I hope, includes nearly all the real punishment – the rest is mainly a matter of waiting for a kind of "radioactive decay" event with a half period of a couple of years or so. I think I can manage to come out not much worse a man than I went in, but that can't be guaranteed. ... Now we settle down to getting through 1947 as quickly as may be. Please remember me to Isobel and your family, and to my Bristol friends. Please thank Mott and Occhialini for me for their cards. Yours ever, Alan May.'

Alan began to find that he had some spare time for reading and then petitioned the Home Secretary for permission to write and on release take out with him the manuscript of a book. This was the project to produce a new version of Hevesy and Paneth, about which Alan had corresponded with Paneth when he was on remand. Alan needed to set about accumulating a stock of textbooks and periodicals, and he received much help from the Principal of the Imperial Training College who borrowed books for Alan from Leeds University Library and who, when he had been promoted to Prison Commissioner, still took a personal interest in Alan's studies. Finally in January 1947 Alan was able to write to Paneth about this. The correspondence continued for a period but eventually the project came to nothing although Alan did quite a lot of work on it, partly because Oxford University Press were unhappy about having a jailbird as one of their authors (this was eventually resolved) and partly because the inherent difficulties of such a collaboration made the other co-authors cooler about Alan's participation.

Alan also continued to discuss with Powell whether to do microscope work for him, and wrote to his brother Ralph: 'Whether I could do this *and* the book is another question – I don't want to get brain fever – but am anxious to keep in practice, and not go out an unemployable scientist with no research to his credit except in the distant past ... I saw in the *Daily Express* under the heading "Atom Secrets Flown to Moscow" that what happened a year ago is still hot news, and the contents of the Canadian Blue Paper a deadly secret – at least to the *Express*. Meanwhile MI5 is hunting down a Central European called Democritus who is said to have revealed some atomic secrets.'

Alan's job in the education office had little to do with education, and he wished to do something to ease the terrible burden of ignorance which he found played a large part in the difficulties of many of his fellow prisoners. He suggested a more general introduction to science, and approval was obtained from the Commissioners, as was the rule before a class was taught by a prisoner. 'I had never taught at elementary school standard, and I found it difficult to express what were to me commonplace ideas in a way which the ordinary man could follow. I started with mechanics, and what I thought would be tangible problems, cricket balls thrown up into the air, cars driven out from a cliff top etc. I soon found that the main difficulty was that the ordinary processes of arithmetic were extremely difficult for some of the class, whilst the whole discussion seemed childish to the others. Transfer to Leyhill supervened, but I learned enough of the difficulties of such teaching to make me feel that the popularisation of science is just as difficult as research.'

Transfer to Leyhill took place in monthly drafts. Candidates were interviewed by the Senior Medical Officer and the ones he considered suitable were listed and their names and records sent to Head Office for the final decision. Dutchy asked Alan whether he wanted to go and he answered 'yes' without any doubt, to Dutchy's evident disappointment; he had given Alan a good job, and done his best to help him, and yet he seized on the first opportunity of leaving Wakefield. But Alan had never reconciled himself to the Wakefield system, and felt that if Leyhill was run in the same spirit as Camp Hill he would be happier there, even in a rank and file position. He also found the 'short timers' poor company as the shorter the time a man was doing the more miserable he was, and the messages he received through the grapevine from Leyhill and his old acquaintances there made him a little homesick for their company.

His interview with the SMO was curiously enigmatic. Alan was not supposed to know the purpose of the call-up, and at first he was asked general questions. 'Then he asked if I thought I could stand a rough open air life. This was a hint at Leyhill. When I assured him that I could stand it better than my sheltered life at Wakefield he took another tack and said "You know, a man of intelligence and education can be a terrible thorn in the flesh for the authorities, especially if he makes bullets for others to fire." This took me aback as I had never fancied myself as a prison agitator and told him so. He told me to ponder his advice. When I arrived at Leyhill I found that a Camp Hill man had carried on an underground campaign against the system just as the SMO had hinted and had been transferred to Parkhurst. However I had early on decided that I wanted to come out of prison as little harmed mentally and physically as possible, and I was well aware that a long spell in the Tough Nicks, Parkhurst or Dartmoor, would have been equivalent to three times as long as in the comparatively easy prisons. Fighting the prison system from within is a heroic task, and the strength required was in my view better reserved for a more worthwhile object.'

Before Alan's draft went he paid what he hoped would be his last farewells to the Wakefield system. The first prisoner they met at Leyhill assured them that it had been ruined, because part of the boundary had been declared out of bounds. Looking round at the view of green fields and trees, and remembering the stone walls of Wakefield, Alan had to disagree. Leyhill (March 1947-April 1948) was a converted army hospital, with wards of about thirty beds against the walls with a space between with a small locker for personal belongings. Wards also had rooms used by the leaders. Heating was by coke stoves under the men's own control, so they could maintain within limits what warmth they liked, subject to having enough coke. There were no locks on doors, except such as the stores and offices, and no bars on the windows. There was a boundary, and anyone crossing this imaginary line thereby rendered himself an escapee. There was a fine view of the surrounding country and it was impossible to imagine a finer contrast to the smoky confinement of Wakefield. Ward 4 was a noisy, cheerful ward, much given to tea brewing in the small hours of the morning and mild practical joking. There was quite a number of Camp Hill acquaintances. Tootie Flootie could always be persuaded to start a recital on the flute of all the popular tunes that he or anyone else in the ward had ever heard. He had started to learn to play the cello, for which he retired into the recess, being shy of his struggles being overheard. Lofty now played the American organ for the Methodist services. The band was in temporary eclipse, and no one seemed to want to revive it.

The reception board told Alan there was no atomic energy for him to supervise, and he was placed in the tailors' shop, which was practically the same as at Camp Hill. The stout, jovial instructor set him to work on a button-holing machine and told him that the task was so many thousand button holes per week. After about a month he was promoted to the cutting table as assistant cutter and then to his own job with canvas aprons. These had a peculiarly shaped bib which presented a nice problem of how to get the required number out of the width of the cloth. Alan devised a scheme which reduced the amount of waste cloth to a third, and thereby found himself in grave danger of becoming an indispensable cutter. Then followed a long session with pillow cases. Alan put his name down for a library job, a post that went strictly by turn with a waiting list. But most men at Leyhill had long sentences – many were lifers – so such jobs took a long time to fall vacant. Fortunately for Alan a reshuffle of jobs took place, and in the confusion his friends convinced the authorities that an extra man was needed in the library – his name was next on the list – and he left the tailors after nearly six months. It had been a trying time for him but no worse than for the other men who were there for far longer.

While in the tailors' shop Alan could do a fair amount of reading, and even some research of a sort. At Wakefield life had been regulated by the ringing of bells so that much of the 'free' time was spent hanging about waiting for these. At weekends after lunch they spent about ninety minutes walking up and down waiting for the bell to ring. In contrast, at Leyhill one could start reading as soon as the shop hours were over. Alan shared a small study room and would stay there until the tally at 9 p.m. At weekends he could spend nearly the whole time there except for meals. Thus outside the shops one was as nearly free as possible, and regulation was at a minimum. This was possible because of the small numbers, 300 compared with over 700 at Wakefield, and because as long-term prisoners they knew that it was in their interest to keep this freedom by not abusing it.

The library at Leyhill came from Camp Hill. There were also books on loan from the extramural department of Bristol University and from Gloucestershire Education Committee for classes, and from the County Library. The library was open every midday and evening, and books could be changed as desired. They tried to make the prison library popular and to lead the ordinary prisoners' reading upwards from thrillers and westerns. Shortly after Alan gained his library job a prison newspaper called *New Dawn* was started, and a sample sent to the Commissioners for their approval. They thought it a good idea and from then on it was produced monthly. The policy of *New Dawn* was frankly to improve and to reform. There was a judicious sugaring of prison news and gossip, criticisms of film shows, and notes on football matches, but the medicine was in the leaders and general articles. Efforts were made to get everyone who was at all capable to contribute or submit to an interview. Alan felt that they managed to avoid any feelings of being stooges for the authorities on the one hand or prison agitators on the other, a delicate balancing act.

Alan then moved to the education office, an excellent opportunity. The classes were run jointly by the prison, the county and by Bristol University. The centre of gravity was provided by the county representative, Mr Leakey, a local schoolmaster, an energetic man who spent nearly every evening walking round the camp, talking to everyone he met. He had the cause of Leyhill at heart, and he worked wonders on its behalf. Suggestions for new classes, criticisms of old ones, schemes for increasing the attendances, programmes for lectures, debates, and film shows were all vigorously discussed, energetically pursued, and surprisingly often came to a successful issue. Alan's job was to provide the office work for all this activity. Much more could be done at Leyhill than in the stagnant Wakefield system, and the work was worthwhile.

Promotion to the education office brought a leader's arm band, and a private room with hot and cold water, wash basin and curtains. Nominally Alan was ward leader and responsible for the good conduct of the other thirty-odd inhabitants, but he took these duties very lightly, and discouraged any efforts to use him as a means of passing on complaints against fellow prisoners. With a room of his own and a separate office he was one of the prison aristocrats, who could arrange his work as he pleased. He had many more books sent in, and spent most afternoons and the whole weekend on physics. Mornings sufficed for the routine office work, and evenings were taken up by the classes, which he had to visit in person to see that everything was in order. Often this idyllic arrangement was disturbed by some emergency but in principle at least a third of his time was available for study. The little instrument maker Alan had met in Camp Hill encouraged him to take up music again and they resumed their watch repairing to a piano accompaniment. In addition there was an outstanding series of lectures on musical appreciation by Brent Smith, someone of great personal charm who knew how to illustrate his points with anecdotes and could put across quite erudite points of musical history or theory.

Alan wrote to Ralph early in 1948: 'I have heard from Paneth that the Clarendon Press has finally agreed to my name appearing on their august title pages, so I have written back agreeing to go on with the book and I am now devoting my spare time to it. I had another visit from the Powells before Christmas. I am doing what is known as a "nice quiet lagging", and having passed the quarter mark – indeed even 0.26 of the way, I am now in the middle half or flat part of the course.'

But events intervened. 'At this time departures from Leyhill were not very frequent. Early in May 1948 a draft came down from Wakefield in the usual way by bus. A rumour circulated through the camp that someone was going back to Wakefield with the returning escort. We discussed this and considered various likely candidates who had made themselves unpopular with the authorities. I am afraid my natural humility prevented me putting my name forward as a candidate. A leader brought a message that the Governor wanted to see me in his office. I noticed that the bus for the Wakefield draft was ticking over outside the office block, but even this ominous sign made no impression of danger. Outside the door the Wakefield screws were standing around waiting for the departure. I went in and found a full committee of officials. The Governor appeared a little embarrassed as he told me that I was to go back to Wakefield, not because of anything I had done. In fact, he said, I deserved their thanks for what I had done at Leyhill, but, he added mysteriously, I should pray to be saved from my friends. Of course, he went on, there was no reason why I should not eventually return to Leyhill. I told him that I had a large number of books in the education office that I would like to take with me, and he agreed to that.

'After I left him I found I was under close arrest. Two prison officers accompanied me everywhere. We borrowed a hand-cart from the engineers and threw all the books and papers into the cart. Then we went to my room and disposed of the few that I had there. My belongings in reception had been prepared and we drove off. There was a Wakefield PO, two screws and a housemaster, so I had a fair amount of company. It was nearly three in the morning by the time we arrived at Wakefield and it took some time to get into the prison as the night officer had to be woken and get himself dressed to let us in. There was a cell already prepared for me, with the bed made and water in the jug. In the morning I was put through the usual routine, changed into the Wakefield brown, and came back to see the reception board. Dutchy saw me and pretended to be surprised to see me "Hello, old boy" he said "Didn't you like it at Leyhill?" This left me speechless.'

The files confirm Alan's suspicion that his abrupt transfer from Leyhill to Wakefield was because of the possibility of an attempt at escape and for him to flee to the East. 'Governor. As a Britisher I know it is my duty to let you know that there is a scheme afoot to organise the escape of Nunn May from the prison, and to safely transport him from the country to the other side of the Iron Curtain the Russian occupied part of Germany. Mr Springhall has the arrangements in hand, which may take some time, but it may not, for our safety as a country this matter should not be taken too lightly, and should be investigated at once.' This anonymous accusation was forwarded to the Home Office. There is also a lengthy letter written two years later to the head of MI5 by the same now-released prisoner. A part reads: 'And what happened afterwards; the punishment received by the two prisoners who were instrumental in reporting to the authorities a conversation overheard between Nunn May and Springhall. The conversation was a discussion on how, after Springhall's release, Nunn May could be taken out of the country, and be placed behind the *iron curtain.* I myself overheard it. I told Thomas what I had overheard. Thomas wanted to tell the Governor at once about the conversation. But after considering the matter a little longer it was decided that we ourselves should anonymously send a letter to the authorities to inform them of what I had heard. We were afraid that otherwise the matter would be silenced there and then. Nunn May and Springhall were the Governor's favourites. (How these communists kiss the hand that they cannot cut off!) ... But one thing I know; that Thomas and I suffered the brunt of the Governor's hate for the part we took in the Nunn May incident.'

19

WAKEFIELD AGAIN AND RELEASE

Wakefield (April 1948-December 1952) appeared even more gloomy than before to Alan, who was suffering from shock, and felt cold and numb all the time. After a week in the mailbag shop he asked for a change of job. There were of course no vacancies in the library, but by a great stroke of luck there was a sudden vacancy in the pay office. Dutchy offered him the job, and remembering the radiator which had saved him from freezing solid in 1946 he seized the chance, although he had little aptitude for the elementary book-keeping involved. So having completed two years in four prisons he started on the remaining four years and eight months in Wakefield. He kept this job until his release, and so had an office in which to keep books and journals, and he had enough spare time to read and write. The job involved going round the prison and collecting the recommendations of the screw in charge of each workshop for the week's pay for each worker. So he visited the kitchens, where there would be a cup of tea waiting, and the tailors, who might provide better fitting clothes, if he could be helpful. All suggestions would then be scrutinised by the industrial supervisor.

When Alan re-read his account of Wakefield nearly fifty years later he felt that his view of it was distorted by bitterness and resentment at his sudden removal from Leyhill. He regarded the system as relatively progressive, with a strong emphasis on giving the prisoners something to do, ranging from sewing mailbags to other jobs that might develop their skills. There was also an effort to improve their level of education by classes and correspondence courses. But the most successful aspect of the system was the way the more able prisoners were encouraged to take responsibilities. This system produced a sort of apparatchiks who were of great help in running the prison.

However, his view of the first Governor he had was uncompromising: 'He was a tall, unsmiling sombre man with a deep ominous voice. He had been badly wounded, and a great part of his face had been burned and replaced by skin grafts. This made him appear even more morose than he really was. He was very deaf, and had the greatest difficulty in hearing what the prisoners said when they made applications or were on report. There was a general feeling that this led to a uniform response "No" to all applications, and "three, seven, seven" (three days bread and water, seven days loss of pay, seven days loss of privileges) for those on report, but in fact by constant reference to the Chief Officer at his side ("What did he say, Chief? You're a bloody fool sir? – "three, seven, seven") he possibly knew something of what was said. He was clearly out of sympathy with any schemes of prison reform, and his reports to the Commissioners, of which they generally printed extracts in their annual reports, always included complaints that the prisoners were lazy, badly behaved, ignorant and disrespectful. One felt that if he really disliked such company so strongly he should not have become a prison governor. The just man made perfect is rare in prison. The feeling of stagnation, and even retrogression at Wakefield was I think largely due to his disabilities. A prison governorship is not a sinecure, even for the most meritorious of the war-wounded.'

The two colleagues who did most to keep contact with Alan by visiting him and writing were Cecil Powell and Nicholas Kemmer. Alan discouraged contact with other former colleagues, believing that it would damage their careers. Alan had written to Kemmer from Leyhill with the germ of an idea that led to him submitting a manuscript to *Nature* from Wakefield (Photo 55). In 1984 he wrote: ' ... In 1948 whilst in Wakefield Prison I submitted a letter to *Nature*, with Home Office permission. This was an attempt to account for the fact that the uranium nucleus splits asymmetrically when undergoing fission, the two halves being roughly in the ratio 3:4, whilst the then current theory (Bohr and Wheeler) firmly predicted symmetrical fission. This letter was duly submitted shortly after November 1948 and then nothing happened for some months. I became rather impatient and got permission to write again to the *Nature* office. *Nature* replied that they had sent the typescript to Frisch to review, and he would write direct to me, having failed to pass any opinion on it to *Nature*. After a further delay, I received the typescript back from Frisch with the comment that he thought it not quite suitable for *Nature*, more appropriate to the *Journal of the Physical Society*. He did not make any real criticism, except that there were some things that he would have expressed differently. Since the *JPS* then had

In replying to this letter, please write on the envelope:—
Number....132.... Name....... May ....
LEYHILL
FALFIELD Prison
GLOS.
June 11th 1947

Dear Kemmer,

Many thanks for the reprints and copies of the Physical Review you sent me. I now have nearly all the books I originally asked for, although needless to say new wants have arisen since. I haven't started seriously on Meson theory yet being still immersed in group theory. I have borrowed Wigner and Van der Waerden from Peierls and am slowly digging my way through them.

Presently most of my spare time (which anyhow is not much) is now given to some calculations on the reason for the asymmetry in Fission, the masses of the fragments being nearly 2:1. As far as I can remember no-one has established this theoretically. The Bohr-Wheeler method lands one in a very involved set of expansions in harmonics.

I have tried the following:— consider only the critical deformation i.e. the "saddle point" in the potential energy plot. Then the saddle energy is stationary for all small deformations. It follows that

$$ \sigma\Theta + V\rho = \text{constant} \quad \cdots \cdots (1) $$

over the surface, where Θ is the

surface tension, σ the total curvature and V, ρ e.s. potential and charge density. This looks simple enough. The snag being to calculate V. I have done this numerically using a home made expansion in series for the potential for a disk, and taking as the form of the drop

$$ r^2 = R^2 + (\alpha - 1)z^2 - \beta z^4/R^2 \quad \cdots \cdots (2) $$

in cylindrical coordinates.

$\{\alpha=0, \beta=0$ is spherical.
$\alpha=1$ gives figure with just no waist,
$\alpha>1$ gives a waist $\}$

I tried as a "spot" value $\alpha=1.5$, $\beta=0.5$ and this is already near a solution of (1) at least the one can find values of ρ, Θ so that (1) is nearly obeyed for the three points

$(z=0, r=R)$, $(1.46R, 0)$, $(0.7R, 1.06R)$

This figure has a bit of a waist and looks quite finite.

The asymmetric form can be got by adding $\gamma z^3/R$ to the R.H.S. of (2).

Indications are that there is a solution near $\gamma=0.7$ and the same α, β. Probably by pure chance this gives near 2:1 ratio for the volumes to right and left of the waist.

All this is very rough and tentative. I intend to try varying α, β more and getting more accurate figures.

(partial differential eqns). Also some graph paper.

I gathered from Powell that lots of exciting things are happening in the meson world. I am still not getting the Physical Review or Science Abstracts so am pretty well out of piano, such things except via "Nature" and "Discovery".

I have just managed to get my papers and books which were sent after me from Wakefield. Among other things this means that I have some piano music to play, and can embark on my five year plan of mastering at least one Chopin study. Amongst other excitements we now have a prison wall newspaper "New Dawn" to which I have contributed some of the less respectable notices. Between all this cultural activity and digging my garden (mostly radishes which seem to be the only vegetables which do really care for my methods) time goes quite quickly, and much more pleasantly than at Wakefield.

With my respects to the rest of Cauldridge

Yours ever
Alan May

P.S. I was very pleased to hear that Frisch was in the Saltsonian.

One difficulty is that I have at only square root tables. I have written to my brother for my copy of Jahnke–Emden and for Peirce's Tables of integrals. There is probably a more elegant way of applying (1) using an expansion, but this is beyond my resources here. I am going to try and borrow Watson Bessel Functions which I suspect may have a clue. I should like to have my Phys. Rev. number containing Bohr and Wheeler, and yet another of the Canadian Govt forecasy note books containing notes on a set of lectures by Wheeler, and some numerical work I did in Montreal.

I saw Powell a fortnight ago and discussed microscope work with him. I shall see how much time I have to spare, and how this work goes, before I accept his offer. I have always had a yen for theoretical work and this seems a good opportunity. It is certainly more feasible in these conditions than doing experiment or even writing books. However I keep being held up by my appalling ignorance of mathematics which is revealed in all its grandeur in these ridiculous course attempts. Before I forget I really should have my copy of Whittaker and Watson, and Bateman

---

55. Letter from Alan to N. Kemmer, 1947

a backlog of a year or more this effectively killed my chance of getting in first with my idea, and in fact a similar paper appeared soon after in the *Phys. Rev.* so that the whole thing would have had to be re-written, and was no longer so brightly original. I was rather bitter and disappointed about this. The Commissioners were also rather put out, having looked forward to their enlightened step in letting me publish ... I was reminded of this episode by reading Bohr's *Collected Works* vol 9 (edited by Peierls) where I found that the same problem worried him a lot, to the extent of drafting a paper which also never got published, being shot down by Wheeler not Frisch this time. A rather similar solution eventually came out, but not till 1950.'

Alan wrote to Ralph at the end of 1950: 'I also heard from Powell, who has just been awarded the Nobel Prize for Physics. In reply to my congratulations (Photo 56), I had a joint letter on his latest results (from him) and how they are spending the prize money (from wife and daughter). As it is about £10,000 that may take some time. I feel that the honour is a bit tarnished by having Bertrand Russell as a fellow prizeman, but that can't be helped. He (Powell) certainly deserves it, having done the only notable piece of physics in this country since the war. I hope to be with you for New Year 1953. This thought is becoming, as you will have seen, almost an obsession – a disease known as Gate Fever when the victim starts working it out in days (750). Freud would trace this obsession to something that a nasty old man did to me when I was younger – and he would be quite right.'

Alan's correspondence with Powell interested MI5 so that in 1952 William Skardon (Note 37) wrote to the prison authorities: 'I am returning the report on a conference on V-Particles and Heavy Mesons which you forwarded. This document is an unclassified one. The sender, Prof C.F.Powell, is not well regarded by the Security Service, and though we realise that the moment Nunn May is released from prison he will naturally reestablish contact with Powell, it is not the sort of relationship we should encourage. We would be most interested to know whether Powell has been in regular contact with Nunn May during his stay at Wakefield, and would like to review the situation in the light of any information you may be able to supply on this point.' The reply gave the dates of letters from Alan (eight) and Powell (three), and of four visits, in 1946, 1947 (two) and 1951.

Alan continued to play as much music as possible, and his memoir describes his attempts at getting access to an adequate piano. There was a

In replying to this letter, please write on the envelope:—
Number..*9.11.8*. Name....*May. AN*.

....WAKEFIELD........Prison

Ⓡ

11 / 11 / 50.

Dear Powell,

Heartiest congratulations! I hope Russell realises what good company he is in.

Best wishes to Isobel and the family

Yours.

AN May.

No. 243   (21442—3-11-42)

56. Letter from Alan to C. F. Powell, 1950
University of Bristol, with permission

musical appreciation class, which listened to gramophone records of classical music. The gramophone was re-wired and improved by the local talent, and a scheme started by which members paid 1d per week and so built up a fund to buy records. An offshoot was a special 'Highbrow' class confined to classical music, at which reading magazines or any other form of inattention was severely frowned upon. There was also the jazz club, which met on Saturday nights. All the jazz boys attended spruced up in 'spiv' shirts and specially pressed clothes. Several members of the Highbrow class were keen to understand more about classical music, and particularly the inner mysteries of sonatas, symphonies, the difference between the first and second subjects and so on.

As usual when recondite knowledge was required on out of the way subjects they came to Alan for assistance. He read all the books he could find in the prison on musical form and history and then offered to give a talk to the Highbrow class on the subject, adding that he could illustrate points on the piano. In this way a second-hand reconditioned Steinway Grand was acquired. The good response to these talks, and the experience he had had at Leyhill with the lectures given by Brent Smith, convinced him that an interest in music is one of the best consolations of imprisonment because it took prisoners out of themselves and released the emotional tension of imprisonment. Many went further and began for the first time to take a serious interest in music itself. Of course the best way for prisoners to develop an interest in music was for them to learn to play an instrument or to sing in a group. At Camp Hill and Leyhill the facilities had been good, and many of the members of the bands there had learned in prison. But at Wakefield the authorities had natural objections to practice in cells. Band members went into the chapel about three nights a week for practice, but it was difficult to gain admittance to the prison band, and even more difficult to get any efficient practice when one was in it.

In addition to that which he describes, Alan took a special interest in a couple of young Polish inmates who were convicted for armed robbery. They had been part of Anders' Army, which had ended up in Britain. Among their problems were those of language and lack of education, and Alan gave them tutorials. When they were released and returned to Poland, both continued their education, and Jan Szewczyck became a professional philosopher.

Alan's letter to Ralph in November 1949 illustrates his efforts to be accepting of his situation: 'This may seem outrageously inappropriate, considering both our circumstances, but could you send me some Christmas decorations? A few lengths of coloured paper and a bit of tinsel would be enough to convert our mess to something between Aladdin's cave and an Egyptian bordello, which makes everyone feel more at home on Christmas Day.'

In March 1949 MI5 had sent Skardon for another attempt to get information from Alan on his recruitment: '… I told May at once that I represented the Security Service and that the Governor had requested me to make the points mentioned above. May replied that he was quite prepared to stay and listen to me, and we thereupon embarked upon a conversation which was by no means one-sided. This lasted for about 90 minutes and was of the friendliest character, but the only real information that I could obtain was that his recruitment, if that be the right word, took place literally a few hours before he left England for Canada, and that the individual for whom I might be looking in this connection was well out of reach. I think it would be quite unfair to infer too much from what he said, but I gained the fairly distinct impression that the individual to whom he referred was a member of the Soviet Embassy, and I also gained the feeling that this individual followed him to Canada. There are however no firm grounds for this expression of view. I put forward various arguments which I thought might perhaps sway May to be forthcoming as to the earlier details of his Soviet associations. In response I received only the meagre details outlined above. His point was that he could not bear to be a squealer. He despises such people and would rather serve his normal prison sentence than gain any advantage by – as he put it – talking out of turn. He is obviously a man of some character; equally he is a difficult and lonely sort of individual, and he was not much impressed by the argument that by indicating the individuals responsible for his defection he might save others. He said that as all the facts have been fully reported in the official publication of the Canadian spy case, anyone was free to learn the lesson for himself. We then got on to the question of motive. May told me that he considers himself as a Socialist, that he is pro-British, has never wished to harm this country and has never been anxious to assist any other country. On his release from prison he hopes to settle down into a useful life in this country and not to be harassed by MI5. He claims that he did no damage to his country or its interests by the actions that led to his imprisonment. He explained at some length how he was sent down to Chicago by his superiors in Canada to work in the American development plant, and how he was told unofficially to keep his eyes and ears open and to report back anything interesting that he might discover whilst in the USA. On his return his superiors told him that he must not prepare a written report on these discoveries as it would be extremely embarrassing to the British Government in their relationship with the American State Department.

'May says that the information which he passed "on a dirty piece of paper, at a street corner", and the samples of uranium which he handed over, were insignificant details connected with his work, and that his only object was to gladden the hearts of the Soviet authorities by telling them that the atomic bomb was really a worth-while weapon and a practical possibility, and not merely the figment of some journalistic imagination. He stressed that it would be quite impossible to impart any useful information on the subject of atomic research even to an expert physicist, in less than six months in a laboratory. The whole subject was of so complicated and experimental a character that a mere message or a chance meeting could provide no information that could possibly be of the slightest assistance. He recognises that to break faith at all was wrong, but is puzzled to know why other people who seem to have been more actively engaged in really subversive activities received much shorter sentences. He quite saw my point that he was a man of specialised training and in an extremely trusted position, and that therefore his sentence was more serious. Perhaps the only argument that affected him in any way was my suggestion that if he did not indicate the persons responsible for his downfall I should be left to browse amongst the names of his friends, associates and colleagues, perhaps to the unfair disadvantage of one of them. He said he had always been sensible of the danger even of communicating with such people for fear that to be associated with him would justify the authorities in purging them from their employment. I asked him whether he could name one person who had suffered in this way, but he was unable to do so.

'At the end of the interview I commenced to ask him, should he reconsider the matter and decide to inform us more fully of his past association with the Soviet Intelligence Service to notify the Governor that he desired a further interview with me, when he interrupted me to say that he had no particular reason for bearing love towards MI5. His first contact with this organisation had led to ten years penal servitude as the result of the admission which he was persuaded to make to Lt Col Burt. His next meeting two years ago (with Mr Cussen and Mr Marriott) had produced in him such a boiling rage that he had found it quite impossible to discuss the case at all with them. After two years he was therefore no more pleased to see me, but he said he hoped he had not in any way appeared rude. At the same time he had no wish to meet me again, and I felt his mind was made up on this point. However, I managed to complete my instructions that he should approach the Governor should he desire to see me. He said he thought it extremely unlikely.

'During the interview I made no promise or suggestion to him that any action of his would lead to a remission of sentence, although I did mention petitions which had been made from time to time by the Association of Scientific Workers for his release. He said he was not allowed to have any knowledge of these efforts on his behalf, although in fact he was told that the Association was currently engaged in an attempt to secure a remission of his sentence. He added that an additional reason for his dislike of my department was his transfer back to Wakefield from Ley Hill. I acted complete innocence in this matter and said that it was no part of our business to arrange the transfer of prisoners, this being a matter solely for the Home Office. I have no confidence that Nunn May will ever decide to tell his story, but there is just the outside chance that upon reflection he will.'

Marriott commented in the file: 'Please see Skardon's account of yet another unsuccessful attempt to persuade Nunn May to talk. The only useful admission which he made is sidelined in paragraph 3, and I am asking B2b whether there is any possibility of their identifying the individual allegedly concerned. I am rather inclined to the view that Nunn May may after all really have very little to tell us, and that his reluctance to talk may be due to the fact that his recruitment was quite casually affected and that he may be rather ashamed to admit having got himself into such serious trouble in a comparatively trivial way.' A year later MI5's Director General (Sir Percy Sillitoe) wrote to the British Embassy in Washington: 'The report that May has now decided to talk runs counter to the assessment which we have made of the man, and to the assessment made by the Governor of the Prison where he is detained. In the meantime, would it be possible for the FBI in any way to amplify the information with which they supplied you? You will appreciate that this may be difficult, but Nunn May is a desperately difficult man to interrogate and if we are to get any prospect of success we want all the help we can get.'

In mid-1952 the authorities began to consider Alan's impending release, due at the end of the year. Alan was entitled to a remission of one-third of his sentence for good behaviour. Their main concern was to prevent him from leaving the country on security grounds, and so there was discussion of finding suitable work for him. The British also did not want to be seen by the Americans as soft on spies. Hollis wrote: 'There is every advantage to us in finding out what Nunn May intends to do when he comes out of prison. ... If Nunn May were to get a job in nuclear physics in industry, he would be constantly brought to the fringe of classified work, while if he were to get a job in a University, there might be adverse comment that the young nuclear physicists were passing through the hands of a convicted Russian spy who has not as yet shown any signs of repentance for what he has done or of a change of views. I cannot think that there would be any serious criticism in this country or abroad if Nunn May were allowed to go to the Soviet Union on his release from prison. Personally I do not believe that he would want to go, and I should think it is unlikely that the Russians would accept him.' Alan wrote to Ralph: 'I mean to apply for my home leave about October, and would like to spend it with you if that is possible. Please say if it isn't, or if you are doubtful.'

Skardon saw Alan again in September: 'I saw the Governor, Mr Ransley, in the first instance. He has been watching Nunn May's correspondence and had been studying the reports submitted by officers present when Nunn May received visits, and as he saw it the position is as follows. Up to a month ago Nunn May was pretty confident that, upon leaving prison, he had sufficiently influential friends to enable him to find a job in some academic field. He thought it would be a matter of simplicity to obtain employment as a lecturer, a teacher or doing tutorial work. He had been advised by his relations that there was still some public feeling about him and his crime and that he ought not to be too optimistic. It appeared, nevertheless, that Nunn May believed that with the small balance standing to his credit at the bank and with his savings certificates he would be able to support himself for the length of time necessary to find a job. Nunn May was proposing to apply for the five days' home leave often granted to long-term prisoners for the purposes of rehabilitation and resettlement and was proposing, with the approval of his brother, to spend this leave and the early part of his life after release from prison with them. The Governor communicated with the Prison Commission and asked for their views as to the granting this leave should application be made by Nunn May. He was instructed that leave of this kind would not be granted in this case, and the Governor had informed Nunn May accordingly when he made application. The Governor has the advantage of reports periodically made by his predecessor and his own observation, and was able to tell me that Nunn May's behaviour in prison has been impeccable. There was a suggestion, apparently contained in a report which some newspaper was proposing to publish, that Nunn May was taking advantage of certain facilities accorded to him in prison to spread the gospel of communism whilst taking classes without any supervision. There is no word of truth in this sort of story for, although Nunn May does take a class in musical appreciation, the classes are always supervised by prison officers either in or out of uniform. So far as the Governor has been able to discover, Nunn May has done nothing to spread any communistic beliefs which he may have retained. So far as he could discover, Nunn May had every intention of settling down to some useful employment in this country and was optimistic as to his prospects of doing so. I thought it would be proper to see Nunn May and I did so, immediately telling him that it had not been my intention to see him, but that owing to some misunderstanding, he had been approached to discover whether he was prepared to see me. I assured him that, whilst I was vitally interested in the past, my concern was to discover what intentions he had for the future. During the course of discussion it became clear that the Governor had a very true picture of the situation as Nunn May sees it himself. Of course he knows that all the newspapers containing references to him are censored, but from his relations he has been given to understand that the public is still interested in his case and is sensible that public feelings have been exacerbated by them … There is no doubt that the Press will make every effort to track him down, for the Governor told me of a recent episode where a reporter found his way into the Prison Officers' Mess seeking a story about Nunn May.'

Alan wrote to Ralph about this meeting: 'My application for home leave was bounced back with alarming speed. No explanation was given, but I imagine the authorities are influenced by publicity which, as you mention, still attends my slightest action. I had a visit from MI5 in the person of Mr. W. J. Skardon (room 0.55, War Office) who assured me that as far as they were concerned I would be completely free after my release. I told him that my chief worry was getting a job, and he made the (I think rather foolish) suggestion that I should change my name! All the newspapers coming in are censored and anything referring to a prisoner is cut out. I am therefore a cause of considerable annoyance to the other inmates, who don't want to read about me, but find the most important football or racing news cut out as well, being printed on the other side of the paper. Thus although I don't know what is printed about me, I do know how much from the size of the hole in the paper and I can guess that it isn't complimentary. I may be unduly optimistic, but I think that after a burst of publicity when I am released the newspapers will lose interest when I am free. There is something romantic about prisons – to those who aren't in them – and a scientist in prison may strike the popular imagination. But a scientist seeking a job is a very prosaic and everyday thing." Ralph replied: '*The Sunday Express* carried a story that you were thinking of changing your name and added the authentic information that you had been disappointed at not being allowed rehabilitation leave. This story could only have come from the MI5 gentleman himself; so you see you never quite know when you may be talking to someone who himself talks to newspapermen!'

Early in December Dick White directed: 'Please get in touch with James of the Ministry of Labour and advise him on the lines of the letter from the Ministry of Supply. ... We naturally do not want our participation or interest in the placing of Nunn May to be known outside the present privileged circle. If James is successful it should appear as a normal action by the Prisoners' Aid Societies and the Ministry of Labour.' Then immediately after Alan's release C. A. G. Simkins wrote: 'It is proposed that Mr Skardon should see Nunn May as soon as possible and endeavour to establish a personal relationship through which he can guide Nunn May's actions. His approach will be on the footing that the authorities believe Nunn May genuinely desires to settle down to useful work in this country, and that the official world will give all the assistance it can to this end. He will explain to Nunn May that the security services have a special duty and anxiety with regard to his future. They do not want on account of this to subject him to a rigorous surveillance but would prefer to enlist his co-operation in avoiding any action which might be detrimental to the national interests or his own future.' In the midst of this Cockcroft had received a request: 'The Security Service are anxious that he shall obtain suitable and harmless employment, since there is then some chance that he will become a useful citizen; while if he feels that every man's hand is against him he will revert to his evil ways. Furnival-Jones asked whether you would be good enough to let me have a note, based on your knowledge of Nunn May and his qualifications.' Cockcroft replied with a list that included medical physics, school teaching and development of scientific products in industry.

The Foreign Service were worried, particularly as Eisenhower was about to succeed Truman as President and the atomic relationship would be re-negotiated. They cabled HM Ambassador in Washington: 'You should know that Dr Alan Nunn May will be due for unconditional discharge from Wakefield Prison on the 29 December.

2. We realise that his release, particularly at a moment when we are hoping for increased Anglo-U.S. collaboration in atomic matters, may not only give rise to anxiety in this country but also evoke unfavourable comment in the United States. Consideration has been given to the possibility of extending Nunn May's sentence to its full term of ten years but to deprive him of the fruits of his good conduct would be open to criticism on the ground that it was arbitrary and unjust, and involved a gross breach of faith; no comparable action has been taken for at least forty years. Moreover, it is considered that on balance security would be best served by releasing him now and seeking to turn him into an honest citizen. To continue to detain him unwarrantably for the full term of his sentence would embitter him and render his eventual resettlement more difficult.

3. The greatest risk from our point of view lies in the fact that on his release there is no legal power to prevent him leaving the United Kingdom for a country of his choice. He is not now in possession of a valid passport and the issue of one to him could be refused; this would hamper but not necessarily prevent his departure. Thus, although his information on atomic matters will no longer be up to date, his abilities could be made use of by a foreign power. His disappearance or departure for the USSR would be a severe set-back for any improvement in Anglo-U.S. cooperation we may hope to achieve with the new Administration. In consequence consideration has been given, at the highest level, to the possibility of securing some reasonable assurance that if Nunn May were released, he would not leave the U.K., at any rate until the expiry of the full term of ten years.

4. It has, however, been found that no effective means can be devised of ensuring that he will not leave the country but there are no positive grounds for supposing that he would in fact do so, and indeed the indications are that he has no such intention. Nunn May is unmarried but it is understood that he is planning to stay with a brother after his discharge. Special efforts will also be made to find suitable employment for him in this country and there are several fields in which it may be possible to do so without prejudice to security.

5. You should accordingly let the State Department know this at once and explain that the release is in accordance with United Kingdom law.

6. As regards United States public opinion, it has been decided that we should not take any initiative in making any communication to the American press but that an explanatory "hand-out" should be available.

…

9. I note that Alger Hiss will be eligible for release for good behaviour in 1954. This is a point you may be able to use in conversation.'

From Washington to F.O. Secret. 22 December 1952. 'Release of Dr May. Though I see no harm in warning the State Department of the fact of May's release, I should much prefer not to confide to them our fears about his future intentions and our inability to prevent their realisation. Our respect for the law would earn us no credit from the Americans and might well invite objections which it would be very difficult for us to ignore without serious damage to our relations and to the prospects of future cooperation. They are at the moment in a hysterical state about disloyalty and their actions show how little they themselves are inhibited by legal considerations when their own security is concerned. Even if they accepted our argument that we are legally debarred from taking action, they would be quite unable to understand why the necessary legislation should not be introduced. Apart from this there is a real danger of leakage to the Press … In general the whole position could hardly be more unsatisfactory. As soon as we get over one security incident another arises and it looks as if this one will be underlined by the approaching execution of the Rosenbergs in the second week in January. Surely there are means of putting dangerous criminals on probation which could be used in this case so that we could at least claim to be taking some precautions.'

F.O. to Washington. 24 December 1952. 'We fully realise that May's release is likely to have a bad reception in the United States and agree with you that from the point of view of Anglo-American relations in the atomic energy field, the position could hardly be more unsatisfactory. These considerations were fully in the minds of Ministers when they took the decisions.

2. Unfortunately there are no means of releasing prisoners conditionally. The Criminal Justice Act 1948 abolished the old ticket-of-leave system when penal servitude was abolished and there is now no power to release Nunn May on licence. For your information only, the Home Secretary has

considered whether any other way of releasing him subject to conditions can be found. He has been unable to find any means by which Nunn May could effectively be prevented from leaving this country after his release if he wishes to do so. It would be quite impractible to introduce special legislation to deal with an individual case. This is the position and we cannot get away from it.

3. On the other hand, there is no evidence to suggest that May intends to leave the United Kingdom for an Iron Curtain country. Even if he did, his information on atomic energy matters is seven years out of date and in the view of those best qualified to judge would not be of much value to the Russians.'

Alan wrote a detailed memoir of his release. The new Governor, Ransley, did his best to help Alan evade the crowd of waiting press at the prison gates, and later wrote warmly to Alan wishing him well. At 3 a.m. on 29 December 1952 Alan was taken from the rear of the prison by squad car to catch a train at Doncaster for King's Cross, from where his sister-in-law Jackie escorted him without incident to their home at Chalfont St Peter. There they were besieged by the press until Alan agreed to provide a statement, which was published in most of the national papers on 31 December:

'1. I do not wish to discuss the details of the action which led to my imprisonment. I myself think that I acted rightly, and I believe that many others think so too. To those who think otherwise I would like to point out that I have suffered the punishment that was inflicted on me by the law, and I hope that I shall now be entitled to at least the consideration normally granted to released convicts: an opportunity to restart life.

2. There is just one of many erroneous statements of fact which have been made about me which I would like to correct now. I was not convicted of treason, nor was this word used by the prosecution or judge at my trial, and I certainly had no treasonable intentions. I was wholeheartedly concerned with securing victory over Nazi Germany and Japan, and with the furtherance of the development of the peaceful uses of atomic energy in this country.

3. My object now is to obtain as soon as possible an opportunity of doing useful scientific work, in which I can be of some service to this country and to my fellow men.

4. Now that my imprisonment is over, I can only wish for the same consideration and fair treatment which I received throughout the long

period of my sentence from the prison officials and my fellow prisoners. (signed) A.N.May'.

Alan received a mixture of mostly friendly and some abusive letters, and village opinion was violently anti-press because of their intrusiveness. On the evening of 2 January an express letter was delivered. It was from a Major McGrath and expressed sympathy and support. He suggested that Ireland would be an ideal place to rest away from the press. The Major had an aunt who would be prepared to look after Alan. The letter ended by saying that he would call at 7.30 that evening, which was the time at which the letter arrived. They had no sooner read the letter than there was a knock on the door, and Jackie answered. After a long discussion Alan was called down to identify Skardon, who was having great difficulty in establishing that he was not a reporter. Skardon said that there was a rumour in Fleet Street that Alan was going to Ireland. Three seats had been booked with Aer Lingus, one in McGrath's name, one in Alan's name, and one other not named, for a flight the next afternoon. Alan assured Skardon that he had no intention of slipping away, that he had never heard of McGrath and that he would certainly not accept his offer. Skardon seemed satisfied but showed a tendency to hang around. Ralph gave him a drink, and Skardon said that there was another man outside. Ralph and he went to collect him; he was called White, and presumably was Dick White, since Alan described him as of Under Secretary-level. White seemed to be principally concerned about the effect such a news break would have on Churchill's talks with Eisenhower, Churchill then being due to land in twenty-four hours.

All this time they had been expecting McGrath, but it began to look as though it was a hoax, or a press stunt, or if genuine that he had developed cold feet. Jackie had been just about to serve dinner, and they felt that they could hardly eat under MI5 surveillance and the trout would be spoiled if it were not eaten soon, so Skardon and White were pressed to stay for the meal. They ate a good share of the trout amidst much banter, Skardon making a point of helping with the table while White preserved a more dignified and distant attitude. They stayed until ten waiting for McGrath, with speculation about who he could be, and Jackie even accused Skardon of having written the express letter himself and engineering the whole thing as an elaborate scheme to trick Alan into incriminating himself. As they left, Skardon took the letter for investigation.

After MI5 had gone they sat talking and drinking and got fairly merry, so that when there was a knock on the door at 1 a.m. and the Major himself appeared, they rashly let him in. They were so surprised to find out that he really existed, and so curious to find out what his story would be that they were thrown off their guard. He talked practically continuously and was very entertaining. In the more serious intervals they made it clear that Alan had no intention of flying to Ireland and finally managed to get rid of him. Jackie saw him out of the gate and took the number of his car.

The next day Skardon sent a message that McGrath was a freelance newspaper man, and promised that there would be an official denial of any story about the plane seats (Photo 57).

57. Alan just after his release, January 1953
© International Press

20

BERTI STRUGGLES IN VIENNA 1947-52

Berti always wanted to return to Austria, in spite of entreaties by friends like Tess to stay in Britain. Much later he wrote to her that having been such an advocate for Austria during the War he felt honour-bound to return. Of the hundreds of Austrian scholars who were helped by SPSL, only seven returned to their homeland; the others had seen a better life elsewhere, and felt they would be unwelcome back in Austria.

In letters to me and to Hilde, he put a brave face on his life in Austria and was optimistic. Another source on Berti's life in Austria was his correspondence with Tess, which started early in 1947. In February she referred to his intention to make his life with Ina, whom he had not yet even met after the War, and this correspondence is the only source I have on Berti's unhappy marriage to Ina. Both Berti's and Tess's letters exist from January 1952, and there are thirty-seven letters from Tess before that, for which the corresponding letters from Berti have disappeared. Among the topics they discussed were the comings and goings of scientists such as Kowarski and Frisch, the nature and problems of their own work, and my development. For both, the letters were an important outlet made poignant because between 1948 and Berti's death in 1983 they only met once, for a few hours in Yugoslavia in 1959. He had expected to be able to visit Britain, but apart from once in 1948 this was not to be. As Berti saw me and heard from me much less than he wanted, Tess was a surrogate who was fond of me from Cambridge days and who could sometimes tell him she had seen me.

Berti joined Ina in Rome after leaving Britain on 22 April 1947. He wrote on 7 May: 'Now Paul, I shall probably marry in a few weeks, and then we move to Vienna and start work there and help to rebuild Austria after all the damage that is the fault of the Nazis. I very much hope to see you soon and to have some nice talks with you.' Then two weeks later: ' You will be interested, and please tell Mummy too, that I have now had an invitation from the Austrian government to work in the University of Vienna. So at any rate I know better now what I am going to do there. But of course, I have always been confident that I should be able to be really useful here, and to teach students and other people, who for many years have been able to learn only whatever the Nazis allowed them to learn. For instance, the Nazis tried to teach everybody that the Germans were far better and cleverer people than anybody else, and that for this reason they must rule at first in Europe and later in the whole world. Specially they also taught them that the Jews are extremely bad people and that they must all be killed. In fact, the Nazis killed all the Jews they could catch, about six million of them. So you see it will be quite a job to tell all these students who have only been in Nazi schools what the truth really is, and I am glad that the Austrian Government now has invited me to teach there.'

On 3 June he wrote: 'My very dear son Paul, I want to send you here a photograph of my second wife, whom I have married some days ago. I hope you will like the photograph; and I very much hope you as well as your Mummy will make friends with her. Her name is Ina. She is of course an extremely nice person – if I did not think so I should not have married her! Unfortunately there have been some very horrible things in her life. She was born in Yugoslavia and used to live there, and had a husband and a very nice little boy – Alexander. But then one day after the war had broken out and the troops of Hitler had occupied Yugoslavia, both the husband and the boy were taken away by the Nazis and killed. So she went to the woods to join the Partisans who fought there against the Nazis, and whose leader was called Tito. Ina worked as a nurse in a partisan hospital. Later she went to Italy. We shall make our home in Vienna, and both Mummy and you will be most welcome there. Ina is now your stepmother – but stepmothers are bad mostly only in fairy-tales. Really Ina is very fond of you even now already after I told her everything I know about you. She even carries some pictures of you about in her handbag together with those of her own dead son. She will *love* to have you to stay with us for as long as possible. She speaks English quite well, and she is very good at writing fairy-tales (clever ones) and stories. We very much hope we shall have children soon – though of course nobody can be certain – and they would be your brothers or sisters. I very much hope there is a chance for you to come for a long visit to us and to your granny this summer. Please give all my wishes to Mummy.'

Berti and Ina entered Austria on 6 June. Vienna and its inhabitants were now very different from pre-war times. There had been 185,000 members of the Jewish community before the War, and of these a third were killed. Most of the others never returned so that in the mid-Nineties, even with new arrivals from further east, the Jewish community only numbered about 7000. Jewish homes and their contents had long before been taken over by others. Many pre-war non-Jewish Socialists and Communists had also been killed. Those who did return included committed patriots and political activists who hoped to have positions of influence. Their reception was largely hostile, both from the many Nazi sympathisers and from others who had endured the privations of war. Austria was divided into Allied Zones, with Vienna surrounded by the Soviet Zone, and itself in four sectors. The Russians had made themselves deeply unpopular both in their capture of Vienna and then their exploitation of Austrian industry for their own reconstruction. The film *The Third Man* is seen as an accurate portrayal of Vienna at the time and the Cold War was very evident.

Berti then wrote: 'The railway station is destroyed, so the train cannot go as far as the end of the line ... About 20% of the houses are destroyed. There is very little coal, so not enough bricks can be made ... Food is very short here ... happily I have still lots of food which I brought from England in a big sack, and some food which I brought from Italy ... I shall teach in the University but shall be paid by the Government, namely the Ministry of Electric Power. I shall have an office in the Ministry with a telephone and a secretary and perhaps a carpet on the floor ...'

On his return Berti met his relatives for the first time in nine years. Viola and Willi Pabst had spent much of the War at Fünfturm, and when in Vienna Viola worked in a plant nursery. Willi's son Peter had been badly wounded on the Eastern Front. Willi, who had worked earlier with Leni Riefenstahl, much favoured by the Nazis, had been wooed by Goebbels to make propaganda films. Instead he got through the War only making two non-political films, but was regarded by some as being tainted. Berti wrote to Hilde with relief that he was no collaborator, but there is still a question for me as to why Willi did not leave when he could, before the outbreak of the War. On my first visit, in 1947, I saw Willi filming *Der Prozess* (The Trial), a powerful film about Jews accused of ritual murder in nineteenth century Hungary. After the War, Christian left the Communists for the Socialists, and also qualified as a lawyer. He became highly successful, and represented his uncle Willi, and also Paul Löw-Beer. The relationship between him and Berti was at first friendly but guarded, but soon the previous alienation took hold again (Photos 58, 59).

Berti's job was in the Ministry for Energy and Electrification under a Communist Minister in the post-war coalition. In December 1947 he wrote that he was in absolutely the right place for work, and that a change of Minister would not change that. In this capacity he was also secretary of the Austrian National Committee for the World Power Conference. This conference in Paris gave him the opportunity to visit Britain in mid-1948. Had the Security Sevices known in time, he would have been questioned and possibly detained, or denied entry. An MI5 source reported in May 1948: 'He visited Cambridge and Edinburgh. The reason for the Edinburgh visit was ostensibly a series of lectures he was to give, but this seems unlikely to be the real reason since, if he had anything new and useful to report, he would certainly not pass on the information to British scientists, whom he must

58. Berti and Ina with Viola, Christian, Hilda and their daughter Johanna, c.1948

59. Berti and Ina (right) with Erika and Maresi Musche, c.1949

regard as his opponents in the next war – it seems more probable that he wanted information from them...'

Berti set up a Radiochemical Section in the University of Vienna. It found its permanent home in Berti's former Institute, and in 1948 he became a Dozent, allowing him to teach and to supervise students. On the stairs to his laboratory one passes a memorial to two predecessors who, as the War ended, were shot dead by a Nazi professor who they tried to stop from destroying scientific equipment. His earliest student was Thomas Schönfeld, who became his long-standing colleague (and a co-author of two books), friend and political associate (Note 38).

When Hilde took me to Austria in mid-1947 she discussed whether she should also move to Austria. Viola wrote to her twice, once before her visit, when she referred to Ina, whom she has just met, as very ladylike. She asked how Berti would do without me, and how it would develop. She hoped that

Berti didn't feel similar obligations as his late uncle Rudi who she said rescued someone only out of altruism. Viola was heard to refer to both Berti and Christian (who also married a widow) as 'widow-chasers'. In her second letter she told Hilde how hard it was for her to say goodbye: 'In almost ten years one lived through a lot, but your presence was so strong and satisfying. I can't think of you as a stranger, as you are in my heart. So, although formally you are no longer my daughter-in-law, you must let me call you my daughter. That is how I always felt.' Viola later greatly enjoyed visits to Hilde, Alan and me in Cambridge.

Berti was struggling on all fronts. He and Ina had a good flat but very little money as Ina had no job, and no income beyond that of a left wing poet and translator. Then in October 1948 Berti wrote: 'I have resigned my position in the Ministry. I was not satisfied with my work there any more, and I am not so pleased with the ideas of the present Minister, who is a member of the Socialist Party. So I am going. I shall now work for the University and be able to do more for my students. Also I shall advise some people about industrial chemistry, and they will pay me for it. We shall see how it will all work out.' Although he taught and built up a research group, he had to wait for many years and for a different political climate before he got a university salary rather than merely a lecture fee. Even so, Berti pledged a quarter of his meagre income to Hilde for my upkeep.

In early 1946 an Institute for Science and Art had been established as a forum for the discussion of the state of cultural life in Austria. In May 1948 a memorandum Berti wrote to the Austrian President resulted in a Commission that reported at a large meeting in November 1948. As with the meeting for Austrian Science in London in 1946, Berti was a guiding force: 'I have arranged here in Vienna Town Hall a big meeting of all the important scientists and University Professors of Vienna and Graz to ask the Austrian Government to give them more money so that they can work better in science …' His thesis was that for a small country like Austria research was important, not only culturally and spiritually but economically. His view that one could not have adequate applied research without a basis in fundamental research showed the influence of J. D. Bernal and his views on science and society. It was one that Berti consistently advocated in his continuing concern for the state of intellectual life in Austria. He instanced how many leading Austrian scientists had had to make their careers away from Austria. The proposals were rejected by a top official in the Ministry, a long-time foe who also blocked Berti's appointment to a real position in the University; in Austria such appointments are made by the Government, not the University. Berti was then excluded from the Institute's council on a procedural ground, but the real reason was that he was a Communist.

In his personal life too, his marriage was not at all that he had hoped for. Realising that there would be no children was surely a part, and I remember at an encounter between my parents in 1951 in Italy when I was transferred from Hilde to Berti that I was struck by their affection and concern for each other. His friends were old friends, and the return of Paul and Ala Löw-Beer in 1951 was very important to him. Their emotional bond remained profound until Berti's death. Other friends were his lawyer, Hugo Ebner, and his wife Rosl. Another friend was Ernst Fischer, who had spent the war in Moscow, was a minister in the post-war coalition, and was the CP's best known intellectual. As such, some years later Berti introduced him to the young Socialist Heinz Fischer, another friend and now (2011) Austria's President. Berti's loyalties were not just to Communists, and in the case of another friend, Peter Smolka, he went directly against Party orders in maintaining their friendship. Smolka had spent the war in Britain on anti-Nazi propaganda, working closely with both Kim Philby and Graham Greene, and was later alleged to have been a Soviet agent. It was he who showed Vienna to Greene and provided him with the basis of the story at the heart of *The Third Man*. Then in 1952 he was accused in a Czechoslovak show-trial of being a British agent, and was therefore to be shunned by comrades. Berti loyally sold *Volkstimme,* the communist paper, on Sundays, but also continued to meet Smolka, himself a loyal friend to many.

One of Berti's ways of earning his living was from consultancies, both for himself and for his research group. He also wrote popular science articles for *Volkstimme*. Between 1949 and 1958 there were about 150 of these, some then collected in widely translated books. His models were the articles written by J. B. S. Haldane for the *Daily Worker* in Britain. He enjoyed this because he believed in the importance of communicating to the public both science and its significance for society. The publication in 1950 of his book on radiochemistry, started in Edinburgh, prompted the following: 'You will be interested that my book is nearly ready ... I have dedicated it to you, Paul. This dedication expresses my warm hope that in your grown-up life you will do work in this field or any other which will be of lasting value. Work that will enrich mankind. ... The fortieth birthday is of course an occasion to draw a sort of balance and to ask oneself whether one has done the right things so far, and also to consider how one should arrange one's future life ... I shall have my fortieth birthday in August, and I trust you will be here ... This summer it will be quite easy to bring you here as I attend a conference of scientists in Paris in mid-July. ... I am proud to be one of the two scientists from Austria to be invited. I shall give a talk there ...' But painfully he was denied a visa for this meeting, eliciting sympathetic letters from Guéron and Tess. His exclusion from Switzerland at the same time, for 'police and political reasons', resulted in years of courteous but fruitless correspondence with the Swiss authorities on this ban. Both bans only ended in about 1960.

Two letters from early 1951 show that Berti had known Cecil Powell slightly: 'The reason I went to St Anton was that my friend Nicholas Miller from Edinburgh was there to do some ski-ing, and I wanted to have a chat with him. ... I am very glad I did go there, as by chance I ran into the Nobel Prize winner Professor Powell of Bristol, a physicist, and I could coax him into visiting us in Vienna. So he will lecture here next week, and he will also talk on the problem of peace, as he is a Vice-President of the British Peace Movement. I used to know Powell in England, though not very well.' Then: 'Very nearly I could not get Professor Powell to Vienna in time. He was due to address two meetings – one scientific and one on peace. The car in which we travelled to meet him got stuck in Upper Styria in snow one metre deep. In the end, however, we got through, happily.'

Berti did succeed in establishing a productive group. Initially he carried on research derived from his war-time radiochemical work. However he then started to apply his radioisotope expertise to biology. His first major success came in 1952: 'I have sent off to a journal a little piece of work of which we can be proud: first synthesis of radioactive tobacco mosaic virus. This will make possible the thorough investigation of the metabolism of viruses ... It's a long term project – if only we have peace.' This was pioneering work, and increasingly his interests shifted to biochemistry. In 1958 he was to publish *Radioactive Isotopes in Biochemistry*; this project was also a way for him to teach himself biochemistry systematically.

In writing to me and to Hilde the absence of letters from us were an almost invariable topic. He could not understand (as he did not when he and

Hilde were a couple) why weeks would go by without a word. In a 1949 letter to Hilde he said he had got no information on whether and how I had returned from Austria, and how my school report had been, and that it had been the same the previous year. He thought this was very bad for me, as in this way habits of thoughtlessness, unreliability and irresponsibility were encouraged. He thought it was obvious that he should be given news from time to time, and he regretted the absence of news, particularly since in Austria I had been given much affection by relatives. Yet on this occasion he had kept me two weeks beyond my school resumption without informing Hilde, until he had found a suitable escort for me.

Things were no better the following year, 1950, when he vented his feelings on me: 'Now I have not heard from you for one quarter of a year. This is not right, and it makes it hard for me to write to you as much as I should want to. You are now big enough to understand that in the long run it is hardly possible to keep writing to a person, even to one's own son, if there is never a reply. You cannot very well just write into empty air.' And a few days later: 'I thank you for your letter of April 3rd ...' and in May: 'Again five weeks have passed, and you have not given news a single time. All this is very wrong.'

Happily things improved somewhat, but reading his letters makes me feel guilty again and I feel for him in his helpless situation; he loved me, he craved more contact with me, he had no other children, he was isolated and he had other major problems. Telephones and telegrams were for emergencies only and he couldn't visit me in Britain. He depended on Hilde's goodwill and her ability to get me to write, and although I was fond of him and admired him, I didn't empathise enough to respond. I think sometimes of his adult life as fifty years of entreating his wife and child, and others, to write to him. A major part of his emotional life until his death consisted of planning and then having my one or two visits each year, later with my own family.

21

HILDE AND PAUL IN CAMBRIDGE 1947-52

In 1947 with the advent of the National Health Service, Hilde's boss wanted her to buy into the practice. She couldn't or wouldn't, and so had to move on. There was a restriction on her going to any other Cambridge practice, so we went to London that September. I was a weekly boarder at a progressive school in North London run by Beatrix Tudor Hart, sister-in-law of Edith. However, in April 1948 Hilde started a job in Cambridge as Assistant Medical Officer of Health, a nine-to-five job such as she needed as a single parent. She then took a course on 'educationally subnormal children and mental defectives' as a preparation for an important part of her new job. I saw out the year at the school, doing a weekly commute from Cambridge, by train and bus. The idea of an eight year old doing this alone did not seem extraordinary then.

Hilde was deeply undecided where we would live. Friends were returning to Austria, and she herself was offered a post at a sanatorium in the Russian Zone, but turned it down. Berti was keen for her to be in Austria as it would mean more access to me but he recognised the arguments for Hilde and me to stay in Britain. To his great credit he did not play the access card, but solely considered my (and her) interests. Hilde was also thinking of Yugoslavia (perhaps because Eleanor Singer had gone there for a time in the war after Sidney Fink was killed) and of Germany. Berti rejected both these options very emphatically, and that seemed to have settled the debate. Then in 1950, through Hilde's job, we got a council-owned flat in a Jacobean manor house with a lovely garden. Hilde wrote to Felix Meyer that it was her thirty-second address in Britain, and that we finally felt settled. Even so, letters just before Hilde met Alan in 1953 suggest that even then the good offices of Litzi Honigmann (Philby) in East Berlin were being used to explore possibilities for Hilde there.

These were the years of the Cold War, and then in 1950 the Korean War.

Hilde was an advocate of peaceful coexistence, and from 1951 until her marriage in August 1953 she was secretary of the Cambridge Peace Council, and on the executive of the National Peace Council. In both she acted in her own capacity, not representing any of the disparate member organisations that included the leftists and also religious and pacifist ones, such as the Quakers, Peace Pledge Union and the Fellowship of Reconciliation. They strenuously organised poorly attended events, notably a concert by Peter Pears and Olive Zorian. The good citizens and students of Cambridge had to decide whether to hear good music under the auspices of a 'fellow travelling' organisation.

Each year I went to Austria in the summer and usually also at Easter. It was interesting, I was with Berti, and Hilde had time for other things, but it was also unsettling and disruptive of my life and friendships in Cambridge. For instance, with a less exotic and itinerant life I might have learned to be more comfortable with girls in my adolescence. Berti's friends, especially the Löw-Beers, made me welcome but I depended on Berti and others, including children, having time for me, so I learned to bury myself in the *Encyclopaedia Britannica* and English newspapers. Berti wanted to have me with him for as long as possible. Apart from his own needs in the context of his failing second marriage, I think he did not trust Hilde to be a good mother, and he wanted to imprint on me as much as possible of his own more earnest persona. Tess and he discussed Hilde's failings, but my father's problems with visas and entry to the UK only gradually emerged. When I saw Tess then and later she never asked me the obvious question as to why he did not visit me, her or England. So I became a solo traveller in 1951.

During this period we met the Newton-John family. Bryn was my charismatic young headmaster at the Cambridgeshire High School for Boys and a linguist who had been at Bletchley Park. His wife Irene was a daughter of Max Born, so she was German and Jewish. Their son Hugh became my best friend and we were in the same class. The Newton-Johns then went to Australia, and Hugh's much younger sister Olivia, the singer and actress, became more famous than her father (later a vice-chancellor) or grandfather. Max Born and his great friend Einstein would have been amazed.

Hilde's friends in Cambridge included a group of bright young biologists. But her first serious involvement was with a visiting Italian astrophysicist, a direct successor of Galileo at the Florence Observatory. However, he had an ill wife at home (and children) and so nothing could be done. Just when Hilde was about to marry Alan, she got a letter from him telling her that his wife had died, and of his feelings for her. The accidents of time and place. Another involvement was with a pharmacologist with a particular interest in mammalian sexual cycles who did important work on Soay sheep on St Kilda, and was interested in other rare breeds and in archaeology. He was fourteen years younger than Hilde, and very nice to me. Hilde and he were prepared to be seen as a couple, and travelled together; he then took a job in London, but they remained friends, and he signed the register at Hilde and Alan's wedding.

Eric Hobsbawm, then a young don at King's College Cambridge, was a particular friend of Hilde's because of their shared German and cultural interests. Another friend was a doctor who had wanted to work on bacterial genetics with my future boss Bill Hayes. As with the others, I was fond of him. In addition, he had a wonderful old sports car, and very much wanted to marry Hilde. He had been a taxi driver in Tahiti and fought in Spain. Eventually he became a GP and County Councillor in Essex. Later he inherited and promptly renounced a peerage, and when I last saw him he gave me some literature that I cherish from his early interest in bacterial genetics. He then went as a volunteer doctor to Jamaica, and died there. Also in this period before Hilde met Alan, we went to Bristol to meet Cecil and Isobel Powell for the first time, I believe at the request of Berti in relation to World Federation of Scientific Workers matters.

Hilde told me that she had avoided relationships that implied a real future. I am certain that it was not because she was waiting for Alan, as some have supposed. Two reasons were her own experience of marriage to Berti and her uncertainty as to whether her long-term future lay in Britain. In some letters Hilde said that she felt out of place in Britain. But I said that I wanted to stay in England, and she made an attempt at naturalisation, thwarted, as the MI5 papers show, by having completed out-of-date forms. I also think that as far as Austria was concerned she had had enough of deferring to Berti, and saw the merits of English life, including our home, since she was well-treated and liked.

At first I was happy in my new school, but a very bad report in late 1951 elicited a detailed letter from Hilde to Berti in which she discussed various possible reasons. Some of these were valid, but it is striking that she made no connection between my problems and her own situation. This included much time devoted to Peace Council activities, her ambivalence about being in Britain, her health (she later underwent an operation), and our relative isolation. The next year Hilde wrote to Berti that she wanted me to be proud of our left wing status, and linked this to her own shame at having dissembled to Sir William Bragg. But the difference was that Berti and Hilde were adults responsible for their own actions, whereas I was a child. Things went much better when I made a new friend whose parents were also very kind to me. His older brother did National Service as an infantry officer in Korea, and was wounded. Naturally he was not keen on my politics, but he too was friendly. My friend's mother made a point later of congratulating my mother on her marriage to Alan.

22

ALAN, HILDE AND PAUL IN CAMBRIDGE
1953-61

After Hilde and Alan married there were some fair-weather Cambridge friends; as usual the CP distanced itself from those who were embarrassing. A sadness for Hilde was that Barbara Sparks broke off the tenuous contact they still had. However, the most serious manifestation of hostility came from an alderman who also owned the local paper. He saw Hilde as a potential indoctrinator of the children of Cambridge whom she saw as school medical officer, and proposed to the County Council that she be dismissed. On the crucial day, the Council decided overwhelmingly to throw out the proposal. The matter was widely reported, and Hilde's MI5 file has the paper's detailed report of the debate. This happy outcome was due in part to her professional standing, but there was also a resolve not to allow McCarthyism into Britain, and as such it had wider significance.

Hilde wrote to Berti that 'many mothers, head teachers, teachers, colleagues etc, also ones unknown to me, have supported me. Mothers have spontaneously not only written to the chairman and various councillors but also collected signatures for their letters. A priest has given a very supportive sermon. The British Medical Association, Medical Women's Federation, Business and Professional Women, National Association of Local Government Officers, Association of Medical Officers of Health, have all spontaneously intervened. The overall political significance was immediately recognised. By the second day the word McCarthyism was used by everybody. The extraordinary turnaround of the press, particularly *Daily Express* and (Daily) *Mirror,* that already before the Council meeting came out very strongly for me. We have reason to believe that this turnaround is a sign of how sensitive these papers are to public opinion. This evening the motion was discussed on the BBC in a Home Affairs programme and strongly condemned as McCarthyism. I have an enormous fan-mail from acquaintances and unknown people who congratulate me over this victory over McCarthyism.' She added: 'Alan's passport was refused. So sadly we can't come. For me that is a real blow.' Alan had also not found work a year after his release.

Alan and Hilde were anxious to have a child, and my mother at one time thought she was pregnant. But it was not to be, unsurprisingly due to her many medical problems. Eleanor Singer, now Barratt Brown, who had a similar job to Hilde's in Essex, arranged the adoption of John, who was born in July 1954 and came to us at six weeks. I wonder what hoops Alan and Hilde would otherwise have had to go through even then. In spite of their late start and precipitate marriage Hilde and Alan were together for over forty-nine years. It was a happy marriage of equals, with much humour, and they kept any disagreements to themselves. Alan was devoted to Hilde, observed lots of courtesies, and was very trusting of her and his place in her life. He was doubtless deeply grateful to her too, but never seemed insecure. She admired him deeply and saw in him a stable, straightforward and open man with whom there were no ifs and buts. The decision to adopt John was a statement of their determination to catch up on lost time and have a proper family-based marriage. Later Hilde had little hesitation in dropping everything to go with him to Ghana. She once told me that she was grateful that they had not met earlier; she might have found it less easy to be faithful. The idea that she was waiting for his release is a pure canard, and MI5's theory that their marriage implicated Berti with Alan misread how Hilde approached her life. Alan and Hilde gave each other an enormous amount; she gave him warmth, devotion and a *joie de vivre* and he gave her stability, and intellectual engagement and clarity without patronising her. As a couple they were admired and loved by my friends as well as those of their own generation. A vital part of Alan's life was his love of music. He rented a grand piano, and at the Senate House we heard Myra Hess play the last three Beethoven sonatas. An iconic place, performer and set of pieces. The sonatas were to remain Alan's most-loved pieces.

On the living room table and in the libraries of Cambridge University Alan set about catching up on physics, and in particular on solid state physics and the problem of metal fatigue. But his attempts to obtain jobs were unendingly frustrating. The files show that his situation was monitored, and attempts by government to place him in work continued after his release from prison. The decision to prevent him from teaching physics in a British university was also adopted by the Association of Commonwealth Universities, the conduit for job applications in the Commonwealth. When the Ghanaian President Kwame Nkrumah later went outside this mechanism, there were attempts by the British Government and also probably by the Association to frustrate this. An outside chance was a research fellowship at King's College Cambridge, and Noel Annan, then Provost, assured Alan that his case would be treated on its academic merits, but later warned him of other strong applications. Eric Hobsbawm recounted that Alan went to a King's Dinner as his guest and was treated impeccably.

Peter and Nora Wooster were left wing Cambridge crystallographers who were pre-war friends of Alan's. They invited Alan to work informally in their private laboratory on instrument design. At this time some approaches were also made to Alan, including the idea that he should go to Peron's Argentina and an attempt by a Chilean associate of Bernal to get Alan a job there. But Alan felt strongly that, as he had served his sentence and was British, he should not be driven into exile. At the end of 1953 the Government found a way to defuse the situation of Alan's joblessness, which was becoming a scandal. Sir Henry Willink, Vice-Chancellor of Cambridge University and a former Cabinet Minister, relayed an offer of support for two years from an Anonymous Benefactor through the University. This was confidential but amusing, since the money clearly came from the public purse, as official minutes later confirmed. We did not realise at how high a level the discussions had been, for £2000.

This grant led to work for which the final report was received very courteously: 'I enclose a brief report of the work I have done since January 1954. It is a non-technical outline which I intend to fill in by publication of my results. I have stressed that the ultimate aim has been to establish means such as consultation for industry, making and designing of instruments, by which I can become self-supporting. Of course if other means should become possible, such as a post in industry or a University I should not regard myself as rigidly bound by these plans. May I ask that in transmitting this to the donor you will also convey my sincere thanks for what he has done, and may I also thank you very much indeed for the trouble and care you have taken in making the arrangements for this donation.' Willink replied: 'My dear May, Many thanks for your letter of 1st July. This is just what I asked for, and I am sure that it will be greatly appreciated.' And then:

'My dear May, I have heard from your benefactor. I am to say what satisfaction it has given to gather that you are on the road to becoming self-supporting, but also to say that the payments will have to cease as originally indicated.' It led to contract research for a local company, possibly funded indirectly by MI5.

In early 1956 MI5 eavesdroppers reported that Alan was reluctant to accept overtures from East Germany to visit (in any case he had no passport) and that he intended to discuss with MI5 any intention he had to leave the country. This might relate to a visit from the Löw-Beers when they all huddled together with the radio on loudly to frustrate eavesdropping. When asked for his opinion Berti said it would be a gilded cage, but by then Alan and Hilde did not need to be told that.

During this time Alan had friendly dealings with Nevill Mott, now at the Cavendish, and his colleagues and remarkably he published three letters in *Nature* in 1960 and 1961. In 1956 MI5 discussed whether to approach Mott about him: 'Although this covers the security aspect, I am more concerned about his possible reactions to any approach regarding a fellow scientist if, as I think, at the outset of any talk, some reference would have to be made to the fact that the Government were interested in seeing Nunn May settled down in suitable employment in the UK which would bring him satisfaction and contentment. Mr (Peter) Wright has known Mott over a period of some fifteen years and, from the picture he drew of him, causes me to think that it would not be a good thing for any direct approach to be made. Mott is apparently a pleasant enough fellow and would appreciate the need for the security of secret papers which may come into his possession, but he is also very forgetful and, on the whole, unpredictable. He is one of that band of scientists who feel that they, and they alone, should determine how the fruits of their labours should be utilised. If at the beginning of any talk with him he did not give the impression of being on-coming, it would be difficult to know how to continue the interview.'

Hilde became an Austrian citizen by marrying Berti, and remained as such until after her marriage to Alan, when she obtained UK citizenship by right. However, when Alan and Hilde applied for passports these were refused in July 1955: 'The Cabinet considered a memorandum by the Foreign Secretary about an application by the wife of Dr Alan Nunn May for a passport to enable her to travel to Austria on holiday. It might be Mrs

Nunn May's real intention to reclaim Austrian nationality and remain in Austria in the hope that her husband would be allowed to join her there on compassionate grounds. From Austria they could both defect to a country behind the Iron Curtain. Defection by Dr Nunn May would be likely seriously to prejudice Anglo-American relations generally and, in particular, the completion of the civil and military agreements between the two countries on the exchange of atomic information. These agreements had been signed on 15th June but had to lie before Congress for a period of 30 days thereafter. The Cabinet agreed that no passport should be issued to Mrs Nunn May before 18th July, when this period of 30 days would be completed. Meanwhile arrangements might be made for Mrs Nunn May to be interviewed in order that a judgement might be formed on the question whether she intended to do no more than visit her relations in Austria or whether she had some ulterior motive in seeking to make this journey.'

This interview duly took place: 'Mrs Nunn May asked if a passport would now be granted to her husband. Rex replied that he understood that this had been refused. Mrs Nunn May then said that she could not understand why her husband had been refused a passport again, because when he came out of prison he had been interviewed by Mr Skardon of MI5 and told that while he could not be granted a passport at that moment he was invited to apply later on when there was a good chance that his application would be granted. Upon applying again, a passport had been refused. At the start of the interview the atmosphere was tense. Mrs Nunn May melted a little under Rex's careful questioning and did not object to any of the questions that Rex put to her. There was a time towards the end of the interview when she even appeared charming, but it was the charm of an Austrian woman who could turn it on and off at will.'

Rex's draft report concluded that Hilde did have an ulterior motive, but the MI5 man did not agree: 'It seemed important that new adverse considerations should not without good reason be put before the Cabinet if they were going to reconsider the case of the Nunn Mays. As I understand it the reason why passports had not been granted them was that it was feared that, if they were abused, the atomic energy negotiations with the USA would be prejudiced. Now that agreement on atomic energy exchanges had been reached with the USA, much of the validity of their reasons seemed to have disappeared. He was amending the conclusions to Rex's report by saying that, while it was possible that Mrs Nunn May might have had an ulterior motive, nothing occurred in the interview with her to lend support to that view.' Several months later MI5 noted: 'Rex told me that a passport was issued to Mrs Nunn May a few days after we had interviewed her and after consideration at the highest level. I told Rex that we had heard nothing about this from the Security Department of the Foreign Office. I understand also from Rex that Alan Nunn May has not been granted a passport.'

In mid-1956 Alan's third application for a passport was rejected by the Foreign Secretary, Selwyn Lloyd, and in 1958 he asked Lord Stansgate to take up his case, which he agreed to do as a matter of principle. In the debate in the House of Lords that followed the Minister said: 'No British subject has a legal right to a passport ... The Foreign Secretary has the power to withold or withdraw a passport at his discretion, although in practice such power is exercised only very rarely and in very exceptional cases ... thirdly, persons whose activities are so notoriously undesirable or dangerous that Parliament would be expected to support the action of the Foreign Secretary in refusing them a passport or withdrawing a passport already issued in order to prevent their leaving the UK.'

Viscount Stansgate: 'Is he aware that what is in people's minds is the undesirability of our following the American precedent, where the withholding of a passport is a definite act of State?'

Earl of Gosford: 'My Lords, this process has been going on for many years. The number of passports withheld annually is one or, at the most, two, as against the many millions which are issued.'

A few weeks later MI5 noted that they had no reason to suspect Alan's motives and it was reported that the Foreign Office asked for an early Cabinet discussion because it was 'embarrassing for them to continue stalling on Nunn May's application for a passport.' Alan was again refused a passport in August 1958 but finally he received one in March 1959, on his sixth application.

This period also covers my own transition from teenager to graduate. My life benefited enormously from having Alan as my stepfather, not only because he helped me with my homework but because of his intelligence, friendliness and wide interests that complemented Hilde's. With a young brother as well, we were a fairly normal family with two working parents. In my later school days I became close to Michael Crick, Robin Butterfield and

William Newman, each of whom happened to have a notable father (Francis, Herbert and Max). My life was changed by an excellent biology teacher, E. F. Holden, I won a scholarship at King's College Cambridge, and effectively left home in 1958. At school and also at college I did the conventional things, which in my case included playing rugby. I was only mildly involved in politics. Then in 1961 I graduated in Biochemistry and went to London.

23

BERTI IN VIENNA 1953-55

MI5 re-examined their file on Berti after Hilde married Alan. Evidently both the British and the Americans had each withheld information on Berti from the other. The Americans believed that Berti had links with Soviet Intelligence before he came to Britain, but the British did not know this. I have not seen the American evidence. Berti once told me that two British agents visited him (I don't know when) and that he declined to talk to them. The reluctance to share information continued after the wedding: 'xxxx telephoned with reference to 862a, and asked whether the information in paras 2-4 could be given to the Americans. I told xxxx that my impression was that the Americans had never been told exactly what information we held on Broda at the time when he was accepted for employment on the Tube Alloy project. The reference in para 3 to Broda's internment and connection with the London group of members of the Austrian Communist Party should not therefore be given to the Americans, nor should para 4.' A part of a long update of Berti's file in October 1953 reads: 'In a US report of 1950 it was said that Broda was an idealistic communist who was associated with the Soviet espionage service prior to 1938 when he fled to England. In the UK Broda is said to have continued his activity for Soviet intelligence and following the war he returned to Vienna where he succeeded in obtaining a position at the University of Vienna where, for the Soviets, he has organised an information network with tentacles in every department of the Chemistry Institute. Broda was tolerated in the Institute because he was the only scientist in the Institute qualified to work with radioactive substances as they are related to the field of chemistry. In 1950 the Director of Scientific Intelligence at the Ministry of Defence suggested that a special watch should be put on Broda if and when he came to this country as owing to his many friends at Harwell he would be in an ideal position for collecting intelligence.'

Another note in October states: 'Your enquiry about the possibility that the Brodas played some part in the espionage of Nunn May came at a happy time, for we were already studying Engelbert Broda's case in another connection. As a result of that study we feel sure that Broda was engaged in espionage during the war, although we have no proof of it. ... On 1st October 1945 Broda wrote asking to see him in Cambridge or London. According to Nunn May's diary he went to Cambridge on the 16th-17th October and amongst others saw Broda. Broda and Nunn May both had lunch with Kowarski on the 14th January 1946. I think therefore that the answer to your question is that Engelbert Broda might well have been the person who recruited Nunn May for the R.I.S. (Russian Intelligence Service). You will remember that one of Nunn May's few admissions in an interrogation which took place at Wakefield prison on 21st March 1949 was that he was recruited to the R.I.S. only a very short while before he left the country for Canada and that the individual who recruited him was no longer within reach. Mr Skardon to whom this information was given was inclined to believe that Nunn May's statement was true. In March 1949 when Nunn May said this Broda was no longer in the country.' A further note states: 'xxxx spoke to me this morning about Broda. He has consulted the scientific section who are reluctant to tell the Americans anything at all and they thought we should say as little as possible. I agreed with xxxx that this generally speaking was our view also and said I would tell him the terms of our proposed reply when it was ready.'

A letter from the American Embassy to MI5 in March 1955 on Berti had some novel points: 'Since his own field demands a knowledge of nuclear physics he knows a great deal about it, but he is not and does not consider himself an expert on nuclear physics. Broda is a member of the Austrian Communist party and a convinced, idealistic Communist. He is an extremely hard worker and has never been known to be objectionable in the presence of his university colleagues who do not share his political beliefs. ... In 1933 he was arrested by the Nazis because he was the leader of the Communist party Students' union in Berlin and had organised a similar group in Frankfurt am Main. ... It is also believed that Broda has been and may be at present connected with Soviet Technical Intelligence as a supervisor of a group of Austrian scientists working in the field of nuclear energy. Certain reports, which to date have not been fully substantiated, speak of Broda as a key man in the transmission of secret atomic data from the United States, Canada and Great Britain to the Soviets.' MI5 responded by listing some of Berti's Austrian contacts as: Edith Tudor-Hart 'this woman is said to have worked for the Russian Intelligence in Vienna and Italy in the early 1930s'; Ilona Suschitzky: taught in a Moscow school 1931-1936; Jacob Wolloch, former husband of Eva Kolmer; Franz Carl West or Weintraub; and Paul Löw-Beer. 'Our own records of Broda's activities in this country include no evidence that he was engaged in espionage in the UK. We are most interested in the suggestion in your letter of 3.3.55 that Broda has past and present connexions with Soviet Intelligence and we should be most grateful to know that facts upon which these suspicions are based and the period to which they relate. ... Since preparing the foregoing we have received yours ... of 28th March and are much obliged for the information contained in it.'

Was Berti involved in espionage with Alan? Alan said that his first contact with the Russians was in late 1942, with the only people directly involved being his still unidentified cell leader and the Russian recipient of the information. Apart from Skardon's 1949 report (see earlier), there is no evidence that anyone recruited Alan in 1942 in a different way. But conceivably in his own later account Alan made up or omitted details of his 1942 actions, for instance to prevent me knowing that Berti was implicated, or implicating Berti even posthumously. However, according to Vassiliev, Berti himself did not start passing information until after Alan had left for Canada. On a hillside in Perthshire in August 1994 I asked Alan directly whether Berti had been involved with his activities. He answered explicitly that Berti had not. Although he could have said this to protect me (this goes for all that Alan and Berti said to me), I believe it to be true.

After Skardon's visit to Alan in 1949 he had reported that Alan said he was recruited just before his departure, and that the recruiter was by then out of their reach. Alan may indeed have said this but he would not intentionally have incriminated a friend. It is more likely that he sought to deflect attention from his activities in 1942, without thinking that he was putting others under suspicion. Alan himself stated firmly in his memoir that he was instructed by his cell leader, probably British and within reach if still alive, so Alan might well have wanted a decoy. Apparently it did not occur to MI5 that Alan had been active rather than just recruited before he went to Canada.

On Alan's account there was no need for him to be recruited since the Russians knew of him already. Why then did the Russians in Canada not come to Alan earlier than they did? He said they came to him then only when they had learned of the secret and separately managed uranium plant, and that although he had regarded himself as a defector from the Russian point of view he had responded then because of his loyalty to the cause and because of what he had learned in Chicago about American intentions after the end of the war. Thus, as in 1942, Alan had a specific motive.

An alternative hypothesis centres on the sending of a postcard, as instructed by his Cambridge cell leader (Chapter 11). He was to send this to an innocent third party, a woman at the Cavendish perhaps, and the card would be seen by the real contact. This implies that a real contact did exist at the Cavendish. However, Alan wrote that he studiously avoided sending any cards. Even so, almost two years later, in September 1944, a card was sent to Berti from Chicago, signed by Kowarski, Anderson, Freundlich and Alan. Berti sent it on to me, explaining what a skyscraper was, and telling Hilde that Kowarski now had a useful role (Chapter 12, Photo 47). It was more in character for the extrovert Kowarski (who addressed it) rather than Alan to initiate such a postcard; Alan would then have had to sign it. How could he decline, even if he realised that there might be complications? It should not have been taken as *the* postcard, because Berti wasn't the innocent woman, it wasn't a card from just Alan, and it was two years on, but it might still have activated a response. Someone might have thought this was the signal they were hoping for, if they were party to this understanding. But again in relation to Berti, we now know that he only contacted the Russians after Alan had departed. It is of course possible that a quite different card was indeed sent by Alan, and then acted on, contrary to what he later wrote. I think that Alan never knew if the Chicago postcard's arrival had triggered the Russian approach, but he regarded it as important since he mentioned it in his memoir.

I doubt that Berti knew of any of Alan's activities until his arrest, but he might then have *believed* that he had had an indirect role in them. For instance, he could have suggested to the Russians that Alan was a sympathiser who could answer their queries in Canada. The Vassiliev papers state that Berti nominated Fuchs to the Russians (and *vice versa*) without either knowing that the other was already active. But the innocence of his meeting

Alan after his return from Canada suggests that he did not know enough to stay away. Meeting was a natural thing to do, given that they were scientific and political friends, and he could hope to get new information from Alan and Kowarski about developments in Canada. Nor do I think that Berti tipped Alan off in 1945, as the Examiners' Board story is credible. Even so, the connection with Alan was a sufficient reason why Berti never came back to Britain after 1948, but it is noteworthy that he felt able to make that one visit. Did something happen after that to make him more cautious, such as Edith Tudor Hart's admission in 1947 that she had worked for the Russians? Berti would never have known of the Skardon interview, unless it was then leaked to him.

My view reading the MI5 files, before the Vassiliev revelations emerged, was that MI5 were right to think that Berti probably gave information to the Soviet Union. His connection with Edith Tudor Hart and Kaspar's report just after Alan's arrest support this. The revelations are plausible, and my presence in London and Berti's Austrian Centre activities both provided him with reasons to visit there. If true, it reflects very poorly on British security in their decision to accede to Berti's appointment and particularly in not following up on their suspicions. His value as a spy might at first have seemed limited since he was excluded from the most secret work, but the files then state that the distinction between more and less secret work had broken down, and also that he could pick up further information. There is no suggestion that Berti ran a network, and of course he was safest not having to trust others.

He did act like someone with something to hide. Thus in 1953 he downplayed his friendship with Alan to Tess, he refused to talk to British agents, and he did not seek entry to the UK. Refusal to talk is not in itself crucial evidence, as he would in any case have felt he would have had to talk about friends to ideological opponents. But not returning to Britain was a high price to pay. His exclusion from France may have come through the Americans, not the British, because of what they apparently knew about his connection with Soviet Intelligence. But that did not need specifically to be about atomic espionage. I became well aware of the non-visiting issue and I am glad that even at my graduation, I never exerted undue pressure on him to come. I felt that if he had a secret, he should not share it with me. In the mid-Seventies an immigration officer let slip to a Broda cousin that Berti was in his Black Book, and that was that. I don't know if Alan and Berti ever discussed these matters on the occasions they met in later life.

Stalin's death in March 1953 caused a change in the political climate for Berti. The occupation of Austria ended in 1955 and Austria adopted permanent neutrality. Berti commented: 'In every way the situation is healthier now, and I have full confidence that ultimately the change in the situation will mean a great advantage to freedom and progress, as it will not be possible any more to shift the blame for everything that is wrong on the Russians.' But he was also dismayed that the right wing was in the ascendant: 'I doubt whether you read in your papers that now practically every Sunday there are rallies of former alpine troops, paratroopers, Waffen-SS etc, where the Nazi generals address their former soldiers who wear their Nazi decorations. All preparations for the European Army.' Also in 1955, a film by Willi on Hitler's final days turned out well: 'It is a great success. I am rather glad, as I like old Willi, as you know, and I should not have liked the idea that he made a mess of the story' and: 'I have seen Willi's film, and though I was sceptical before, I readily admit now that it is excellent. He has captured the atmosphere of the last days of Hitler's Reich. Especially, I am pleased that the generals, like Keitel and Jodl, by no means get away well. I think the effect of this film on everybody, especially on young people who have not experienced consciously the Third Reich, must be very good.'

Late that year, at the time of the Einstein-Russell Open Letter on the nuclear threat (Note 17), Berti proposed a resolution against atomic war at a meeting of the Austrian Physical Society. The motion that passed was so weak that he found himself unable to vote for it. This began the passionate involvement in issues of war and peace that was central to the rest of his life. He saw Austria's neutral status and location as of great value for efforts in discussing detente. The Pugwash movement was founded in 1957, and he was involved almost immediately, becoming an active member and eventually president of Austrian Pugwash.

He also became involved in debates on possible medical benefits of radioactivity, advocated for instance by those running the spa of Badgastein. His position was that: 'theoretically I am sceptical whether radioactivity can have any beneficial influence at all, so I am inclined to think that Gastein works only because of the heat of the water, the clean and thin air, the good food, the rest and the daily bridge game.' However, as time passed he became exasperated by the ever-more ill-founded claims made, and spent much time arguing against such misinformation. Another ongoing campaign that was ultimately successful was to ban the use of the carcinogen butteryellow as a food additive.

As mentioned in the Prologue, Berti was very supportive to Hilde of marrying Alan, although he had been given no inkling that this would happen, and foresaw the public reaction that would ensue. Hilde wrote: 'I am very happy about your positive attitude to the changed situation, but of course I have always known what a dear person you are, Bertilein. We are very sure that we have made the right decision, as if we had tried it out for 100 years. Instead, it will have been only 4 weeks on Saturday!'

His own second marriage had just ended in divorce, as he wrote to Tess in September 1953: 'I have not replied to a long and very nice letter from you many months ago. The reason is that in some ways I was in a very bad shape. You know of course that for some years there has been serious trouble between Ina and me. In June, 1953, we were divorced. It is difficult to explain these personal things in any case, and even more so by letter. I shall not attempt it. I just want to tell you as an old and good friend – I hope I may still call you that – one or two things. The divorce was carried through on my initative. I had very thoroughly considered the question for years, and had come to the conclusion that there was no other way out, though naturally I hated to do it. There are differences and contrasts in temperament (and age) which nothing in the world can bridge. We are both to blame to have married without knowing enough of one another, and later probably both of us behaved foolishly in some ways in the relations with each other, but given the state of tension which existed, it could perhaps not have been much otherwise. As things were, I am sorry to say that Ina suffered a great deal, and so did I. As far as this personal side of life is concerned, the last few years certainly for me were among the blackest. No purpose would have been served in dragging on an intolerable and impossible situation. Perhaps I should add that no third persons were involved. I have come to appreciate many fine qualities of Ina, and I maintain, as before, that she is a very gifted, and very decent, and very charming human being. But this does not help. NB there were no political disagreements! We both have to pay dearly for our rash, though well meant, action. If you think now that I do not take marriage seriously enough, I am afraid I cannot do much about it. I cannot explain by letter or, perhaps, at all. But I should be happy to know that you do not think so, because it would not be the truth. I believe marriage is one of the two most important things in life. No use saying more. I want to add that Paul was here, as usual. I am most happy to see how well he develops. ...'

He continued: 'About Hilde you will have read. You know that I knew the husband only slightly in 1942, and have met him only once in 1946, but he always appeared to me, as a person, as pleasant. So I hope the two of them will be happy together, and I am very glad to think that Hilde can now steer a quiet course for the future. Paul is on good terms with his stepfather.' Thus Berti seems to down-play how well he knew Alan; as MI5 knew, Berti had sought him out on his return in 1945.

In her reply Tess showed her concern for Berti and Ina (whom she had still not met) and also her strong disapproval of Alan and her poor opinion of Hilde: 'It was with great distress that I read your last letter. I was not as well informed as you imagined ...You say there were no political disagreements. I wish there had been – and maybe at bottom, there are, for Ina is a poet, with a poet's understanding and intuition that belong to a different realm of knowledge than mathematical, or chemical formulae. I wish Ina could rejoin the friends of her youth, whom she understands and who understand her. I am glad you are so pleased with Paul, and I wish with all my heart that he can be happy and fulfilled. I don't know his stepfather and I can't be wildly enthusiastic about this addition to the family. You see, while I know that he acted according to his own code, I believe that code to be fundamentally wrong, disruptive of human relationships which can only be based on truth, on personal integrity. I believe his action to have been utterly wrong – really in the category "sin", not a mere contravening of a regulation. Thinking as I do, you can't expect me to be enthusiastic at the idea that these values, which I consider to be so wrong, should be put before Paul as the correct ones. I know that you don't take marriage lightly – I wish I could honestly say the same for Hilde. I can only hope, for everyone's sake, not least for the stepfather himself, that this marriage is more than a gesture of bravado on her part. ... Love, Tess.' Perhaps her friendship with him was too important for her to allow herself to think that Berti might also have been a spy. In my own friendship with Tess I always had to balance my appreciation of what she had done for Berti and her fondness and concern for me with my dislike of her antipathy to Hilde and Alan, and the thought that she was applying double standards.

Berti's reply covered several topics: 'I cherish your letter more than I can say now. I want to reply to you in detail by talk or letter, but I find I am too dejected about it now. The whole problem has taken up a very large part of all my energy in recent years. I have felt, I still feel, and I shall always feel that I could not act otherwise than I did if there was not to happen complete disaster. Ina is living in our old and very nice flat. She likes the flat though she does not like Vienna particularly. I understand it. Not only Vienna is tied up with our problems, but in many ways, regarding the general outlook of the people, it is not a very pleasant place for sensitive people. I am not thinking of politics, though the outlook does express itself in politics too. It is rather a general cynicism, crude egotism and callousness, which one can feel so often. You would have difficulties in recognising the Viennese though the outer appearance has changed little. I am living provisionally in a sort of hole in the 2nd district.'

He continued: 'Money problems are difficult, as I support Ina, of course, also (partly) my mother, and when he is here for his holidays, Paul. The Government has always refused to pay me, except for the "Lehrauftrag" which amounts to the equivalent of £6 a month, admittedly on political grounds. "To give him a regular job would be an affront against the Americans", as an official put it. So I must get both the money I need and that I need for our work from other sources. So far it could be done, but at tremendous cost in nerves. For myself, I got the money by writing and as an industrial consultant; for my work from not less than four sources. We shall see how it goes on, McCarthyism is spreading here rapidly. I almost wish I had not written this, do not worry, I shall manage somehow. The work itself is making progress, and in some ways we have opened up really new paths. ... Paul is a source of delight. He is exactly as I should want him to be, interested, keen, intelligent, good-natured, warm-hearted, friendly, modest, tactful. I am very much in love with him … So it must be said, that whatever Hilde's great weaknesses, she has certainly done well with Paul in difficult circumstances ... Meanwhile, all love from Bert.'

Seven months later, in June 1954, he wrote again: 'Now I have also seen Frisch (and the pictures of his children), who also told me about you. I should have written to you a long time ago, if I had not had before my mind that in my last letter I promised to write to you more about the Disaster. I am afraid I cannot say much more about it, however. There are private things in life, about which it is better to keep silent. However, in the period which has now passed, my conviction has grown that I should have perished as an active human being without the step I have taken. I should have faded away. The step has made my life immensely more difficult in many ways, and it makes me sad to have jeopardised even the affection of a friend like you, not to speak of more distant and less important people, but the older I am the more I am sure that one has to do what one thinks is right, whatever people may think. Of course, I am trying to do for Ina what I can. Paul is on very good terms with Alan. I did not doubt it as they are people of friendly character. In fact, Alan is very nice to Paul. Their home seems altogether happy, which is a great thing. My mother visited them last spring. May I send you my love?' Ina then divided her time between Vienna and Zagreb and Berti continued to support her until her death shortly before his in 1983. In March 1953 he moved in with Viola 'for a few months' at the family flat, and he stayed there until his death so, in all, the family were tenants of the Schwartzenberg Estate for 101 years.

Late in 1953 his grandmother Ella died, and in the letter he wrote to me he was very critical of what he saw as her narrow and self-interested life. This was one of several occasions when he blamed his personal problems on his childhood experiences, which seem to me to add up to a feeling of being deprived of affection: 'I felt old time pass away as the coffin was lowered into the grave. ... There is not a single member of her generation left. They were people who reached the peak of their lives in the last century, in very different conditions. I hope, Paulie, you will appreciate that I was not much attached to her, but that I think one cannot and should not feel enthusiastic about people just because they happen to be close relatives, if one does not like their ways. ... She had considerable gifts, as intelligence, energy and even some interest in the lighter arts. However, I did not like her selfishness. She extended her selfish outlook also to her family, and she certainly liked to see her offspring successful. However, she had no moral standards. She would never have lifted a finger for anybody outside her own circle ... She never understood that there are higher things in life than an outwardly successful career. Or that in furthering a career there are things one should not do. With all her intelligence, she could never see beyond her own nose. She had no conception of a greater world, she never felt a need to do something for a better world, or to devote any part of her energy to any good cause. So it is not surprising that with all her intelligence and eagerness to push forward her children etc, she did not earn much love. She was very cruel and malicious against my father, because he was not efficient and successful enough for her. I also think she also made her husband very unhappy. I think my mother has never really forgiven her her behaviour both to my grandfather or to my father. That's why there was so much quarrel. Of course, my grandmother often looked after me as a child, and no doubt she fed me and dressed me when others were out, but I cannot recall a single thing I have learned from her, a single thought I owe to her although, as I stress again, she used to be very clever. There is a silly Latin saying *de mortuis nil nisi bonum*. I am afraid I cannot endorse it. There are people who do not leave a good memory. Of course, ultimately there must have been reasons in her own upbringing etc why she developed as she did, but this does not alter the fact.'

With the Cold War deepening, the Socialists systematically excluded Communists from positions and influence, and in 1953 Berti was expelled from the Institute for Science and Arts, in relation to a lecture he arranged for a Marxist philosopher. It particularly upset Berti that among the Socialists who were involved in this were Christian and their uncle Leo Zechner, in charge of schools in Vienna and a member of Parliament. Berti referred to 'his former brother' several times to me and others, and their estrangement deepened. By then Christian had bought Fünfturm from Willi Pabst, whose last important films were released in 1955 and who had no money, and so Berti did not visit when Christian was there, calling it 'a lost paradise'. An American research grant from the Damon Runyon fund was ended, it seems on State Department advice. But at least Berti and then I had been introduced to the world of Guys and Dolls. Also most bookshops in Vienna refused to display his popular science books, though they sold well elsewhere. Nevertheless Berti did receive two tokens of recognition in 1955, a prize for his research and the title of *Extraordinarius* (titular professor), but no salary was attached to this. Even so, the award of the title was greeted with much surprise because of the politics, and so Berti felt that he had to deny to his friends that favouritism or deals were involved.

In 1954 Berti wrote that he had been grossly overworked, but he seemed always to have been able to work through personally difficult times. He had eleven full-time workers in his group, all supported by soft money, and he had to do all the fundraising, reports, and accounts. As well as running several projects he had a general review article on the work of his group published in *Nature.* He also had four books on different topics on the go. One was a new edition of a popular book on Atomic Energy and another was on the applications of radioactivity to technology (with Thomas Schönfeld). These looked back to past interests, but the other two looked to his future. One was on radioisotopes in biochemistry, referred to earlier, and the fourth was a biography of Boltzmann. He referred to these books as numbers 5-8, and in 1955 he mentioned in relation to Einstein's death 'What a man ... remember that I translated Infeld's biography of Einstein ...'

Since his time in Britain Berti had studied the work and life of Boltzmann. He had corresponded about him with Lise Meitner, a student of Boltzmann, who by then was frail and in retirement. She agreed to write a Foreword to the book, which pleased Berti greatly. However, after much delay she then wrote that she had changed her mind, citing ill-health. Berti was deeply upset and wrote both to me and Tess, who knew her, asking himself and us whether politics was the real reason. Meitner might also not have accepted the picture of Boltzmann that Berti drew. The question was never resolved to Berti's satisfaction, but Boltzmann's successor Hans Thirring obliged with a Foreword. Berti wrote to me in early 1955: 'I am finishing the book on Boltzmann, in my view the greatest Austrian thinker who ever lived. He is the author of the famous relationship between "entropy" and "probability", which is quite fundamental to physics, and which I may attempt to explain to you next time. I trust you will be interested. The relationship can be expressed in the simple mathematical terms $S = k \log W$. This relationship is engraved on his tomb in Vienna Zentralfriedhof. I am quite fascinated by his personality. He was a very progressive man, and fought with much fervour against the reactionaries ("obscurantists") of his day for Darwinism. He applied the ideas of Darwin also quite successfully to the problems of the development of science. He was in some ways a follower and in all ways an admirer of Maxwell, the Cavendish professor.'

Berti recognised that my letter-writing manners had improved, but the pressure to write did not let up. There were exhortatory letters, for instance pointing out on my fourteenth birthday that others had to leave school and get a job at that age. One year later he set out the perils of smoking, including lung cancer. Early on he had accepted the link between smoking and cancer, but another reason harked back to his own experience: 'Smokers get so very dependent on their habit, and are most unhappy when they cannot get tobacco e.g. in prison. They are often quite ready to do wrong things for fear to lose tobacco. I have seen in prison what pressure can be applied on smoking prisoners by withholding tobacco from them.' Another concern of his was however allayed: 'I am very glad with Paul's choice of subjects. It would not be a pleasant thought to me if Paul had chosen English and History, although I appreciate both subjects, precisely because there is no future in them.'

24

BERTI IN VIENNA 1956-61

Krushchev's speech on the crimes of the Stalin era at the 20th Party Congress of the Communist Party of the Soviet Union in early 1956 appalled Berti and he had vigorous discussions within the Austrian CP. Because of his reticence and his Party loyalty, I don't know how much he already knew from his time in Russia or later. My guess is that from the pre-war period he knew of isolated examples of the disappearance of comrades that could be put down to misunderstandings, that in the war he knew nothing, and that after the war he would have attributed the obvious repression to the Cold War. He was very worried specifically about Soviet Genetics. Of all the questions I wish I could ask him, the first would be how much he knew, and when. Like others, he then had undue optimism on how a thaw and improvements would develop in the Soviet Union. As I and others saw, this led him to continue to put the best construction on what he saw and read, well into the Sixties.

The Hungarian Uprising later in 1956 occurred on his doorstep, but because of his party loyalty he still did not speak out, still less leave the CP. He wrote to me: 'The days here are foggy and dark, and this adds to the general gloom. I agree that Hungary is a disaster of the very first order. The question must be faced: here you have had every chance for many years, all your information has reached the people, you could take any measures you liked ... and what is the effect? It appears that dissatisfaction or even hatred is very widespread. Very serious thinking is required now, and it would be the worst to gloss over events and seek easy explanations. I suppose you and I have similar views about the attack on Egypt too. I wish we could have a chat.' In reply to me he then wrote: 'In many ways, I am in full agreement with you. I hope that the fact that the terrible things of the past are coming into the open now will have its profound influence on the future. There is no return. So, after all, I am basically optimistic. A situation where horrible facts are out in the open is preferable and more hopeful than a situation where they are covered up and carried on. However, very far-reaching changes are needed. Incidentally, recent events have in no way induced me to take a milder view of the imperialists, to use an understatement.' Then six months later in 1957: 'Hungary has also been a shock to me, and my views have changed in some ways, though still I cannot (and never shall) make peace with capitalism, or be satisfied with words …' Implicitly he did not accept that having failed, the Communists should allow another government to take its place.

Berti sent his Boltzmann book to Moscow, hoping that it would be translated into Russian, as Boltzmann was highly regarded in the Soviet Union as a materialist on whom Lenin had written. Eventually he received a provisional 'yes' subject to eight suggestions for modifications along ideological grounds, including making references to both Engels and Lenin. Berti gave reasons for resisting most of the suggestions. In the end a shortened form was published with due reference to Lenin. For Berti the most important thing was to make Boltzmann known as widely as possible.

In early 1957 Berti took a step that put him at odds with many CP comrades. He published in the Party's theoretical journal *Weg und Ziel* a critique of the Soviet biologist Lysenko, who under Stalin had been the instrument of the destruction of genetics in the Soviet Union that also led to the deaths of Nikolai Vavilov and other notable scientists, and who was still in favour. Berti wrote: 'I sent you and the rest of the family a copy of *Weg und Ziel* with an article against Lysenko etc. It is, so to speak, my Krushchev speech. Only it is not secret. Nevertheless, it will be, and should be, a bombshell.' He later wrote: 'I think it will do a lot of good, but has greatly enraged certain people.' One comment in *Weg und Ziel* on this article was 'What's good enough for the Soviet Union is good enough for Bert Broda'. This step was the beginning of the process by which Berti abandoned party politics in favour of a number of consensus-seeking activities such as nuclear disarmament, through Pugwash, and the environment. Also in 1957 he resigned from *Volkstimme* because they were cutting staff, but he continued to write occasional articles.

By late 1958 he could visit the Austrian President on behalf of the Peace Movement: 'We were received in the Burg and had a rather pleasant talk. In the end, I gave him the Boltzmann and invited him to my lab. He said he would consider it. He underlined that he welcomed any initiative, from wherever it comes, which would lessen the danger of atomic war and help to end bomb testing. The radioactivity of the air, or water, of Prater grass and Neusiedl reeds, of peas and beans, in short everything as measured in the lab with our scintillation spectrometer is now staggering. All visitors are deeply impressed.' He wrote of his feelings about party politics in 1959: 'Tomorrow is May Day. The Communists will presumably be fewer than last year. I feel that Communist influence here is very low now – most working class people do not seem to feel a need for them. It is all very serious. At the same time, the Socialists less than ever represent a struggle against capitalism, for a better world. ... No trace of any clear ideas or any militancy among them.'

In the post-Hungary period Berti visited all the Eastern bloc countries. In 1957 he wrote to me: 'The thought comes to me what a wonderful country the old Empire was – and how foolishly it was squandered by the reactionary Habsburgs.' A visit to Prague gave him grounds for optimism, but in Poland friends who were Communist Jewish returnees confirmed his fears about the anti-semitism there. He ardently tried to persuade them to stay there and disapproved when they moved to Israel. Berti wrote to Tess after a visit to Moscow in 1957: 'I participated in the symposium on the Origin of Life. The spirit of the meeting was excellent, very cordial, and we all parted as friends. No trace of pseudoideological interference with the discussions, and all were frank – not only on scientific subjects. Altogether I left with the hope that *fear* is a matter of the past – maybe I am overoptimistic. (What we learned about many things of the past, was not pleasant, incidentally). Of course, there would be many things to tell, and I hope there will be a chance. On the material side, life has improved greatly in Russia, from all accounts. Though, for instance, the housing shortage is terrifying. It will take decades to create enough living space. However, I have been far more interested in the mental and intellectual side than in the material side, and it is precisely here that I am hopeful, though much remains to be done. What do I mean, if I say, I shall not make peace with capitalism? Well, I think it is not difficult to explain. By capitalism I mean private property in means of production on a large scale, with all it entails – privileges of every kind for the "haves". I do not think we shall ever have a decent human society, and certainty of peace, unless the social inequality has been removed. And I am afraid this problem has never been tackled seriously by Socialist parties. Though much progress certainly was made in England after 1945, and indeed was inevitable on account of the mood of the people, the basic question whether there should be capitalists and capitalists' children on the one hand, and workers and their children on the other hand, has not been posed. Nor did the Labour Party say it wanted to pose this question. So, you see, many things have been shocks to me in recent years, and there are many things where I must say "no", but I cannot help looking at the question of the division of society into have and have-nots as the fundamental question, even in conditions where the have-nots are, absolutely, quite comfortable, as in Scandinavia, and often in Britain. This applies, of course, also to the division between "have" and "have not" countries. I was invited by Unesco to be chairman of one of their sections at the present Paris conference, but this has been prevented by our Minister of Education. On the other hand, all Nazis are back in their positions of influence.'

In 1959 Berti and Tess resumed their discussion about his personal difficulties after their only meeting, in Jugoslavia. Separately, she had met Ina for the first time, in Zagreb. Tess wrote: 'My dear Berti, It was a lovely day we had yesterday but too short. … I was so grateful that after all these years we could still talk freely. When you told me about your mother, it seemed to me that the description you gave fitted Hilde. And today I saw Ina again, and understood better what you were talking about. You have married two extremely feminine wives. Ina has a completely feminine approach to problems, and when it comes to personal relationships you have a masculine one. This morning there was lots of opportunity for Ina to talk – she knows that I saw you yesterday. One thing you didn't tell me, that Ina still loves you very much. Ina must have been jealous of your work, your friends, your interests, and what your reaction to that would be I know. On the other hand, Berti, there may be some ways of withdrawing from an intolerable situation that are less cruel than others. Ina had thought she was starting a new life with you. She took an interest in the entirely new world of science you revealed to her, and made your family – particularly Paul – hers. In the long run it was stifling for you and you acted accordingly. But from her point of view it was a brutal withdrawal by you of precious gifts you had given her, leaving her high and dry, and more desolate than before. I admit she does not seek the reasons why there was this withdrawal she finds so devastating. For myself, when I made that break, it had to be complete forever – that was my bad character – but I'm grateful for it, even though the deadly sin of pride was at the bottom of it. I'd like to say a lot more, though – to beg you not to invest people with qualities they haven't got and then be disappointed. With all love, dear Berti.' The allusion to her own emotional life is unique in her letters to Berti.

Berti replied: 'I made my mistakes because I could not break in good time the circle into which faulty upbringing had locked me. It is a pity as I could have made a family happy, but I am afraid it is not a terribly interesting story objectively. What worries me most at the moment is the thought how much Paul will be affected by his misfortunes in his childhood. From one generation to the next … Ina is a remarkable woman and has many fine qualities, and is indeed a great poet. But I fear that in her neighbourhood I shall never feel at my ease, and shall always be on my guard. The Ehrlich sisters like it if people are at their service. In the case of Ina, this applies not only to assistance in every step she makes, but more subtly to the things of the mind. She will always ask me to be at her disposal with what I think and feel and say. And she will try and try and try to check. She does not understand that one cannot order feelings and thoughts. I am afraid there is no other possibility than to stay away as far as possible.'

Within her next letter Tess wrote: 'I realised very quickly that she was vastly different from the idea I had of her before I met her. That was based on your account of twelve years ago, on her letters to me, and on my own incurable naïvete. … There is an intolerance of another point of view which I find unsympathetic and alarming. As I now see it, the first mistake was yours, and a ghastly one. It is one I should have made myself, in the naïvete I have mentioned. You were in love with an idea of Ina; you added to your recollections, and your admiration, attributes that in your conception should have been there, but weren't. In your special circumstances, you had a desperate need. You let hope, and artistic imagination, be a substitute for a scientific approach. You made up your mind to marry Ina, without knowing her – you knew only your own idealised image of her. You persuaded her to marry you, and in doing so you took on a tremendous responsibility. … That Paul should have his difficulties is not surprising; indeed, I have always thought it a miracle how free he is of them in view of all he had to go through. It is vitally important for Paul to learn to be independent of mind. I was always afraid that he would be conditioned in his thinking.'

Later in 1959 Berti reported to Tess that the incoming Director of his Institute intended to start a determined action to regularise Berti's position, saying that it was better to be rejected for being a Communist than to give up from the start. The focus of the letters then shifts to me: 'That Paul is doing well, on the whole, in his studies is no great surprise, but I have been afraid that he may have difficulties in finding the right coordinates for himself. In fact, I ascribe his unevenness in work partly to these difficulties, to partial failure to find solid ground under his feet. It is so important for him to develop in a normal direction, and human warmth will help him a great deal. On the other hand, I think he could be a very good and valuable friend for somebody who appreciates his gifts of intelligence and character. Of course, I have no objection against Paul becoming very English – in the sense of the many great English traditions. Nor do I mind it if he decides to come here less often at the present stage of his life. I understand him, and I am confident that our contact will not suffer from it.' Had I seen this letter at the time I would have said that the unevenness in my work at college and the lack of confidence to which it was linked were specifically due to having been poorly prepared at school in mathematics and also chemistry. I also consider that I was rather immature, particularly in comparison to other students who had done National Service.

Tess replied: 'Paul and I had an evening together. I was tremendously relieved to find him relatively unaffected by the dark spots that could have led to emotional complications. He accepts his environment, but in a natural way, not aggressively, as might have been the case if he were consciously rejecting something else. By some miracle he has developed into a normally happy young man. This does not mean he has been uninfluenced; he certainly has, but the influences have been good, and have tended to make him be himself ... It is good too that Paul accepts his home. He is fond of his stepfather, and of the little brother. There could have been so many snags there.' Berti responded: 'On the whole, I agree with what you wrote about Paul though I fear you are slightly over-optimistic. There are hidden difficulties in Paul, which can be traced to the various events of his childhood, but I hope he will be able to deal with the problems. It is an important fact that he sees them fairly clearly. ... Certainly I shall come to London before long one day.' Perhaps his policy was to hold out to Tess the possibility of a visit rather than to risk a discussion or worse following a flat 'no'.

Before my graduation in 1961 he wrote to me: 'Now about my not coming this time. I think we know one another well enough, and we need not make many words now. Practically to the last moment I have pondered again and again whether I could manage now. ... When you are here, we can talk about all aspects of life in this world of ours.' Instead, he asked Tess to represent him: 'My dear Tess, I thank you so much for being in Cambridge on Friday. I cannot tell you how I much appreciate this act of friendship. ... I pondered practically to the last moment whether I should go this time, but ... I so much hope we can have a good chat in London in autumn. All love, especially, Bert.' She replied: 'I wished all the time you were there ... I met Alan for the first time. He is a very gentle person, as of course you know.' Berti's anxiety about Tess's view of him is shown in a note to me: 'I hope you had a nice evening with Tess. I imagine that you had some exchange of views about me, as indicated in your card in advance, but I trust that excesses were avoided.'

At this time, when he was fifty, he was admired, liked and accepted in his social circle, but seen as apart and private. He only wrote once to me about his isolation, in 1960: 'I find it awfully difficult to have a really close and confidential relationship with my compatriots because there are just no people who look at things in a way which I can appreciate. It is not that I do not know the right people. I have met hundreds and hundreds of them one time or the other, Bourgeois, Catholic, Socialist, Communist, but they all share a certain prosaic and narrow attitude which chills me. Do not misunderstand me. Of course, there are heaps with whom I am on good terms and friendly and with whom I gladly pass a few hours or even days, but there is nobody, except Ala and Paul (Löw-Beer), with whom I could really speak my mind.' Tess realised this isolation, and both Hilde and Ala knew it well. The context of this letter was his fear that I would in turn have similar difficulties.

Berti remained interested in the Lysenko issue, and altogether in the state of Soviet and Eastern bloc science. He collected material for a book on Lysenko that in time he felt was rendered unnecessary because of an article written by others. One theme would have been the link between the economic situation in Russia and the promises that Lysenko made. Another was the tradition of physiology as distinct from biochemistry that existed in Russia, derived from Pavlov and others. As Berti got more involved in biochemistry himself, he marvelled at the specificity of biological reactions and wrote to me: 'In fact, it is the main fault of those who have fallen for that Lysenko, that they do not know the sharpness and precision of biochemical reactions and were ready to let everything fall into a bog of ill-defined "physiological" mechanisms. ... The exact formulae can be written down now, though the chemists learned about them only a few years ago.'

In line with his thinking, he reported in early 1960: 'I am to lecture on physical chemistry all year for biologists and biochemists, also for such medical students who are interested. This is an important and congenial task, which will also help to make me indispensible here. But I must admit that I view the prospect with concern. I never taught thermodynamics, kinetics, electrochemistry, photochemistry etc and I shall need extremely careful preparation. It will serve to tidy up my own thoughts, but the difficulties will be very great. Think alone of the mathematics. Moreover, in the summer of 1961 there will be radiation chemistry – also a new subject to me.' Late in 1960 he wrote: 'Learning thermodynamics. ... It costs a great deal of work to study my subject deeply enough to be able to teach it properly, but as it is to me the subject of all subjects, I do not mind devoting many days a week to it, literally. During this time, I am not to be spoken to. Of course, not the whole days, but many hours at predetermined times. ... This class is, for the time being, primarily for my own enlightenment. At the age of fifty I must really get to the depths of the matter.'

This teaching led directly to the flowering of his own scientific work in the area of bioenergetics, and he was able to concentrate on this: 'For me, there is a thing of utmost interest: I fulfilled my year's plan, completed the MS on Technical Applications on Saturday, 31st December and sent off the parcel at 20.45 p.m. I am relieved. It was drudgery. I was not so interested in the subject but before completing the work I could not really turn the full force to essential things. Congratulate me.' I hope that I did. A month later there was a real new beginning: 'Perhaps the most important thing is that I have decided to write, *sooner or later,* a thinnish book *Thermo-dynamics of Living Matter* or so. Do not worry, it is not for the near future. But it is a kind of intellectual need to me to explain these things which are so important and which I understand so well now, I hope.'

Meanwhile the feud with Christian had continued, so Berti wrote with relish early in 1957: 'There has been a comic incident on New Year's Eve.

When I was told that Christian would be in Prinz Eugenstrasse, I naturally decided to stay away. My mother phoned to persuade me to come, or else they would be thirteen. The person who dreaded this number was Christian, he got quite hysterical about it, and when I declined he threw out Dr Stern (a tenant) who had been invited. The poor chap had to withdraw to his own room and listen to the noises made by the party next door. Amazing.' But Berti kept contact with Christian's daughter Johanna. He also had good relations with his cousin Liesl, who had fed him from the back door of the Austrian Legation in Prague and was an ardent Catholic moving in high circles: 'Yesterday, blutwurst at Liesl's. She wants to arrange a talk between the Cardinal Archbishop of Vienna and me about Faith and Truth. Perhaps I accept.' He did. However, his real devotion was to his cousin Erika. It was a real grief to him when in 1961 she died after illness brought on by overwork, stress and smoking. Maresi was left an orphan, but continued her studies and married. Her growing family gave Berti an environment that he cherished, and one that he would have wanted me to provide for him too.

Berti wrote extensively to me with news of himself and also seeking to shape my future. It was all well meant but it was difficult for me because it was so asymmetric. His letters often had an air of slight disapproval and he belaboured the obvious. A clue to his underlying mindset was that when I turned seventeen he remarked that it would be more difficult to maintain the illusion that I was really a child, and even in 1960, when I was twenty-one, he rejected a photo of me sent by Hilde saying that he preferred photos that made me look younger, and even went to the trouble of copying and circulating one such photo. He found it hard to accept that I needed to disengage emotionally from him, and this led to serious conflict in 1964.

His ambivalence on the privileged life associated with Cambridge had led to a lack of empathy from him about my strong desire to do well in my school examinations, and he was lukewarm in his reaction to my getting a place and then a scholarship at King's College. After a four month period between school and university which I spent with him and Viola in the Prinz-Eugen-Strasse flat, working menially in the lab of a colleague of his, going to the opera and reading novels, I went to Southern Italy with Michael Crick and started college in 1958. He then wrote wishing me well, but his main thrust was to remind me that the world was not fair and just, while stating that there was no disagreement between us: 'In reminding you of your privileged position, only in part due to merit, my sole motive is my wish that you should keep in mind that in our social conditions many are deprived of the opportunities they ought to enjoy. Of course, you are aware of this fact in any case. In my view, everything possible should be done to remove this injustice.'

My response that I was aware of these issues and of my good fortune, but then by also trying to hold my tail up, I gave him another opportunity to make me feel that I was insufficiently politically aware and engaged for his taste. His views on criticism were set out in a subsequent letter: 'Incidentally, speaking of self-criticism and the power to stand frank criticism. You know that I am all in favour of it, and I shall always be. No intellectual honesty is possible without it. But perhaps it is worthwhile to point out that no other movement ever dreams of promoting or even allowing (except in narrow limits) self-criticism. Has one ever heard of the Pope repenting the burning of Giordano Bruno? Or the Social Democrats criticising the support of the Kaiser's war? Or the British Government dissociating itself from the methods with which the colonial empire was built? Of course not, and no-one expects any of these powers to be frank. In the case of the Communists, one does expect it, and rightly one is disappointed if they are not – because higher moral standards are valid here than for the Churches, the other political movements or for the Bourgeois governments. But all this is not meant to revive political discussion between us now – I am sure this is no controversial point between us.'

Unfortunately he criticised himself sparingly to others and received little criticism from his friends, who knew that he was both sensitive and fixed in his attitudes, such as his view of the superior claims of Socialism and his personal puritanism. There followed an exchange based on a critique in *The Observer* of the East German leader Ulbricht that I sent him, which again showed my attempts to engage with him and show that I too was thinking about the world, and how his life and views were deeply affected by his historical sense and experience: 'I hesitated somewhat whether I should answer your strongly worded letter. As you well know, in general I do not mind reading the literature issued by the press Lords or their equivalents in other countries. In fact, I read about ten papers a day, or glance through them. At the same time, I do not fall into the trap of believing that the attacks against Socialism launched by the Capitalists and those paid by them

– ever since a Socialist movement started more than a century ago – are in the least motivated by concern for the well-being of the nations or for liberties. However well they camouflage themselves, what matters to the Capitalists is of course the maintenance and extension of the privileges of those who own the Capital. This applies also to the Lords Kemsley, Astor, Rothermere, Beaverbrook etc etc and who pays the piper calls the tune. Second, as regards my opinion of Ulbricht and *The Observer* I suppose I should prefer some problems to be treated differently in the DDR, and to that extent there are differences of opinion. I am also very willing to admit that a few things I have heard of Ulbricht personally do not please me over much; other things about him I appreciate. However, this cannot be the main point. The fact is that Ulbricht has worked consistently all his life, first as a plain working class trade unionist, later as a prominent leader of the militant wing of the working class movement, for Socialism, against Wilhelm's militarism, against Hitler's Fascism, and against Capitalism in general. He and his friends have courageously suffered tremendous losses at the hands of the Nazis, and are engaged now in a different struggle against the Adenauer policy, which aims at the restoration of a Germany of the traditional kind, and includes the rehabilitation of the Nazis. The not-always-pleasant features even of progressive movements in Germany are, in my opinion, conditioned partly by the fact that Germany is so deeply ingrained with reactionary traditions. The average German is still proud of the power of the Nazi army. On the other hand, I very well recall the role of *The Observer* during the heyday of the Nazis – "the eminently sane and intelligent newspaper", as you put it. Sunday after Sunday J. L. Garvin preached collaboration with the Nazis and the support of Hitler's drive to the east in the interest of the unity of Western, Christian civilisation. Sunday after Sunday the Nazis were encouraged in their aggressive policy against Austria, Czechoslovakia, Spain and others. Monday after Monday we could read in the Nazi newspapers triumphant accounts of what one of the leading newspapers of the British Empire had to say. *The Observer* used to blurt out frankly what Chamberlain and Halifax, for diplomatic reasons, had to cover up with hypocritical reservations. As one of those who have suffered from the effects of the policy of HM Government, as put so clearly by *The Observer*, I may perhaps be excused for not taking too seriously what advice the same paper has to offer now. If I remember correctly, I wrote to you in my previous letter that I did not expect *The Observer* to do justice to Ulbricht. Perhaps I may now say more explicitly that – comparing the records of comrade Ulbricht and of *The Observer* – I do not hesitate in my choice though I may not agree with Ulbricht on all points. Perhaps you will reply now that *The Observer* has changed its spots, has a new editor etc etc. I do not know who the new editor may be, but it matters only to a limited degree. Editors are appointed by the owners, who are of course prominent members of the British plutocracy, to further their interests. One editor may do it more discreetly and cleverly, the other less so. But what ultimately matters to the capitalist press, is not, of course, truth.'

In 1959 I arranged to go with Alexis Vlasto, a notable amateur botanist and Old Church Slavonic don at Cambridge, and his student to collect plants for Kew and to see Serbian churches in Old Serbia, Macedonia, and Montenegro up to the Albanian border. Berti himself had in the Thirties been with Hilde to Lake Ohrid, where we also went, but he was very much against this project. Perhaps I did not consult him earlier partly because I anticipated his reaction. When I resisted his pressure to let down my companions and myself, he re-iterated his view: 'It makes me sad that you did not reconsider your ideas about Macedonia, and also, incidentally, that you did not ask me at the start. I hope you will not be angry with me, but I still think that you approach a very different country with Cambridge ideas. The frontier is not a line which must not be touched, but rather a whole sensitive area. Foreigners who claim to look for grasses or stones will be looked on with extreme suspicion. The fact that the expedition has been widely advertised in Cambridge, as you say, will count for little with Sergeant XX, who has been urged to shoot on sight at certain points, or even less with irregular fanatics from one or the other side of the frontier. Incidentally, ordinary bandits, for whom a few pounds are a fortune, are not to be forgotten. Perhaps you will take my views more easily if I frankly tell you that I did all kinds of nonsense at your age – but there was nobody to warn, or even to care. Perhaps it is still not too late to step back ...' In the end he accepted that I was going. In later life he remained unhappy about my travels, seeing them as foolhardy and frivolous compared with being in the lab or with him, but he himself felt free to travel.

That summer I received a much more affirming letter from Berti on the back of winning a national prize with an essay on *The Chemical Basis of*

Inheritance (which brought me to the attention of Sydney Brenner, to my later benefit (Note 39)). 'I am *very happy* about your success with the essay. It is a well deserved success, as we all know that it was solid work, and really your own work. Altogether perhaps, this award will serve to cheer you up and to remind you that you fulfil all conditions to be a smashing success in life – not only because of your intellectual power, but also because of your pleasant ways, which will attract general sympathy, and because you are, after all, a very decent chap. Just one thing needed: to overcome your own doubts and inhibitions, and be cheerful, frank and forward-looking. Good luck, you will do it, and not only in the sciences, but equally in life … Of course it is right that it is better to be a good botanist than a moderate chemist, and it is also right that there are still huge areas open for the not-so-chemical biologist. You quote, much to my delight, microbiology – a very fine subject, I think, and I mentioned, I think, genetics. By all means, go this way if you come to think it is the best.'

The next summer I joined a college friend in Cornwall on a dam construction site as a pneumatic drill operator. This surprised him: 'Many thanks for your most interesting letter. You will have guessed that I am very pleased with the whole enterprise and that I think that it will be a most valuable experience for you … You may remember that I spent a fortnight in rather similar conditions, and with similar purposes, in an East German opencast lignite mine in 1929. General conditions may have been even harder (-8C, working day started at 6 a.m., there was a longish way to work on foot) but probably the work itself was less heavy. In any case, I gave up earlier than I had meant to, and I am still sorry about this defeat which was due to moral rather than physical weakness. It is an experience for life, I am sure. Do you appreciate why Krushchev insists that the Soviet students have a long time in factories etc before they are admitted to higher education?'

I decided to get away from Cambridge to do a PhD elsewhere in Britain, a decision with profound consequences for me. These thoughts elicited the expected responses and also some helpful opinions on possible supervisors. Berti was very pleased when at Brenner's suggestion I applied to and was accepted by William Hayes (Note 40) to work on microbial genetics in his Medical Research Council Unit in London: 'I am pleased to hear that you intend to leave Cambridge for a time at least. Nothing against Cambridge, which is one of the finest places in the world in many ways, but of course

Cambridge is a very specialised case. I do not mind if you ultimately settle in Cambridge but you should do so only after getting to know the world outside Cambridge, so to speak the rest of the world. Not be a Cambridge don *all* your life. That's also why I am happy to know that you are thinking about doing your thesis in London. Not that you think I have forgotten about the visit to Cambridge, in spring perhaps.'

I was very happy about my choice because I took to both the project and my new colleagues, and because being in London was liberating for me. Berti was delighted for me and in spite of his very modest means he offered to supplement my meagre studentship, and eventually I accepted this offer. Even so, at the end of the year Berti wrote me a letter that showed that in spite of the positive appearances, for him all was not well in our relationship: 'Now it is the old year's last day, and naturally the thoughts go back somewhat, as indeed they have been doing now for some time. Will you forgive me if I say a thing which has been on my mind, increasingly. It is my feeling that our relations have deteriorated (is the word too strong? Should I say, they are not what they used to be?) and not only recently but maybe for the last three or four years. I imagine you have felt the same. Certainly I am very unhappy about it. The reason for it? Of course, I have my thoughts about it but I think it would not be good to have details on paper. If one were to speak about them there would have to be the possibility of direct reply and explanation. In writing, misunderstandings are unfortunately certain to crop up. And in any case I do not know to what extent I am right. I am sad about some things you are doing or not doing. I think it would be good if you could think about your attitude to me. Of course, as far as I am concerned, I shall always be ready to do anything which will bring back the relations to what they were. I shall be very happy when it comes to it. There were many pleasant and enjoyable stretches last summer (Note 41). It would have been even better if we could have had the opportunity to talk about various problems in our minds. But more warmth is needed for that, I feel – less coldness. As I say, perhaps you should consider your attitude. And maybe it is also good to take a little time for it. ... All success and particularly all happiness to you for 1962. Love Dad. Yours faithfully, in the original sense of the word.'

He was never more explicit to me but in 1964 talks between him and both Hilde and Ala led each of them to write to ask me to be more attentive to him, while reassuring me that the problem was mainly his rather than mine. Hilde believed that he missed my previously less critical view of him, and allowed herself to refer to having thought a great deal about his psychopathology and his inability to love anyone for themselves rather than to improve them. Sadly, I was unable to meet his emotional wants from me in spite of trying quite hard, and I believe that his needs could not and should not have been met by me if I was to live my own life. In 1965 I went to the US for three years and at the start of 1966 Berti wrote to Tess, seeking reassurance: 'We are both happy with his development, aren't we?' My absence and my marriage while there helped to put our relationship on a new basis.

25

EPILOGUE

Berti's faculty voted in 1959 that he should be given a personal chair, but the Ministry sat on this until 1964. In 1963 he became a salaried Assistent, and wryly explained to Tess that this was a position usually gained at the age of twenty-five, so it was about right ... with the digits inverted. He finally became a full professor in 1968. The task of teaching physical chemistry to biochemists and medical students had made Berti learn the subject systematically, with a decisive effect on his research and scientific writing. His magnum opus *The Evolution of the Bioenergetic Systems* (1975) concerns how organisms evolved to be able to obtain the energy they require for growth and metabolism, including photosynthesis. It was a product of very wide reading, correspondence and discussion (Note 42). In 1977 Berti published a paper entitled *Two kinds of lithotrophs missing in Nature* which in 1994 led to the discovery of a novel mechanism, anaerobic ammonia oxidation (*ammonox*), by which elemental nitrogen returns to the atmosphere in the nitrogen cycle, in parallel with the long-studied process of de-nitrification. One of the organisms mediating such production of nitrogen was then named *Scalindua brodae* after Berti. Such organisms were first seen as having potential in waste-water treatment, and have now been shown to be very important in nitrogen flux in the oceans. His abiding interest in photosynthesis led him to become a strong advocate of solar energy as providing the best long-term solutions to the world's energy problems.

He also continued his interest in Boltzmann and in Einstein, and wrote extensively about them and on Max Planck and other contemporaries of theirs. His interest was scientific, philosophical and historical, and he was always eager to provide the context of a particular topic. Frequently he would circulate copies of manuscripts of articles and update them over a period of years (Note 43).

Berti held to his Marxist view of history and politics, and kept his emotional loyalty to the cause. Although he disengaged from the CP, it seems that he never left it; not for him the very public recantation of some friends, notably Ernst Fischer. Instead he devoted his energies to less partisan issues, notably peace, the environment, and energy issues. He was recognised as an informed and honest participant in debates, and his opinion was valued privately by Chancellor Kreisky and President Kirchschläger, and by several Socialist ministers. In Austria Berti was identified with three public issues. In 1969 he became executive vice-president of the Austrian branch of the Pugwash organisation, and was an assiduous participant at its international meetings and a spokesman in Austria on issues of detente and disarmament. He later became president. Second, in 1973 he alerted the mayors of the communities in the Wachau, the most scenic stretch of the Danube, to a scheme for dams there to make navigation easier and for power generation. This would have meant the loss of an important part of Austria's heritage. He was tireless in mobilising opinion in a coalition against this scheme, which was ultimately dropped. Third, in 1979 the Austrians voted on whether to commission a first nuclear power station, on the Danube quite close to Vienna. Berti came out against the scheme, on the basis of 'not here, not now', arguing that the hazards of the plutonium that would be produced outweighed the benefits. The outcome of the vote meant that the station was left uncommissioned.

By 1968 he had become reconciled with Christian, because they shared a concern for Viola and because Berti respected what Christian achieved as Minister of Justice. A card from Christian from this time laments the years of strife between them. Then in the mid-Seventies he formed a new relationship. His companion (they never lived together) was Gitta Deutsch, whom he had first met when she was a young Austrian refugee in Cambridge. She was the daughter of Otto Erich Deutsch, best known for his catalogue of Franz Schubert's works. After she was widowed she had returned from England to Vienna, and worked there for the UN. Like Ina she was a poet and translator of poetry and after her retirement and then Berti's death, she became well known for this.

Berti retired in 1980, and received a high decoration from the Austrian Government (Photo 60). He had also been a foreign member of the East German Academy of Sciences, and received an honorary doctorate from his old university, then in East Berlin. He then spent most of his energies on peace issues. One of his last articles on the arms race has the title *The*

60. Berti, c.1980

Gadarene Swine of the 20th Century. He did not live to see the collapse of Communism, but he did see the increasing burden on the Soviet Union brought about by the arms race, which had a major role in its ultimate collapse. Then in 1983 he died very suddenly on a solitary walk in the Danube wetlands, on 26 October, Austria's National Day, a few days before he was to address a demonstration on disarmament and then go to another Pugwash meeting. In his wallet was a poem by Erich Fried, another Austrian refugee in England, ironically enumerating all the reasons why one should not become involved in political activities. Berti has a grave of honour near those of Boltzmann, Beethoven, Willi Pabst and Christian, who died in 1987, in Vienna's Central Cemetery. Family and some friends of Berti's still meet each year where he died on that day, to remember him and to maintain the ties of family and friendship that were central to his own life.

In 1961 President Kwame Nkrumah took up a suggestion by J. D. Bernal to invite Alan to Ghana as a Research Professor. Nkrumah resisted strong pressure from the British to withdraw the offer, Alan accepted and Hilde and John joined him in Ghana in 1962. A year later the departing Head of Physics recommended Alan as his successor, he applied and was appointed. The Vice-Chancellor, Conor Cruise O'Brien, wrote of this episode in his *Memoir.* Meanwhile Hilde happily switched to tropical medicine, which became the most fulfilling part of her career. In the early years she took the infant outpatients clinic at Accra's main hospital. I witnessed how each day there were over two hundred mothers with their sick infants, and how she first picked out the ones who would have died before they reached the head of the queue. The clinic continued without a break until everyone had been seen, with no air-conditioning and conducted in a mixture of several languages. Later Hilde was at the University Hospital, dealing with everything from road accidents, minor surgery, malaria and family medicine to the psychological problems of students on whom the expectations of whole villages were placed (Photos 61,62).

As well as his research into the physics of Ghanaian diamonds and his teaching, Alan created a science museum. Together with Thomas Hodgkin (Note 44), husband of Dorothy (with both of whom they became close friends), he attempted unsuccessfully to resolve a confrontation between Nkrumah and O'Brien on issues of academic independence. Here he placed his job on the line, though he knew he would not find another job easily. When Nkrumah was ousted in 1964, a number of the expatriates who were closely linked to him and his ideology were deported. However that same night Alan was visited at home and asked to stay on, which he and Hilde agreed to do. About three quarters of their stay of seventeen years was post-Nkrumah. Much of that time was difficult, through various coups, inflation, shortages and increasing crime, but it was also fulfilling for them professionally and also socially. John spent some of the earlier years in schools in England, with me as a surrogate parent (Photo 63).

61. Alan with Kwame Nkrumah, c.1964

Alan remained as head of his department, and struggled with the problems of low numbers and quality of students, as physics was in competition with law, medicine, accountancy and other more lucrative options for students. Other problems common to African countries were poor teaching in schools (he introduced a foundation year in science in response), good students going abroad and the brain drain of qualified scientists. He served as Dean of Science and on his retirement in 1976 he became a government adviser on science education until 1978, when he and Hilde left Ghana. They lived in Cambridge, where Alan used the libraries. At first they were very worried about money, since their pensions were very modest. Then Hilde was given an Austrian pension as a victim of Naziism,

62. Hilde with nurses, Legon Hospital, c. 1970

and they could get by comfortably and give some help to John when he returned from the Ivory Coast, where he had worked. They were determined to enjoy their retirement, and did so even though Hilde had colon cancer in 1982.

Alan steadfastly declined to talk to the press, and was careful to avoid any eavesdropping even to the end. However the dangers that he had foreseen, of the extreme danger of relatively easily made dirty bombs and of a monopoly of nuclear capability by the US, both made him quietly convinced that his actions had been justified. He read extensively on atomic energy matters and drafted the memoir that is the basis of much of this book, but did not discuss

63. Paul with John May, 1965

either his war-time actions or his subsequent time in prison unless asked (Note 45). He only appeared in print with reviews in *Nature* of books on Klaus Fuchs. Alan's political involvement was confined to joining and then leaving the Labour Party (the latter on a pensions issue). But he read *The Guardian* carefully and continued to have independent views on contemporary politics, especially on Third World development and on disarmament (Photo 64). He was also interested by intelligence issues, and this led to occasional letters to authors including Lord Annan, whose *Our Age* annoyed him to the extent that solicitors became involved. As he and Hilde approached ninety their own generation were dying off, and they became frail, but a family rota of support allowed them to stay in their own home until Alan's death. Hilde then moved into a nursing home and died a year later. Their combined ashes were scattered on Ben Cleat on the Isle of Skye and at the University campus in Ghana. The latter event was in 2006 on a family visit to John, who had terminal cancer and was spending some months in Ghana, where he grew up and which he loved.

64. Alan and Hilde in Scotland, 1994

My own career was uninterrupted in a way that made me aware of what both Alan and Berti had not had. I had left Cambridge at the same time as Alan and Hilde went to Ghana, and with no family home to visit I often spent weekends with friends, including Cecil and Isobel Powell in Bristol, so that I came to see in Cecil the exceptionally humane, modest and supportive friend who was so loyal to Alan. He would recite Housman as we walked the hills. In 1950 he had received his Nobel Prize and met Bertrand Russell, who received the Prize for Literature that year. Russell had a couple of years earlier discussed the use of nuclear weapons pre-emptively against the Russians, but the meeting with Cecil was important in his revising his thinking. Cecil told me that after he had used a speech at a banquet in Stockholm to point out what scientists could and should do for humankind, Russell had said to him that it was the speech that he himself ought to have given. Their meeting was one of the events that led to Russell's joint letter with Einstein and nine others who included Joseph Rotblat and Cecil (the Einstein-Russell letter), that contained the immortal phrase 'remember your humanity and forget the rest', the last thing that Einstein signed before his death in 1955. This in turn led to the Pugwash movement, of which Cecil was a founder and driving force (Note 17).

The PhD work I had done in London led in 1965 to a fellowship at Berkeley in California. My stay there was scientifically less satisfactory, but interesting for other reasons. There I met and married Linda Chase, who came from New York. I had resolved to return to the UK because of my attachment to Europe and particularly the Britain that had been decent to Alan and Hilde and gave me a free education. So in 1968 I re-joined Bill Hayes' unit, now in Edinburgh at the newly-created first university Department of Molecular Biology in Britain. Linda and I had a daughter and a son, and now have grandchildren. During the Edinburgh years Hilde and Alan were regular visitors to Edinburgh and Vienna, and on one memorable and sometimes tense occasion they, together with Berti and also Maresi and her family, had charge of our children on a holiday in Austria.

My own research was in two main areas. First I worked on plasmids, small supernumerary chromosomes that turn out to be ubiquitous in bacteria. In nature they provide a means for genetic material to transfer between strains and species of bacteria, providing new combinations of genes for natural selection to act upon to give bacterial evolution. One result is the inevitable appearance of resistant bacteria in response to antibiotic use. My principal interest was in bacterial evolution, and I wrote a book about plasmid biology. Plasmids also provide tools for genetic engineering and thus for the biotechnology industry. Among the pioneers of genetic engineering were Ken and Noreen Murray, colleagues of mine in the department (Note 46). The parallels between the wider issues raised by research on atomic energy in Berti's and Alan's time and genetic engineering in the Seventies, both characterised as Pandora's Boxes, were obvious.

In 1980 I took the founding chair of Applied Molecular Biology at UMIST (University of Manchester Institute of Science and Technology), an institution with its own distinguished history and ethos that, some years after my retirement, was absorbed into Manchester University. The early years involved the hiring of new staff, and together with them the design and commissioning of new laboratories and the creation of new courses. In terms of my research, I used this new start to begin a programme on the fungi that re-cycle plant material. The durable and largest component of wood and straw is lignocellulose, a complex of three polymers, cellulose, hemicellulose and lignin. Because of the complexity of lignocellulose, particularly the lignin component, studying its biodegradation was a technically intractable problem, but potentially one with great biotechnological importance. Our strategy included the first application of molecular genetics to the study of lignin degradation, and we had generous long-term funding from Research Councils and the innovative Venture Research programme run by Donald Braben for British Petroleum.

After fifteen years in which I had the usual distractions of teaching and a heavy administrative load, I felt that I had insufficient day-to-day contact with the research of my own group and that this would not improve, so I took early retirement, and left UMIST. Early in the Eighties I had put Joseph Rotblat forward for an honorary doctorate at Manchester University, but my proposal was rejected. Happily the next year, again at my suggestion, UMIST gave him its own honorary fellowship, one of the first forms of recognition he and Pugwash received in Britain (Photo 65). For thirty years I have participated in the work of Tess's SPSL, which had helped Berti so many years before, and its successor, the Council for Assisting Refugee Academics.

It is with my parents as human beings that I want to conclude. Alan's two memoirs tell of his life until he met Hilde, and they ring true to me

65. Joseph Rotblat, c.1995. The Royal Society, with permission

concerning his intellectual life in both physics and politics. He had friends but I can say little about his emotional life before his conviction, other than that he was self-contained and shy, and wrapped up in his work, with music as a vital outlet. When I knew him, he was calm, balanced and philosophical, and his uncomplaining account of prison revealed his inner dignity. His lack of self-pity at his lost career and freedom was strengthened by seeing others in worse situations in prison and because of his remorse at having been involved in the Atom Project at all. He had done his time and emerged as a whole person, and could live a relatively open life, unlike for instance Anthony Blunt, for whom he had no respect. He and Hilde were very close as a couple and had good friends, and we all loved his sense of humour. Hilde was emphatic to me throughout their forty-nine years together that she was very happy with him. I could not have wished for a better parent for myself or grandparent for my children.

Hilde was lively and charismatic, and she kept her positive attitude, her *joie de vivre* and her interest in people and places almost to the end. Only when I reconstructed her earlier life through the letters to her did I fully realise how far she had been from the confident and self-possessed woman I knew. On the surface she had managed her unusual childhood, except for what I see as her need for a father-figure. I have to ascribe much of her unhappiness in her twenties and thirties to the way her relationship with Berti developed under the pressures they were under and their incompatible personalities. This was especially the case because Berti was politically in the eye of the storm all the time they were together and later, when he continued to affect her deeply. In contrast, with Alan she was with a man she trusted and who cherished her as she was. She never made anything of what he owed to her.

As a twenty-one year old Hilde had been abruptly cast into the world of Gottfried Kühnel, medicine and politics, estrangement from her uncle Felix, and then being with Berti. This was a life very different from that which Felix had envisioned for her, but could she ever have had a peaceful life? She had a will of her own, and besides, being half-Jewish, she would have been a target for the Nazis. Berti was also charismatic and to be admired for his intelligence, drive and commitment, he was very attracted to her and he believed that will power would get them through her still-raw feelings for the unattainable Gottfried. The pity seems to me that she felt she should accept Berti, and did not wait for someone whom she could truly love. Perhaps I am going too far, but late in life Hilde told Maresi that she had always felt guilty towards Berti because at that time emotionally she had never been able to truly free herself from Gottfried.

It is a great loss for me that Berti no longer had Hilde's letters from before his return to Austria when he died. Did he destroy them as being too painful, or when he married Ina? The affair that Hilde had while Berti was interned was a symptom rather than the cause of their separation, as his letters to her then, and her one surviving letter to him a bit later, indicate that real problems existed between them. Also if Hilde's remark about this is correct, Berti himself had been unfaithful to her when I was born. I don't know whether either of them had other affairs. That she chose not to go to Austria too, as the first Mrs Broda, had the consequences that were later so major for all of us.

In her own way Hilde did become fully engaged. She got Berti and Paul Löw-Beer out of prison, she escorted a hunted Communist leader for many weeks, she helped people to cross borders illegally, and she stuck by Berti after he had escaped to Czechoslovakia and then went to Russia. Her alleged alias as Dr Faber, which I don't understand, suggests that in London she was an intermediary for others. But in the Austrian Centre she was regarded as a foot-soldier who did not meet Berti's standards, notwithstanding the MI5 agent's assertion that she was one of the Inner Circle. However valuable the Austrian Centre was for others as a social centre, she, as a mother and doctor whose marriage to one of its leaders had collapsed, found her residence there very unpleasant. She could not submit to Party discipline and instinctively she did not accept the Party line on the capitalist nature of the war.

How was it then that Hilde, having been married to one to-be atom spy (whom she never knew to be such), then knowingly married another? For some this coincidence has had to have some connecting explanation. But I can assert that her second marriage was undertaken for love. The point seems to me to be that the circles of acquaintance for both Hilde and Alan were limited, and that these circles overlapped. Yes, she probably did admire him before they met in early 1953, so perhaps in that sense she might have felt a mission to be with him, but it was not just bravado, as Tess suggested to Berti.

The suggestions that Hilde was a poor mother include her own despairing question to Barbara Sparks and Berti's opinion for much of the time. The letters between Tess and Berti after he returned to Austria allude to Hilde's defects, while Berti himself seemed beyond criticism. But until I started to research and write my memoir this notion simply did not occur to me. I saw her as a loving and supportive mother who treated me as well as she could, and I still think that she did her best. She was interesting and fun, and I have always been proud of her. The closest that I come to criticism from my own experience is from the period just before she met Alan, when she was deeply involved in Peace Council work, and made no connection between her apparent depression and how I was coping with my own problems. I don't think that she ever felt that I was resentful or angry at her. When she and Alan had difficulties with my brother John she was nostalgic for my childhood. Hilde and I had a loving and trusting relationship to the end.

A Sword of Damocles hung over Berti for forty years but he kept his big secret. This was partly because he was lucky, but also because he was a master at compartmentalising his life. He was difficult, mostly lonely, and never found real contentment. I wonder if things might have been different for him had he not had to live with his secret. The clues to his feelings that he left in his letters and conversations hark back to his family and youth. They include his dislike of his grandmother, his ambivalence about his mother, his lack of respect or empathy for his father, and his deep problems with Christian. On the other side were his admiration for Pabst, Schönhof, and later Hermann Mark, and his happiness when he was fostered in Norway. Berti could be forward-looking and optimistic, but his personal attitudes were conservative and nostalgic, as if he was looking back to a lost childhood.

In my opinion the relationships with both Viola and Christian were love-hate ones. Berti saw Viola as superficial and pleasure-loving, and not sufficiently loving of him as a child, whereas Hilde and then I saw her as a life-giver for her circle, cultivated and theatrical, and she made the best of many difficult times. But I also remember him in tears at Viola's death, the only time I saw him thus. His reconciliation with Christian was also very important to him. It was achieved through a tacit agreement not to fight old battles again, but it also involved positive acts and was moderated by late middle age and, among others, by their companions Gitta Deutsch and Maria Strasser, a formidable and aristocratic Hungarian who for years had been incarcerated in solitary confinement in Communist Hungary. I have wondered whether Christian had been frightened by his older brother's intensity.

In his personal life Berti was frugal and after Viola's death left him as sole occupant of the family flat (but with many guests) he cared little for its maintenance. He was generous with both time and money, even when he had little himself but especially after becoming a securely-salaried academic. He was always interested in the younger generations in his family and the children of his friends. Thus he considered taking them to Venice for the first time as a rite of passage, and whereas Saturdays generally involved lunch with the Löw-Beers, Sundays were set aside for trips to museums, often without being sure that they were wanted – he assumed it. For instance, Maresi was unable to tell him otherwise, since she knew it was well-meant. He preferred children to be serious and studious. In all this was the sadness that I, his own child, was so inaccessible.

Berti was attractive to women, and was attracted to them. He always craved a secure relationship, but it eluded him, first with Hilde and then with Ina, and with other women too. His tendency with women was to come to the rescue and to see that as the basis of a relationship, and in the cases of Hilde and particularly Ina he acted impulsively, imagining that beyond the initial attraction willpower would make things right between them. But he was also restless, as seen in both his marriages. Perhaps he also lost interest or at least took his partner somewhat for granted with the urgency and importance to him of his other activities. His traits of being judgemental and not taking people as they were made all his relationships more difficult, although he also commanded much respect, loyalty, and affection.

Everyone who knew Berti as a scientist recognised his ability, his effectiveness, his prodigious memory and his broad vision. He came closest to doing something truly original with visual purple, and later his situation prevented him from exploiting advances such as his synthesis of radiolabelled tobacco mosaic virus, the fruit of his early realisation of the power of radioactive tracers in biology. He had to content himself with writing a series of excellent books rather than having a powerful laboratory. So the synthesis of ideas then became his forte, and what colleagues most valued him for. It bore striking posthumous fruit in his prediction on anaerobic ammonia oxidation. I have been told that he would have been elected to the Austrian Academy of Sciences had his politics been different. But he was philosophical about the political discrimination, so long as he was able to work. In his unattached state, he had a freedom that he used to work hard and travel. He regarded his office as his real home and after his retirement he kept it as his base. I never saw him not busy at something, and this energy and ability to focus and pigeonhole his activities was chastening for others.

Berti was scathing about religion as a social prop, but could later form coalitions with the Churches on issues of Peace and Disarmament. To the end he proudly kept his own formal affiliation with the distinctly minority Protestant Church, because he saw its dissident voice as important for Austria. His own faith remained in Socialism as expressed in Marxism, and in this he never wavered. This was partly intellectual, and of course he was well read in the fundamental texts, and was very well-informed about the world about him. But the emotional and idealistic underpinnings, from listening to Egon Schönhof and Willi Pabst as a child, were as important. I feel that he later tended to idealise those, especially in science, whom he admired, perhaps here too seeking father figures. This in turn led me to have a life long scepticism about heroes of any kind. He never, that I recall, talked or wrote in those terms about Stalin, but concerning the Soviet Union, and also Communists, he went rather easily from recognising their sufferings, courage and sacrifices to thinking they had to be right.

Berti's internments, the bombing, the separation of my parents, the residential nursery and the illnesses were known to me in outline, but other details of my early childhood were new to me. Bowlby's Attachment Theory seems helpful in explaining why Barbara Sparks found me so traumatised and why Berti and Hilde then found me so difficult. But I also tell myself that very many children suffered in the War through separation and loss, whereas I never lost the love of either Berti or Hilde. The long-term damage that Berti referred to is hard for me to characterise or comment on. Yes, I do seek security and affection, fear rejection, and have a pessimistic streak. I also try hard to please others. This does not seem unusual! These traits are most directly traced back to Berti, and in thinking about myself it is usually in relation to him rather than to Hilde or Alan.

Others see me as carrying a filial burden, but it is one I have shouldered gladly. From an early age, I was told a lot about my parents' concerns and treated as a young adult. I was a witness, shaped by them and events, and with this came a knowledge that some things were confidences. I have felt lucky to have had such interesting and committed parents, and the process of researching and writing this memoir has made this feeling deeper. I accepted much from all three, helped by the mutual respect and friendliness of Alan and Berti. My attitudes were shaped on science, on history, on music, on speaking out, and on support and help within a family as being supremely important. I have had a sense of obligation to use the professional opportunities given to me, but have often felt that I lacked Berti and Alan's single-mindedness. Moreover, I have always been diffident in making professional judgements on others. Even so, science was a fulfilling and I think a constructive career for me. I have also lacked the passion and certitude on political issues that Berti had, so I have also been diffident about public debates and arguments in general. Perhaps this was my reaction to my parents' lives or just that times are different; Hungary and then college came at a critical time. Naturally I have wanted to live my own life and be judged on that, and especially I have wanted the generations after me to have a normal upbringing.

CHRONOLOGY

1896 Marriage of Walter Nunn May and Minnie Kendall

1906 Marriage of Ludwig Gerwing and Elsa Meyer

1909 Marriage of Ernst Broda and Viola Pabst

1910 Suicide of Pauline Meyer

29.8.1910 Berti born

12.3.1911 Hilde born

2.5.1911 Alan born

1916 Christian Broda born

13.2.1917 Suicide of Elsa Gerwing

1919 G. W. Pabst returns to Austria from internment

1921 Egon Schönhof returns to Austria from Russia

1921 Ernst and Viola buy Fünfturm

1922, 1924 Loss of Broda family fortune

1926 Walter and Ted Nunn May removed from own firm

1928 Berti completes school; starts at Vienna University; meets Paul Löw-Beer

1928 Berti studies in Berlin

1928 Berti joins Social Democrats

1929 Hilde studies at Freiburg; meets Andrew D'Antal

1929-1930 Hilde studies at Munich

1930 Hilde studies at Bonn; meets Gottfried Kühnel; goes to Berlin

1930 Berti joins Austrian Communist Party

1930 Alan starts at Cambridge

6.1931 Semmelmann affair

1931 Berti transfers to German Communist Party

14.9.1931 Berti arrested at demonstration in Vienna.

1931 Hilde starts studies in Berlin

1932 Berti and Hilde meet and become couple

12.7.1932 Berti described as 'Reichsleiter of German Student CP'

1932 Berti starts thesis

(1932 Berti may have been in USSR)

30.1.1933 Hitler becomes Chancellor

2.1933 Dollfuss suppresses Austrian Parliament.

1.5.1933 Death of Ernst Broda

5.1933 Berti detained for two weeks and then expelled from university and from Germany

1933 Berti at Mark's Institute in Vienna; starts second thesis

1933-34 Hilde studies in Würzburg

1933 Alan graduates and starts as postgraduate in Cavendish Laboratory

2.1934 Austrian Civil War

1934 Berti and Hilde travel in Corsica and in Balkans

20.7.1934 Dollfuss murdered

1934 Berti obtains PhD; Privat-Assistent to Mark

1934-35 Hilde studies in Graz; then moves to Vienna

7.5.-7.6.1935 Berti in prison

29.7.1935 Berti escapes twice from arrest; goes to Czechoslovakia

5.9.1935 Berti and Hilde marry; Berti returns to Czechoslovakia

9.1935 Anti-Jewish Nuremberg Laws in Germany

10.1935 Italy invades Abyssinia

12.1935 Berti travels to Moscow

early 1936 Hilde enters sanatorium in Black Forest

7.3.1936 Hitler marches into Rheinland

5.6.1936 Popular Front in France

7.1936 Olympic Games in Berlin

1936 Alan appointed to King's College London; joins CP; visits USSR

mid-1936 Hilde visits Berti in USSR

16.7.1936 Franco revolt in Spain

18.8.1936 Trial of Kamenev and Zinoviev and others in Moscow; executions 25.8.

10.1936 Berti leaves USSR for Czechoslovakia

9.1.1937 Berti re-enters Austria ; then imprisoned for two weeks

5.1937 Berti visits England with Mark

10.1937 Berti gets job in patent lawyer's office

3.1938 Anschluss; arrest of Egon Schönhof (murdered 4.10.1942)

3.1938 Berti leaves Austria for Switzerland, then France

7.4.1938 Hilde qualifies as doctor; goes to Aachen

10.4.1938 Berti enters UK

10.5.1938 Hilde has obtained visa for UK

7.1938 Berti and Hilde visit Isle of Wight; Kühnel visits London

23.7.1938 Initial Special Branch report on Berti and Austrian CP group in London

8.11.1938 Goodeve hires Berti to work on Visual Purple

5.12.1938 Berti and Hilde move to 6c Oak Court, Highgate

1.1939 Discovery of Fission

11.2.1939 Special Branch report on CP meetings at Oak Court

3.1939 Berti visits France

15.3.1939 Paul born, Hitler enters Prague

23.8.1939 Molotov-Ribbentrop Pact

8.1939 Alan with radar group on East Coast

1.9.1939 Bohr and Wheeler paper on U235

3.9.1939 War declared

14.9.1939 Comintern declares that the war was Imperialist on both sides

9.1939 Alan sent to Bristol

10.1939 Cecil Powell invites Alan to join him

6.10.1939-13.2.1940 Berti's first internment

4.1940 Oliphant, Frisch and Peierls visit Bristol

10.5.1940 Invasions of Low Countries, Denmark, and Norway

5-6.1940 Fall of France; Dunkirk; Berti strives to finish Visual Purple work before internment

13.5.1940 Special Branch interview with D'Antal

6-9.1940 Berti's second internment, at Huyton, Liverpool; loses MRC grant; released 24.9

26.9.1940 Oak Court bombed; Berti and Hilde separate

1-10.1941 Hilde is House Physician, QE Hospital for Children, Hackney Road

4.1941 Berti works for R F Reed

3.1941 Paul in home in Hitchin

4.5.1941 Paul established at Sparks family

5.1941 Seaborg and Lawrence show that plutonium is more potent than U235 for fission

6.1941 Hitler invades USSR

8.1941 Fuchs becomes source for GRU; at end of 1941 Cairncross starts informing to Russians

7.12.1941 Pearl Harbor; US enters War

12.1941 Wigner-Smyth report on fission products

10.1941-1.1942 Hilde is House Physician at Stoke Mandeville Hospital

20.12.1941 Berti joins Tube Alloys at Cavendish

early 1942 Chadwick calls Alan to Liverpool; Alan moves to Cambridge in spring

1-8.1942 Hilde is House Surgeon, North Middlesex County Hospital, Edmonton

9.1942-7.1944 Hilde is Assistant MO Middlesex County Council

29.8.1942 Alan completes his radioactive poisons report

27.9.1942 Berti removes Paul from Sparks family; Paul with Berti for 8 weeks; then with Hilde at Austrian Centre until 7.1943

29.9.1942 Churchill in Moscow; secret agreement on weapon information between UK and USSR

1942 Murder of Erna and Meta Meyer

10-11.1942 Alan passes Atomic Project information to Russians

11.1942 Alan departs for Canada

2.12.1942 Fermi reactor at Chicago achieves criticality

22.12.1942 Vadim reports that Berti has provided initial report

1.1943 Berti meets Glan from KGB

31.1.1943 Capitulation of von Paulus at Stalingrad

7.1943 Last German offensive, Kursk-Orel

8.1943 Quebec Conference between Roosevelt and Churchill

8.1943 Berti described as main source of information to KGB; increases information flow in 1944

1.1944 Alan attends Chicago conference with Fermi team

10.3.1944 Alan's memorandum on ZEEP

5.1944 Cockcroft replaces Halban as Director of Montreal laboratories

8.1944-3.1945 Hilde is Resident MO, Culduthel Fever Hospital and TB Sanatorium

11.6.44 Berti 'at all costs not to be sent overseas'

24.8.1944 ZEEP given final approval

30.8.1944 Postcard sent to Berti in Cambridge from Chicago

8 or 9.1944 Alan visits Chicago; reactor poisoning incident; Alan receives U233 and U235 samples

9.1944 Bohr meets Churchill; Churchill and Roosevelt discuss Bohr and secrecy

early 1945 Alan meets Angelov

27.3.1945 Hilde and Paul move to Cambridge

6.1945 Compton, Oppenheimer, Fermi, and Lawrence recommend use of Bomb without warning

7.1945 Successful nuclear test (*Trinity*) of a plutonium bomb

8.1945 Bombs dropped on Hiroshima (U235) and Nagasaki (plutonium)

8.1945 Smyth Report published

9.8.1945 Alan gives U233 and U235 samples to Angelov

5.9.1945 Gouzenko defects; Cockcroft summoned to Ottawa

16.9.1945 Alan leaves Canada

19.9.1945 Alan contacts Blackett; they meet on 20.9.1945

1.10.1945 Berti writes to Alan

16.-17.10.1945 Alan sees Berti and others in Cambridge

20.11.1945 Philby warns Russians that Alan will be questioned

14.1.1946 Alan lunches with Berti and Kowarski

7.2.1946 Cockcroft meets Alan

15.2.1946 Alan's first MI5 meeting; Canadian arrests

20.2.1946 Alan's second MI5 meeting

4.3.1946 Alan arrested and charged

8.3.1946 Kaspar reports on Edith Tudor Hart

13.3.46 Berti visits Edith Tudor Hart

1.5.1946 Alan tried and sentenced

1.5.1946-7.1946 Alan at Wormwood Scrubs

7.1946-10.1946 at Camp Hill, Isle of Wight

24.8.1946 Berti and Hilde's divorce becomes absolute

9.1946 Berti moves to Edinburgh

10.9.1946 Berti-Simpson correspondence starts

10.1946-3.1947 Alan's first stretch at Wakefield

11.1946 Alan meets Cussen and Marriott from MI5

24.12.1946 Cecil Powell visits Alan

3.1947-4.1948 Alan at Leyhill

3.1947 Berti travels to Rome to meet Ina Jun

4.1947 Berti leaves UK; marries Ina at end of May

6.6.1947 Berti returns to Austria with Ina; takes post in Ministry of Electric Power

11.6.1947 Alan writes to Kemmer on his theory on fission

1.8.1947 Deputation to Home Secretary on Alan's behalf

10.1947-10.1962 Hilde is Assistant MOH, Schools, Cambridge

4.1948 Berti represents Austria at World Power and Energy Conference in Paris; his last visit to UK

4.1948-12.1952 Alan's second stretch at Wakefield

1948 Berti becomes Dozent; 10.1948 resigns from Ministry

11.1947 Berti arranges meeting on Austrian science

1948 Alan submits paper to *Nature* from prison

21.3.1949 Alan meets Skardon at Wakefield

29.8.1949 USSR detonates A-Bomb

1950 Berti publishes *Advances in Radiochemistry*

1951-53 Hilde is Secretary of Cambridge Peace Council

15.9.1952 Skardon reports on visit to Alan about his release

11.1952-1.1953 Cabinet discussions on Alan's release

29.12.1952 Alan released and goes to Ralph and Jackie May's house in Chalfont

2.1.1953 Skardon and Dick White visit Alan at Chalfont

early 1953 Hilde meets Alan at Chalfont

5.3.1953 Stalin dies

6.1953 Berti and Ina divorce

19.6.1953 Rosenbergs executed

1.8.1953 Alan and Hilde marry

1.1954-12.1955 Anonymous Benefactor provides grant to Alan at Wooster laboratory

1.1954 Cambridgeshire County Council discuss Hilde's employment

20.7.1954 John May born; adopted 9.1954

1955 Berti as *Extraordinarius* (title only)

3.1955 Berti moves back to Prinz-Eugen-Strasse

7.1955 Hilde interviewed at Passport Office; receives passport

1955 Berti refers to Christian as 'my former brother'

10.1955 State Treaty establishes Austrian neutrality

1955 Berti's *Ludwig Boltzmann* published with foreword by Hans Thirring, not Lise Meitner

2.1956 Krushchev speech at 20th Party Congress of CPSU

7.1956 Suez Crisis; 10.1956 Hungarian Uprising

2.1957 Berti's *Weg und Ziel* article on Lysenko and others

8.1957 Berti in Moscow for *Origin of Life* Symposium

1958 Berti publishes *Radioactive Isotopes in Biochemistry*

3.1959 Alan receives passport on sixth application

1958 Paul spends spring/summer in Vienna with Berti and Viola; enters King's College Cambridge

7.1959 Berti meets Tess for only time after 1948, in Yugoslavia

12.1959 Faculty vote for Berti as Professor *ad personam;* Ministry does not act on this

1960 Berti starts to teach physical chemistry to biochemists and biologists

1960 Christian becomes Minister of Justice; serves 1960-66 and 1970-1983

1960-61 Three notes by Alan in *Nature*

9.1961 Paul takes postgraduate studentship in London

10.1961 Alan appointed Presidential Professor in Ghana (later appointed to university chair)

31.12.1961 Berti's letter to Paul on their deteriorating relationship

1962 Alan goes to Ghana; Hilde and John follow

1963 Berti appointed Assistent; 1964 appointed Professor

1965 Paul gets PhD and goes to Berkeley, California; Hilde visits in 1966

2.1966 Nkrumah ousted

1966 Berti is President of Chemical-Physical Society

12.1967 Paul marries Linda Chase

4.1968 Berti appointed *Ordinarius*

8.1969 Cecil Powell dies

1969 Berti becomes Executive Vice-President of Austrian Pugwash

10.1971 Berti writes letter to Wachau communities

12.1973 Christian's penal code adopted

1975 Berti awarded Ehrenkreuz 1st Class

1975 Berti publishes *The Evolution of the Bioenergetic Processes*

1977 Berti predicts anaerobic ammonia oxidation

1978 Alan and Hilde retire and leave Ghana

1980 Berti retires

26.10.1983 Berti dies

2.1987 Christian dies

1999 *The Haunted Wood* is published

12.2002-1.2003 Alan dictates his last statement and dies

2004 Hilde dies

2006 The National Archives release files on Berti

2007 John May dies

2007 The National Archives release files on Alan and Hilde

2009 Berti identified as 'Eric' in *Spies*

ACKNOWLEDGEMENTS

My principal thanks go to Alan for his unique draft memoirs of his life until his arrest and of his years in prison, and for his letters from prison that were returned to him after his release. He had wanted to put his own version of events before the public, and a third of the main text of this book is based on these. In that sense we are co-authors, and I have often felt that he was at my shoulder as we placed his spying within the wider context that had so concerned him. Partly because he refused to divulge some details, his few attempts at interesting publishers in his memoirs came to nothing. So did his idea of finding a ghost-writer. Towards the end, approaching ninety, Alan had neither the drive nor the time away from his family and health concerns to do more.

Just when events allowed me to make decisions on how to proceed with Alan's papers, MI5 placed the files on Berti and then on Alan and Hilde in the public domain. Then I knew, rather than merely surmised, that Berti had been a prime suspect for espionage. Moreover, the files had new material on Alan's arrest, imprisonment and release, and on his life with Hilde in the Fifties. I saw that writing about Alan, Hilde and Berti together would be the best way forward, so that as well as the need for time at The National Archives I had pressing reasons to re-visit all Berti's papers and to read carefully his letters to Hilde, which she had kept. Then in 2009 there came the Vassiliev revelations. My memoir in the 1984 anthology (Note 43) had sought to give the essence of the man, but there was now much more to tell; the world has changed so much, Berti was known to have spied, and I knew more about his personal life in the Thirties and Forties, mainly through these letters.

Tantalisingly, Berti had written 'memoiren?' in his diary for a day shortly after the day on which he was to die so suddenly. I had known that, like Alan, he did want to set down thoughts on his life, but at some future date. For him it was a matter of finding the time, since he was so busy with Pugwash and other peace activities. He was insistent that the historical context was all in seeking to understand the actions of individuals, and he would have tried to explain his own actions in the context of what he himself knew at the time. Such an account would have reflected his Marxist standpoint, but it would also have been rich in anecdote, personalities and family lore. He would have tried, even before the fall of Communism, to face up to its failures and to Stalinism, as he had done with the Lysenko issue. But it is too much to expect that he would have revealed his spying, he had other loyalties, and he would have continued to be his reticent self on personal matters. Hilde shared this reticence about their relationship, but she would have wanted Alan's and Berti's voices as well as her own to be heard. Thus I owe it to her too to describe how her life unfolded.

In placing Hilde's and Berti's actions in the context of their personal lives I have had to overcome my own reticence on family matters, but if the book was to be written at all it had to be as open as I could make it, and I hope that it comes across as balanced and fair, and also as being written with love for them and for Alan. I have thought about them and their actions every day of my adolescent and adult life, and I am glad that I can now, one hundred years after their births, set down my thoughts and feelings on them as parents too. In this, I thank Linda Chase Broda, Cleo Broda and Steve Crosher, Andrew Broda and Karen Corless, Marietheres (Maresi) Frauendorfer, Beat Steffan and Fran May for their support. I also thank John and Nickie Fletcher, Sara Macaulay, Claire and Alex MacLeod, George McQuitty, George Nuki, Ruth Stungo, Gabrielle Syme and Robert Ibberson, Claudio and Penelope Vita-Finzi, and other friends for their interest and encouragement.

On Berti's death, Wolfgang Kerber, director of the Central Library for Physics of the Austrian Universities in Vienna, gave me a room in which to keep his many books and extensive professional papers. This allowed me and others to start to put these papers in order, and the first fruit was the book cited in Note 43. Together with his colleague Peter Goller, Gerhard Oberkofler, the Archivist of Innsbruck University and an indefatigible student of the Left in Austria, produced an invaluable documentation on aspects of Berti's life in 1993, when an exhibition on Berti was also held. During 2008 I put Berti's papers in sufficient order to give them to the Library for archiving, with open access. I am very grateful to Wolfgang Kerber, his successor Brigitte Kromp, and Peter Graf from the Library, and Gerhard Oberkofler, Helmuth Springer-Lederer, and Peter Markl for their continuing interest, help, support and friendship during this process. The late Gitta Deutsch and Thomas Schönfeld were devoted to Berti's legacy and memory and I am grateful to them too. My cousin Maresi gave me a home-from-home, as she had done for Berti, and I am deeply grateful to her for that and for the many very helpful readings and discussions we have had. Others in Austria whom I wish to thank are Traudl Schmidt for access to her thesis on Paul Löw-Beer, Barry McLoughlin for the material described in Note 8, Peter Ebner for his knowledge of Berti and his circle, Kitty Löw-Beer for discussions on our parents, and Robert Rosner, who knew Berti, Thomas Schönfeld and Paul Löw-Beer well.

My translations from the German originals of letters to Hilde from Berti and from Felix Meyer are more literal than literary. Although the absence of Hilde's letters to Berti before 1947 is a great loss to me, I am fortunate about what else survives. These include all the letters that Berti wrote to me between 1943 and 1983, and letters between him and Tess Simpson. Berti's letters to her from 1952 are held by the Brotherton Library of Leeds University, and I thank the Library and Richard High for access to the Esther Simpson Archive, for help, and for permission to quote from Tess's letters from 1946. Tess wrote to me after Berti's death that she had his letters from 1952, but did not mention his earlier letters, and they are not in the archive. Ruth Boreham very kindly gave me her own transcripts from Berti's file in the Society for Protection of Science and Learning archive at the Bodleian Library of Oxford University.

Hilde and I were fortunate to establish contact with Peter Sparks shortly after his mother's death in 1998. In time he and I exchanged the letters from which I include extracts, and I am most grateful to him for allowing me to quote from hers. They came with his warning on her sharp tone, but they also show her warmth to us and how things actually were for her and 'our crazy trio', as she put it in one letter to her husband. I also thank him for providing me with photographs.

I acknowledge extensive use of the MI5 and other Government files on Alan, Berti and Hilde that are held in The National Archives, as made clear in the text. The relevant volumes of material are: KV 2/2209-2226 and KV 2/2563-2564 (Alan), KV 2/2349-2354 (Berti), and KV 2/2553-2555 (Hilde). Files AB 2/653 and AB 4/130, referred to in the text, have also been cited.

I thank Yale University Press for their generous permission to make extensive quotation from *Spies*; Dr Dana Z. Anderson and his brothers for their agreement to quote the letter to Alan from their father Herbert L. Anderson, present as a photostat in Alan's file in the National Archive; The Churchill Archives Centre (Dr Lynsey Robertson) for permission to reproduce a letter from Sir James Chadwick, CHAD I 24/2 in the Chadwick Papers; *The Morning Star* for the quotation from an article by J.B.S. Haldane; and Oxford University Press for the quotation from A. J. P. Taylor.

Alan has been poorly served by some of the published photographs of him. I thank Alan's niece Mrs Diana MacDonell for the photographs of the May family and of Ralph Nunn May; Trinity Hall, Cambridge and Dr John Pollard for Alan's matriculation photograph from 1930; and Library and Archives Canada for their 1945 image of Alan. I have been unable to trace the current holders of the rights on the images of Alan in the early Thirties and in 1953. I thank Daniel Pabst for providing me with the photographs of his grandfather G.W. Pabst. The image of Edith Tudor Hart with her son, and permission to use it, were generously given by her brother Wolfgang Suschitzky. I also thank the following for providing me with images and/or permissions: Anne Meitner and the Meitner-Graf Archive; the Master and Fellows of Trinity College Cambridge (Sandy Paul); The Royal Society (Joanna Hopkins); The University of Bristol (Hannah Lowery); and the Special Collections Research Center, University of Chicago. Credits and copyrights are given individually with the images.

I am most grateful to Gino Segre, a physicist and friend over forty-five years who has written with distinction on the physics of the Twenties and Thirties (*Faust in Copenhagen,* 2007, Pimlico), for his comments on the manuscript, and to Jenny Brown for her critical insight on how to improve this book. I thank Susan Lendrum for help in reading a crucial draft letter, Stephen Hopkins for excellent advice on the intelligence literature and on publishing, and Sara Macaulay and Ruth Stungo for their thoughtful readings of the manuscript. Roddy Simpson has helped greatly with computer advice and preparing the photographs for publication. I am most grateful to Peter Brawne for his gift of the cover design. I thank Jeremy Thompson and his colleagues at Troubador for their professionalism. By no means least, I thank Tam Dalyell for his insightful and generous Foreword.

NOTES

These brief Notes concern what is relevant to this memoir. Because of the internet and other sources, much more information is usually readily available on these subjects, including the later careers of individuals. Thus, for instance, titles conferred later on some British personages are generally omitted.

1. James Chadwick 1891-1974 studied at Manchester, Berlin and Cambridge. He discovered the neutron, a neutral particle with about the same mass as a proton. He was awarded the Nobel Prize for this in 1935. He moved from Cambridge to Liverpool in 1935 and built the UK's first cyclotron there. In the War he was Head of the British Mission in Washington linked with the Manhattan Project in the US.

2. As will be set out in more detail, the war-time Atom Project started in Britain when the MAUD Committee was set up following the Frisch-Peierls report that Oliphant forwarded to Sir Henry Tizard in 1940. The Tube Alloys project at the Cavendish Laboratory in Cambridge (1941) was mostly moved to Montreal in late 1942. The US Manhattan District project (directed by General Leslie Groves 1896-1970 and J. Robert Oppenheimer 1904-67) was based at Los Alamos in New Mexico, the Metallurgical Laboratory in Chicago (Enrico Fermi 1901-54; Nobel Prize 1938) and elsewhere. Joseph Rotblat 1908-2005 was at Los Alamos. Some Tube Alloys staff at Montreal were Free French from the Joliot-Curies' Paris laboratory.

3. John Cockcroft 1897-1967 studied at Manchester and Cambridge. In 1932, with E. T. S. Walton, he effected the first disintegration of a nucleus by proton bombardment, by means of the first successful use of a particle accelerator (Nobel Prize 1951). In the War he directed air defence research at Malvern and then the Montreal project. He became the first director of the UK's Atomic Research Establishment at Harwell.

4. Oppenheimer, Fermi, E. O. Lawrence 1901-58 (Nobel Prize 1939), and A. H. Compton 1892-1962 (Nobel Prize 1927) constituted the scientific committee that recommended the use of the Atom Bomb on Japan without

warning. Leo Szilard 1898-1964 was one of those who opposed this. In 1934 he had taken out a patent on a nuclear fission chain reaction as an energy source. In 1939 he drafted the letter that Albert Einstein sent to President Roosevelt on the possibility of creating an atomic bomb. For a biography of the many-sided Szilard see: *Genius in the Shadows,* W. Lanouette, 1992, Scribner, New York.

5. *Spies: the Rise and Fall of the KGB in America.* J. E. Haynes, H. Klehr, and A. Vassiliev, 2009, Yale University Press, New Haven and London; *The Haunted Wood: Soviet Espionage in America – the Stalin Era.* Allen Weinstein and Alexander Vassiliev, 1999, Random House, New York.

6. G. W. Pabst 1885-1967 began film directing in 1923, using a darkly realistic documentary style. His approximately 35 films included *The Joyless Street* (1925), *Pandora's Box* (1929) (both silent), *Westfront 1918* (1930), *The Threepenny Opera* (1931), *Kameradschaft* (1931), *Don Quixote* (1933), *Der Prozess* (1948), and *Der Letzte Akt* (1955). He returned from France to Austria in 1938, and made two films during the war. His last film was released in 1956.

7. Christian Broda 1916-1987 was a lawyer and Social Democrat politician. He was Austrian Minister of Justice 1960-66 and 1970-83. He had particular interests in the reform of criminal law, family law and asylum law, and was awarded the European Human Rights Prize of the Council of Europe in 1986.

8. As this book was about to be typeset, I was kindly given items concerning Berti by Dr Barry McLoughlin. They come from a larger Communist Party dossier on him held in the Russian State Archive for Political and Social History. I have used information from a secret official precis in Russian, dated early 1942, and two items written by Berti. The first of these is a short political biography he composed after his arrival in Russia in December 1935; the details are consistent with and amplify what I had inferred from other sources. The other, written from Austria and dated 21.7.1937, concerns his political conflict with his brother Christian. Plainly there is much more to be seen and assessed from Russian sources about Berti's activities in the Thirties.

9. Alan's brothers were Edward 1897-1964 who earned a Military Cross at the front in the Great War, and Ralph 1902-1980 who was Executive Secretary of the National Union of Students until the War, when he joined the Crown Film Unit of the Ministry of Information; at its winding-up in 1952 he was its General Manager. Whereas Edward cut Alan off completely, Ralph was Alan's main support during his trial, imprisonment and release. His sister Mary 1908-2000 was a medical secretary. Like their father, she also visited Alan in prison.

10. P. M. S. (Patrick) Blackett 1897-1974 was educated at Dartmouth Naval College and saw action in the Royal Navy in the Great War before studying physics at Cambridge. He won a Nobel Prize in 1948 for his development of the Wilson Cloud Chamber as used in nuclear physics and cosmic rays, and for its use with Occhialini to confirm the existence of the anti-electron (positron). They also showed that a photon could produce an electron anti-electron pair. Blackett became President of the Royal Society. Occhialini also worked with Cecil Powell, and was a friend of Berti's. E. C. Bullard 1907-80 was a pioneering geophysicist.

11. This can be found with much other interesting material on Paul Löw-Beer in a thesis based on oral accounts provided by him very late in his life. Traudl Schmidt, 2005, *Das Schicksal hat mich verschont … Versuch einer politischen Biographie. Die Lebens- und Familiengeschichte von Paul Löw-Beer (1910-2003).* Master's thesis, Faculty of Social Sciences, University of Vienna.

12. Hermann Mark 1895-1992 served as a much-decorated Austrian officer on the Italian front in the Great War. He was a pioneer of the use of X-ray diffraction on high molecular weight molecules. He worked in Germany on polymers in I.G.Farben's laboratories, but because his father was Jewish, with the rise of the Nazis he moved to Vienna as professor of physical chemistry. In 1938 he and his family made their way to the US, where he built up yet another research laboratory in Brooklyn and was recognised as one of the fathers of polymer science. When Mark received an honorary doctorate in Vienna in 1980, Berti's presentation address contained a vivid picture of how Mark created a vibrant and informal group around himself, and of his generosity of spirit. Berti regarded Mark as his most important mentor and role model, and proposed him for a Nobel Prize.

13. Some of the major steps on the road to Fission were: Rutherford's initial discovery that radioactivity involved the transformation of one chemical element into another; Chadwick's discovery of the neutron; the Joliot-Curies' discovery that radioactive elements could be made by neutron bombardment; Fermi's use of slow neutrons to effect nuclear disintegrations; and Hahn and Strassman's finding that uranium gave rise to the medium-sized element barium, interpreted by Meitner and Frisch as fission having occurred and yielding much energy.

14. The Academic Assistance Council was founded in 1933 by Sir William Beveridge, Lord Rutherford, Archbishop Temple and others. Leo Szilard had had a crucial meeting with Beveridge in Vienna that started the process. Esther Simpson 1903-96 soon joined it as Assistant Secretary, and devoted much of her life to it and its successor from 1936, The Society for the Protection of Science and Learning (SPSL). It continues as the Council for Assisting Refugee Academics (CARA). Szilard also helped AAC in London in the Thirties as a volunteer. An estimated 2600 refugees from Europe were helped at this time, including 16 who won Nobel prizes. Moreover, in the internment periods of 1939-40 Esther Simpson had a major role in effecting the release of over 600 internees. *In Defence of Learning. Academic Refugees: their plight, persecution and placement,* 2011, S. Marks, P. Weindling and L. Wintour, eds. British Academy and Oxford University Press, follows a symposium held at the British Academy. It includes articles on the contributions of Beveridge and Szilard, and one by the author on Tess Simpson's personality and beliefs, seen through her side of her correspondence with Berti. In *Refugee Scholars: Conversations with Tess Simpson,*1992, R.M.Cooper, ed., Moorland Books, Tess gives her own account of her life and friends, and includes the anecdote on helping Berti travel to Italy to meet Ina Jun in 1947.

15. Edith Tudor Hart (sometimes Tudor-Hart) 1908-73 was born Edith Suschitzky in Vienna. She was expelled from Britain in January 1931, but in 1933 she returned as a British subject, having married Alex Tudor Hart. While he worked in general practice in the South Wales coalfields, she began to establish her reputation as a photographer of working people, industrial decline, refugees etc. She then separated from her husband and

lived in London. In February 1947 she admitted to MI5 that she had worked for Russian Intelligence in Austria and Italy in 1932-3. It is alleged that she had a crucial role in the recruitment of Kim Philby by Russian Intelligence.

16. Georgii Flerov 1913-90 wrote in April 1942 to Stalin to point out that since 1939 no work had been published in the West on fission, and that the leaders in this field had not published at all. This was a trigger for the Soviet Atomic Project.

17. Cecil Powell 1903-69 obtained his PhD at the Cavendish under Rutherford and C. T. R. Wilson in 1927. He was at Bristol University from 1928 until his retirement very shortly before his death. He won the Nobel Prize in 1950 for his development of the photographic method of studying nuclear processes and his discoveries regarding mesons made with this method. The pi-meson was a theoretically-predicted heavy sub-atomic particle. In 1955 he was a signatory of the Einstein-Russell letter, and was involved in the preparations for the first Pugwash Conference on Science and World Affairs in 1957. Rotblat said: 'Cecil Powell has been the backbone of the Pugwash Movement. He gave it coherence, endurance and vitality'. Powell chaired the meetings of the Pugwash committee, often standing in for Bertrand Russell. His research with balloons on cosmic rays depended on multi-lab collaboration, and this became a stimulus for the emergence of CERN, the European Organisation for Nuclear Research at Geneva, of which he was one of the founders.

18. A. J. P. Taylor, English History 1914-1945, p559. Pelican, 1975.

19. Bohr and Wheeler were so influential because although Frisch and Meitner had realised that uranium underwent fission, they had assumed it was true for all uranium. Shortly after, Bohr made the important observation which finally appeared in print in the Bohr-Wheeler paper, namely that only U235 underwent fission, and U238 did not. Since ordinary uranium is 99.3% U238, the uranium would have to be refined to make a bomb, but since the two isotopes are chemically identical this seemed to be prohibitively difficult.

20. R. E. Peierls 1907-95 and O. R. Frisch 1904-79 were working in the Physics Department at Birmingham in 1940. Its head was M. Oliphant 1901-2000, who forwarded their report to Sir Henry Tizard 1885-1959 in his capacity as chairman of the Aeronautical Research Committee.

21. Tizard established the MAUD committee in April 1940 in the wake of the Frisch-Peierls report. It represented the start of the British Atomic Project, and its members were G.P. Thomson 1892-1975 (Nobel Prize 1937) as chairman, Blackett, Chadwick, Cockcroft, Philip Moon, and Oliphant. 'MAUD' was a codename, based oddly on the first name of Bohr's children's former governess. A research programme on isotope separation (see Note 18) and fast fission was agreed on, so that in June 1940 Franz (Francis) Simon was commissioned to work on isotope separation through gaseous diffusion; by December he had concluded that such separation was possible. Using new American data Peierls re-calculated a new critical mass for U235 at 4-5 kg. This information was sent to the Uranium Committee in the US, but its secretary simply locked away the information without informing the committee's members. In July 1941 MAUD approved their final two reports and disbanded. One report was on uranium for a bomb, and the other was on uranium as a source of power. The British believed that uranium research (also in Germany) could result in the production of a bomb in time to affect the outcome of the war. The second report concluded that a nuclear reactor had promise for future peaceful uses and recommended that Halban and Kowarski should move to North America where more heavy water would be available.

22. Dick Goldsmith White 1906-93 became Director of MI5 1953-56 and of MI6 1956-68.

23. Frédéric Joliot-Curie 1900-58 (Nobel Prize 1935), Hans von Halban (later no 'von') 1908-64 and Lew Kowarski 1907-79 were respectively French, Austrian-Jewish and Russian by origin. Halban graduated in Switzerland, and worked with Bohr in Copenhagen, where, together with Frisch, he showed that deuterium absorbs neutrons poorly. Kowarski trained as an engineer and joined Joliot in the early thirties, supporting himself until 1938 by working part-time for a gas pipe company.

24. Nicholas Kemmer 1911-98 was born in St Petersburg and educated at Göttingen and Zürich. He worked in Tube Alloys from 1940 and proposed the names Neptunium and Plutonium for elements 93 and 94. He was in Canada from 1944-46. He succeeded to Max Born's chair in Edinburgh.

25. The Smyth report was published shortly after the use of the atomic bombs on Hiroshima and Nagasaki. Its full details are: *Atomic Energy. A General Account of the Development of Methods of using Atomic Energy for Military Purposes under the Auspices of the United States Government 1940-1945. H. D. Smyth. Written at the request of Major General L. R. Groves, United States Army.* It was also published by the British.

26. J. B. Conant 1893-1978 was a chemist who was President of Harvard 1933-53, and chairman of the National Defense Research Committee 1941-46. Harold Urey 1893-1981 won the Nobel Prize in 1934 for his isolation of deuterium and then heavy water. In the War he worked on the separation of U235 from U238. Later he was a pioneer of studies on the primitive atmosphere and the origin of life. Edward Teller 1908-2003 was born in Hungary, did his doctorate with Heisenberg and went to the US in 1935. He was in the Manhattan Project at Los Alamos in the War, and became one of the strongest initial proponents of the fusion 'Hydrogen' bomb.

27. ALSOS (a pun on the Greek word for 'grove') was initiated by Groves to investigate how much atomic research the Germans had achieved. Its staff followed the advancing Allied troops first in Italy and then in France and Germany searching for evidence. It also organised the seizure of German nuclear resources, materials and personnel for the benefit of the US and to stop these being acquired by the Soviet Union. Samuel Goudsmit was the technical leader, and in 1947 he published an account *'ALSOS'* of their work and conclusions.

28. Wallace Akers 1888-1954 was a physical chemist and research director of ICI. He was director of the Tube Alloys project 1941-46. Michael Perrin 1905-88 was another ICI chemist, who had developed the production of polythene. As Akers' deputy, he was involved in the liaison between Tube Alloys and the Americans. He also was responsible for the war-time British assessment of the German effort.

29. Douglas (Dave) Springhall 1901-55 was a founder member of the Communist Party of Great Britain. He was discharged from the Royal Navy in 1920 for political agitation. He visited the Soviet Union in 1924 and 1926, and was gaoled for activities in the 1926 General Strike. While Political Commissar of the International Brigade in Spain, he was wounded in 1937. He edited *The Daily Worker* in 1938-39, and then served as British representative at the Comintern in Moscow. He brought back from Moscow the edict that the War was imperialist, and became one of the three who then formed the collective leadership of the CP. In 1943 he was tried *in camera* and convicted of passing classified information to the Russians. He was released in 1948, went to China in 1950, and died of cancer in Moscow.

30. George Placzek 1905-55 worked with many other leading physicists, including Frisch, Peierls and Bohr on fission and a possible role of U235 for a nuclear chain reaction. He also worked with Landau in Kharkov around 1937 (the year after Alan visited there), and thus knew the reality of the Soviet Union at first hand. Bruno Pontecorvo 1913-93 was Italian-born, the brother of a noted geneticist and of a noted film-maker. He was an early assistant of Fermi, and participated in his slow neutron experiments. In 1936 he joined the Joliot-Curies, and remained there until the Nazis entered Paris, when he and his family made their way to the US. After working in the oil industry he joined the Montreal group in 1943, and from 1948-50 he was at Harwell. In 1951 he and his family abruptly and secretly went to the Soviet Union, where he lived and worked until his death.

31. Herbert L. Anderson 1914-88 was a member of the team that first demonstated nuclear fission in the US. A close associate of Fermi, he was one of those responsible for Chicago Pile-1, which achieved the first man-made nuclear chain reaction on 2 December 1942. He also worked at Los Alamos and as a consultant for the Hanford reactors, which generated fissionable plutonium. He was to be Director of the Enrico Fermi Institute in Chicago 1958-62.

32. Roger Hollis 1905-73 joined MI5 shortly before the War. He was Deputy Director-General 1953-56 and Director-General 1956-65. He was

alleged by Peter Wright in *Spycatcher* and also by Chapman Pincher to have been a double agent. Christopher Andrew in his authorised history of MI5 concluded that Hollis was not a double agent.

33. Max Born 1882-1970 taught at Göttingen University 1909-33, when he was associated with many key figures in mathematics and physics, including Einstein and Heisenberg. He then left Germany for Cambridge, and was professor at Edinburgh 1936-1956. He made major contributions to the development of quantum mechanics, solid-state physics and optics, and eventually received a Nobel Prize in 1956. He was the predecessor of Nicholas Kemmer and then Peter Higgs in the Edinburgh chair.

34. The idea of creating a bomb in which an initial fission explosion triggered a fusion reaction of hydrogen isotopes, the principle of the H-bomb, may have come from Fermi in 1942. It was then discussed with Teller and Oppenheimer among others. There was a conference on the topic in 1946; Fuchs was present and passed the information to the Russians.

35. Gerald Gardiner 1900-1990 was Lord Chancellor in Labour Governments 1964-70, when he introduced many reforms into British law, including the office of Ombudsman. Although over conscription age, he served in the Friends' Ambulance Unit as an alternative to military service from 1943-45. He fought for the abolition of capital punishment, and was defence counsel at the *Lady Chatterley* trial in 1960. He believed that even as Lord Chancellor he was subjected to surveillance by British Intelligence.

36. Sir Hartley Shawcross 1902-2003 prosecuted Alan as Attorney-General in the Labour government of 1945-51. He led the British prosecution at the Nuremberg War Crimes tribunal. His approach there was to focus on the rule of law, and to show that the laws the defendants had broken were ones to which pre-war Germany had been a party through international treaties and agreements. He maintained that each of the defendants was a party to the common murder of those who were old or mentally ill, and those killed in the gas chambers or by shooting. He is quoted as saying: 'There comes a point when a man must refuse to answer to his leader if he is also to answer to his own conscience'.

37. William James ('Jim') Skardon 1904-87 went from the Special Branch to be an MI5 interrogator. Fuchs confessed to him but he had much less success with Philby, Blunt, and Cairncross.

38. Thomas Schönfeld 1923-2008 was from a left-wing Viennese Jewish family that spent the war in the US. After service in the US army he returned to Vienna in 1947 and became Berti's first graduate student, obtaining his doctorate in 1950. His professional life was as an inorganic radiochemist, and he became a full professor at the University of Vienna in 1972. His close intellectual relationship with Berti covered co-authorship of books on the application of radiochemistry in microchemistry and in technology. He was an editor of the anthology referred to below (Note 43). He remained deeply committed to the Communist Party and to working on issues of peace and disarmament until his death.

39. Sydney Brenner b.1927 is a pioneer of molecular biology. His early work, partly with Francis Crick, established fundamental features of the genetic code and of gene expression. Later he made the nematode worm *Caenorhabditis elegans* a model for studies of multicellular animals, and won a Nobel Prize for this work.

40. William Hayes 1913-1994 was a medical microbiologist at Hammersmith Hospital, London, who showed that the basis of the sexual system of the bacterium *Escherichia coli* is F, a self-transmissible mini-chromosome that is the archetype of 'plasmids'. Plasmids have great importance in nature e.g. as the carriers of multiple genes for resistance to antibiotics in bacteria, and more generally in bacterial evolution. They are also essential tools for gene cloning.

41. This refers to a long journey we took together. After my graduation I accompanied Berti to an International Congress of Biochemistry in Moscow. We drove from Vienna via the North Cape, Finland, and Leningrad, and returned via Minsk and Warsaw.

42. An interesting example of Berti's extensive and engaged correspondence was with Harold Urey in 1969 on the geochemistry of sulphur in the

primaeval ocean. Berti was sceptical for several reasons about Urey's view that sulphate was present, but Urey replied that he saw no reason to add to or detract from any of the contents of his recent article, which contained a value of 10^{-14}. Berti then sent his own calculations that showed the value of the equilibrium constant was about 10^{14}, and there was no such sulphate. He added 'Please forgive the bad typing. I got a little excited about the matter, and wanted to reply as soon as I could. …' Urey wrote back thanking him and stating that Berti was quite right, also in his stoichiometry, and that his own discussion of sulphate oxidation was very wrong.

43. A book published in 1985 contains an anthology of Berti's less-technical articles, together with introductory articles, a personal memoir, and chronological lists of 647 of his publications ranging from books to newspaper articles. It is: *Engelbert Broda. Wissenschaft, Verantwortung, Frieden, Ausgewählte Schriften* (Science, Responsibility, Peace, selected writings) edited by Paul Broda, Gitta Deutsch, Peter Markl, Thomas Schönfeld, and Helmuth Springer-Lederer, and published by Franz Deuticke, Vienna. Springer-Lederer was Berti's closest colleague for many years and Peter Markl has been an analytical chemist and a writer on scientific and philosophical issues.

44. Thomas Hodgkin 1910-1982 was a pioneer in the study of African history. He joined the Palestine civil service in 1934, resigning in 1936. He then taught and administered in adult and extra-mural education, latterly in Oxford, until 1952. He had visited the Gold Coast (later Ghana) in 1947, befriended Kwame Nkrumah in 1951, and developed interests in African history and in contemporary nationalism. In 1962-65 he headed the new Institute of African Studies at the University of Ghana, before returning to a post at Oxford. In 1937 he married Dorothy Crowfoot, the Nobel Prize-winning X-ray crystallographer. Dorothy Hodgkin was President of the Pugwash Movement 1976-88.

45. Among Alan's sources was Margaret Gowing 1921-1998. *Britain and Atomic Energy 1939-1945,* Macmillan, 1964, was the first authoritative account of the part played by Britain in the development of the first atomic bombs. Her 1978 Rede Lecture *Reflections on Atomic Energy History,* Cambridge University Press, provides a succinct, clear and accessible account

of the issue of secrecy in the Anglo-American relationship during the war and in its aftermath, and its consequences for Britain in both the military and civilian areas.

46. Kenneth and Noreen Murray b. 1930, 1935 pioneered the use of the bacterial virus λ in gene cloning. A direct application was the development, production and use of the first vaccine produced by genetic engineering, against hepatitis B, produced by one of the first biotechnology companies, Biogen. The Murrays' Darwin Trust has supported many foreign postgraduate students in biology in Edinburgh and other universities.

LIST OF PHOTOGRAPHS

1. Alan and Hilde at the time of their wedding, 1953
2. Viola Pabst as an actress, pre-1907
3. Young Willi Pabst
4. Ernst Broda 1923
5. Willi Pabst, mid-1920s
6. Berti and Christian with their cousins Erika and Gerd Obst, c. 1924
7. Berti at 16
8. The Meyer family, 1889
9. Felix Meyer in his prime
10. Elsa and Ludwig Gerwing, c. 1910
11. Hilde and her Meyer cousins Margot and Claire, pre-1917
12. Hilde, 1923
13. Maria Lesmeister ('Mutti'), 1933
14. Sister Benedikta, c. 1926
15. Felix and Marguerite Meyer undated
16. Hilde, c. 1931
17. Paul Löw-Beer, c. 1932
18. Alice Rabinowitch, later Löw-Beer, c. 1932
19. Fünfturm
20. Hilde and Berti, Fünfturm 1932
21. May family, c. 1917
22. Alan at Matriculation, October 1930
23. Alan, c. 1932
24. P. M. S. Blackett
25. Lord Rutherford
26. James Chadwick
27. John Cockcroft
28. Hilde, Berti, Christian on Gross-Glockner, c. 1933
29. Hilde at St Blasius 1936
30. Hilde, Berti and Øle Prestrud, Moscow 1936
31. Berti 1937
32. Berti and H. Mark in London, 1938
33. Esther Simpson. c. 1946
34. Edith Tudor Hart with her son Tommy, 1938

35. Berti, Hilde, and Paul at Watlands 1939
36. Berti, Hilde and Paul with Gwendolen Caroe and Sir William Bragg 1940
37. Cecil Powell, Bristol 1948
38. Niels Bohr
39. Otto Robert Frisch, c. 1970
40. Mark Oliphant
41. Peter Sparks and Paul, 1942
42. Berti, Peter's aunt and grandmother, Peter and Paul, 1942
43. Barbara and Jack Sparks, 1938
44. G. P. Thomson
45. At Montreal: Seligman, Pontecorvo, Goldschmidt, Guéron, Halban, Auger
46. E. Fermi, L. Szilard, H. L. Anderson et al, 1946
47 and 47A. Postcard to Berti from Alan, Kowarski, Freundlich and Anderson in Chicago 1944
48. Alan on departure from Montreal, September 1945
49. Berti and Paul with Kowarski family, 1943
50. Berti and Paul c.1946
51. Berti, c. 1946
52. Ina Jun Broda, c. 1947
53. Felix Meyer, c. 1948
54. Ralph Nunn May, c. 1946
55. Letter from Alan to N. Kemmer
56. Letter from Alan to C. F. Powell
57. Alan, January 1953
58. Berti and Ina with Viola, Christian, Hilda and their daughter Johanna, c. 1948
59. Berti and Ina with Erika and Maresi Musche, c.1949
60. Berti, c. 1980
61. Alan and Kwame Nkrumah, c. 1964
62. Hilde with nurses, Legon Hospital, c. 1970
63. Paul with John May 1965
64. Alan and Hilde, Scotland 1994
65. Joseph Rotblat, c. 1995

Index

Information in Notes is indexed with the suffix "n"